Women and Social Class –
International Feminist Perspectives

Women & Social Class

Series editors: Pat Mahony and Christine Zmroczek
(Roehampton Institute, UK)

This new series aims to address a relatively neglected area of feminist theory, women and social class. The series is intended to analyze social class in relation to women's lives, to theorize it by highlighting personal experience and to understand it in ways which move beyond the macro analyses provided by male, 'left' oriented accounts. In developing feminist understandings and analyses of how class continues to operate across and within diverse contexts, the series is committed to evaluating the ways in which social class combines with other social forces to produce inequalities for women in the present and in the future.

Already published:

Class Matters: "Working-Class" Women's Perspectives on Social Class
Edited by Pat Mahony and Christine Zmroczek

Class Work: Mothers' Involvement in their Children's Primary Schooling
By Diane Reay

Women and Social Class –
International Feminist Perspectives

EDITED BY

Christine Zmroczek
and
Pat Mahony

First published 1999 in the UK and the USA by UCL Press

UCL Press Limited
11 New Fetter Lane
London EC4P 4EE
UK

The name of University College London (UCL) is a registered trade mark used by
UCL Press with the consent of the owner.

UCL Press is an imprint of the Taylor & Francis Group

British Library Cataloguing-in-Publication Data
A Catalogue Record for this book is available from the British Library.

Library of Congress Cataloging-in-Publication Data are available

ISBNs: 1–85728–929–3 HB
           1–85728–930–7 PB

Typeset in 10/12pt Times by Graphicraft Limited, Hong Kong
Printed and bound by T.J. International Ltd, Padstow, UK.
Cover design by Rob Steen

Contents

CONTENTS

Notes on contributors

Maher Anjum was brought up and educated in Bangladesh, Libya and Britain. At present she works at Stepney Housing and Development Agency and is a lecturer in social policy and sociology. She is currently completing her PhD from the University of Greenwich in which she explores the influence of anti-racist policies on the life chances and opportunities of Bangladeshi women in Britain. She is the co-author with Lesley Klien of "Involving black and minority women in regeneration initiatives: a case study of Bethnal Green City Challenge" in Rosa Ainley (ed.) *New Frontiers of Space, Bodies and Gender* (London, Routledge 1998).

Anita Franklin is a senior lecturer in sociology at the University of Central Lancashire. She teaches and writes in the areas of race and ethnic studies, gender and women's studies, and development studies. Anita Franklin has lived and worked in the UK since 1984. She is currently writing a book on the state of Equal Opportunities debates in the US and UK.

Laurel Guymer is a radical feminist, women's health activist, critical care nurse, midwife and women's studies lecturer at Deakin University, Geelong. She first became interested in issues of class while living as an exchange student in Nashville, Tennessee in 1979. Since then she has completed a graduate diploma in midwifery and women's studies, a Master of Arts (women's studies) and is currently working on her PhD. She is an active member of FINRRAGE (Feminist International Network of Resistance to Reproductive and Genetic Engineering) and is involved in the international campaign against population control and abusive, hazardous contraceptives. Her current research includes feminist investigations of class, new provider controlled contraceptives, sexual coercion and the sex industry, and the implications of the pro-euthanasia movement for women.

Elizabeth J. Hatton is professor and Dean of Faculty at Edith Cowan University South West Campus (Bunbury) Australia. Her research in the sociology of teaching and the sociology of teacher education is driven by a concern for issues of equity including social class, ethnicity, gender, sexual orientation and rurality.

Hana Havelková is a sociologist and political philosopher by training. She is an associate professor at the Institute of Humanities, Charles University in Prague, where she teaches social theory, feminist theories and philosophical readings. She has edited four books in Czech on gender and feminism since 1989. She is a member of the Board of the Gender Studies Centre in Prague and of the Board of the International Association of Women Philosophers.

Susan Hawthorne is a lecturer in the Department of Communications and Language Studies at Victoria University, St Albans Campus, Melbourne, Australia. She teaches novel writing and editing and publishing in the postgraduate area of professional writing. Also a novelist and poet, her books range across many fields. She is author of *The Falling Woman* (Melbourne: Spinifex Press 1992), *The Spinifex Quiz Book* (Melbourne: Spinifex Press 1993) and has recently co-edited two anthologies, *Car Maintenance, Explosives and Love and Other Contemporary Lesbian Writings* (with Cathie Dunsford and Susan Sayer; Melbourne: Spinifex Press 1997) and *Cyberfeminism* (with Renate Klein; Melbourne: Spinifex Press 1999). She is also an acrobat and aerialist in the Women's Circus and the Performing Older Women's Circus.

Ronit Lentin is an Israeli-born feminist sociologist and writer residing in Ireland. She is course coordinator of the MPhil in Ethnic and Racial Studies at Trinity College Dublin, where she also lectures in sociology and women's studies. She has published extensively on the gendered relationship between Israel and the Shoah, feminist research methodologies and auto/biographies, Israeli and Palestinian women peace activists, and on gender and racism in Irish society. She is the editor of two volumes of *In from the Shadows: the UL Women's Studies Collection* (University of Limerick: Department of Government and Society 1995, 1996) and of *Gender and Catastrophe* (London, Zed Books 1997). Her latest novel is *Songs on the Death of Children* (Dublin: Poolbeg Press 1996).

Leela MadhavaRau has lived differing versions of ethnicity, "mixed ethnicity" and racism in England, Canada and the United States. Recently, she has moved away from employment in the field of anti-racism and, while contemplating a career change, is writing and researching these same issues. She is exploring other new realities through the eyes of two young sons, Sanjay and Rohan.

Frances A. Maher is Professor of Education at Wheaton College, Norton, Massachusetts, USA where she also teaches women's studies courses. She is the author of numerous articles on feminist pedagogy and is co-author (with Mary

Kay Tetreault), of *The Feminist Classroom* (New York: Basic Books, 1994). She is currently at work on a comparative study of women's studies in England and the United States, having recently spent several months in London visiting women's studies programmes there.

Pat Mahony is Professor of Education at Roehampton Institute London. She has worked for many years in the areas of "equal opportunities" and teacher education and is currently engaged in a number of research projects exploring the impact and significance of government policy in these areas. She has written extensively in the areas of gender and schooling and, more recently, on the effects of "new managerialism" on policy and practice in teacher education.

Changu Mannathoko is a senior lecturer in the Department of Educational Foundations, University of Botswana, in Gaborone, Botswana and the director of the annual regional gender and development course. She has published widely in the areas of teacher education, educational management and gender and education. She also works with NGOs involved with education, publishing and women's rights.

Bandana Pattanaik is currently a postgraduate student in women's studies at Deakin University, Melbourne, Australia. Back home in India she has taught English language and literature at the tertiary level. Her areas of interest include women's writing and cultural studies.

Janice G. Raymond is Professor of Women's Studies and Medical Ethics at the University of Massachusetts in Amherst, Massachusetts, USA; the co-director of the Coalition Against Trafficking in Women (a feminist human rights organization) and the author of five books and many articles, the most recent of which is *Women as Wombs: Reproductive Technologies and the Battle Over Women's Freedom* (San Francisco: Harper 1993).

Miri Song is a lecturer in sociology at the University of Kent. Her research interests include debates around ethnicity and cultural identity, migration, and children's labour.

Valerie Walkerdine, **Helen Lucey** and **June Melody** all grew up working class in various parts of Britain. They collaborated on the research reported in their chapter while working on the ESRC funded project "Transition to Womanhood in 1990s Britain", at Goldsmiths College, University of London. Valerie Walkerdine is presently Foundation Professor of Critical Psychology at the University of Western Sydney, Nepean; Helen Lucey is Research Fellow at the School of Education, Kings College, University of London and June Melody is training to be a psychotherapist in London.

Gaby Weiner is Professor of Education in Teacher Education at Umea University. She is co-editor (with L. Yates and K. Weiler) of the Open University Press series Feminist Educational Thinking (1994–9). Her most recent books are: *Feminisms and Education: an introduction* (Buckingham: Open University Press, 1994, reprinted 1995), *Equal Opportunities in Colleges and Universities* (Buckingham: Open University Press 1995; with M. Farish, J. McPake and J. Powney) and *Educational Reforms and Gender Equality in Schools* (Manchester: EOC 1996; with M. Arnot and M. David). Other current research interests include academic writing and publishing practices, and European and global issues affecting education policy.

Christine Zmroczek is Senior Lecturer in the Department of Women's Studies at Roehampton Institute London and Editor in Chief of *Women's Studies International Forum*. Together with Pat Mahony she has edited *Class Matters* (London: UCL Press 1997) and is editor of the series Women and Social Class for UCL Press. Her other research interests centre on twentieth-century women's history, oral accounts of women's lives, ethnicity and migration. Currently she is at work on two books on second and third generation daughters.

Introduction

Christine Zmroczek and Pat Mahony

This volume presents new ideas about class within an international context. Its particular focus is on women's theorized experience of social class from a variety of feminist perspectives, contextualized in relation to the countries and regions in which the authors live. The contributors write about their experiences of class in Australia, Bangladesh, Botswana, Britain, Canada, Czechoslovakia and the Czech Republic, India, Israel, Korea, New Zealand, Poland and the USA. Many of the authors have lived in more than one country or region and are able to make comparisons and illuminate differences and similarities between them.

The contributions reveal how varied entire class systems can be from one country to another, from one generation to another in the same country and from region to region. The authors analyze their own understandings of class and the implications for their feminism and for feminist theories in an historical period when capitalist market economics have claimed a globalizing influence and class has been said to be dead.

In editing this collection it was our aim to explore how class appears and operates by using experience as the basis of analysis. In particular we wanted to spotlight social class while retaining a focus on its interconnections with other defined and defining social and political categories.

The need for a book

Our interest in producing such a book came from two main sources. First, our earlier work on women and social class concentrated on the ways in which women from a range of working-class backgrounds, now in middle-class occupations, had experienced social class (Zmroczek & Mahony 1996a; Zmroczek & Mahony 1996b; Mahony & Zmroczek 1997b). Through that work we became increasingly aware of the need to widen the debates about how class works in

1

order to include the contributions of women from middle- and upper-class back-grounds. In learning how women from working-class backgrounds thought and felt about the classed nature of the rules and codes against which they had been and continued to be judged, we knew we had exposed only part of the story. What we still did not know is how these rules and codes were perceived by middle- or upper-class women, whether they were actively taught, how their functions were understood and how visible they were. We had known that there was a wealth of information to be gained ever since a friend who had been educated at a prestigious fee-paying girls' school remarked to one of us: ". . . your naiveté is quite astonishing. Of course they're actively taught – they're to sort out the hoi-polloi like you dear."

We recognized the need to raise wider issues about women and social class across classes and national boundaries. We also realized that some of the issues raized by contributors to our book *Class Matters: "Working Class" Women's Perspectives on Social Class* (Mahony & Zmroczek 1997b) had implications and linkages for women across class divisions. Such issues include power, dis-crimination, racism, sexism, political aims and activism, stereotyping and sexuality as well as feelings of anger, pride, guilt, solidarity and isolation. The authors also wrote about their disappointments, frustrations, pleasures, laughter, dramas, crises and triumphs, many of which we thought might be recognized by and resonate with women from different social class backgrounds. Because of this we wanted to explore "the other side of the coin" in greater detail in order to become clearer about how power, discrimination and stereotyping operate.[1] In other words we wanted to know how class discrimination is taught, how far it is explicit, how far, for example, a middle- or upper-class feminist might be con-scious of the impact of her classist behaviour, how far therefore she could be held responsible for it and what the nature of the problem might be in trying to persuade her to modify her attitudes and actions. Our experience to date had led us to believe that some middle- and upper-class feminists, such as the contribu-tors to this volume, do try to understand the implications of their class location, the power relations entailed in it and the potential impact of some of their attitudes or behaviour. Others have seemed unwilling or unable to do so, react-ing with expressions of guilt, defensiveness or denial. A third group has seemed genuinely unaware of the classed nature of their comments and behaviour. We have also been told that social class is not a useful category, that it is an old fashioned, out of date topic.[2]

Given the importance of social class in the differential impacts of social transformations across the globe (Mahony 1998), opportunities to discuss and theorize class in new and meaningful ways seem to have been remarkably absent from some academic disciplines in recent years. One of our aims in editing our first collection on class and the resulting series in which this new volume ap-pears, was to renew feminist debates and recover them from the worn arguments of the 1970s and 1980s. We continue to be astonished to read of the "death of class" (Pakulski & Waters 1996) and would agree with Beverley Skeggs's trenchant remark that "to abandon class as a theoretical tool does not mean that it does not exist any more . . . ; only that some theorists do not value it" (1997: 6).

It is important to ask whose interests are served by the obliteration of the theoretical premises of one of the major categories around which societies are ordered. It is not difficult to understand why politicians and ideologues might want to argue that class no longer exists. How could the widening gap between rich and poor (Lean & Ball 1996) be legitimated other than by the pretence that the failure to maximize opportunities for social mobility is the fault of the poor themselves? How might governments ignore their responsibilities to address structured discrimination organized around the axes of class, "race", gender, sexuality and disability other than by declaring them not to exist? But as the contributors to this volume demonstrate, experience shows that such discriminations continue to exist.

The difficulties for middle- and upper-class women in trying to carry out what is, in effect, an excavation of the ground on which they stand, should not be underestimated. It may involve recognizing material and cultural privilege. This can be particularly uncomfortable or painful for feminists whose politics have led them both to analyze how power relations are constructed and maintained and to challenge these. However, as this volume demonstrates, such excavation is possible. It is also important. Women from working-class backgrounds might be pleased to have their insights and analyses about how they are discriminated against confirmed by middle-class women describing how they have been trained to discriminate. Women from middle- and upper-class backgrounds may find it easier to "hear" the critical voices of other women from similar locations – and hear them they must if they are to move beyond "doing class" to engaging critically with its politics.

We also wanted to understand what might be shared by feminists across differences, so we determined to try to expose how class works, how it is maintained and by implication what it would mean to challenge it.

A second major impetus which was influential in our decision to concentrate on the international aspects of our project came from a chance remark at a conference. We had just presented some of our research on working-class women's experiences of class in Britain when, during the subsequent discussion, a woman commented that in her view our work was "interesting but parochial" since "class is a purely British phenomenon". We listened carefully to the responses of members of the audience who were from, or had experience of, countries other than Britain. It seemed that while the particular markers of class and even whole class systems might be different, the analysis which we had presented could easily be recognized and translated into other contexts. We left the conference excited by the prospect of contributing further to deepening understandings of class.

As part of a feminist project, we were, and remain, keen to encourage women to view class through the prism of experience. As a result of our previous work based on theorized experience, we had built up a picture of class experience as deeply imprinted, rooted and retained through life. This, we argued, is a more helpful way of understanding how class works than the more conventional notion of class as a social category left behind or newly entered as one moves up (or down) the "ladder of success" (Mahony & Zmroczek 1997a). We wanted to continue in a feminist tradition of scholarship in which experience is made explicit, in order to move beyond the blunt instrument of the traditional statistical survey. We agree with Bertaux and Thompson (1997) who argue that, while statistical analyses can be of immense value for the large picture, there is a need for other ways of exploring class if the fine detail is not to be missed. This fine detail may throw light on areas hitherto hidden and result in the recasting of theories which no longer fit. Our dissatisfaction with traditional analyses and descriptions of class is that they do not speak to the experiences of people, particularly women. We would argue that it is essential to begin with theorized accounts of experience if the detailed processes through which individuals become classed are to be charted. From the reader's perspective such accounts may offer new insights, challenge old certainties or provoke yet more questions (as the chapters in this volume have done for us). Equally the reader may disagree with the meanings or analysis the author attaches to her own experiences. Such is the nature of theorized experience which aims to contribute to an ongoing process of understanding rather than claim the last word.

Understanding past experiences of class, mediated through family, work or education, often provides contextual clues for understanding the present. It allows political connections to be made between ourselves and other women and shows how (beyond the factor of wealth), even the less obvious signifiers of class such as accent, clothes, housing, style, qualifications or body language have set parameters around our opportunities (Giles 1995; Hey 1997; Reynolds 1997; Skeggs 1997). Only if there is an understanding of the myriad ways in which, intertwined with other oppressive political realities, class works to determine the distribution of life chances through daily, "simple" acts of discrimination, can a repertoire of challenges begin to be developed. The development of such challenges is important in moving this class project away from a preoccupation with personal identity and towards a commitment to political engagement.

A purely British phenomenon?

In seeking contributions to the book we approached feminists we knew to be interested in the subject and published a call for papers in two feminist journals. We posed a series of questions which were intended to be "'prompts", aimed at helping women get on the inside of those issues on which we wanted them to reflect. These included:

- How do you define yourself in terms of social class, and why?
- Is definition important, why/why not?

- What have been the effects of your experiences of social class?
- How have these experiences shaped your expectations?
- What part have social institutions, e.g. education played in your understanding of class?
- How has class affected and been affected by (dis)ability/nationality/health/ "race"/ethnicity/religion/relationships/sexuality?
- What opportunities/barriers have been presented by class?
- How has it affected your feminism? How has feminism affected your understandings of class?
- How should feminist debates around class develop?
- Are there other important issues not represented above?

From the wide range of countries, regions and cultures about which the contributors write, it is clear that class is not just a British phenomenon. This does not mean that it works in identical ways nor that its markers are the same around the globe. On the other hand neither do the particularities of class mean that it does not exist, for as Avtar Brah argues, it is possible to

> . . . focus on a given context and differentiate between the demarcation of a category as an object of social discourse, as an analytical category, and as a subject of political mobilisation, without making assumptions about [its] permanence or stability across time and space (Brah 1996: 110).

Within the major themes that emerge through the chapters in this volume, some of the reasons for differences between women's experiences and trajectories begin to be more clearly defined. Authors begin to identify the ways in which class positionings (including their own) are constructed and reconstituted on a day-to-day basis and the variety of ways through which they came to understand these processes. They make it clear that how to "do" class is explicitly as well as implicitly taught and that this knowledge is used in accomplishing the politics of class acts. It seems to us that it has become increasingly difficult to define class adequately, or to provide an answer to the question about what are its interconnections with other categories of oppression and discrimination. Paradoxically, though, it becomes easier to identify the particular mechanisms through which class discrimination operates and is mediated through and by gender, sexuality, ethnicity and racism. Avtar Brah has summarized the dilemma of recognizing the complexity of social relations while still being able to act politically.

> The search for grand theories specifying the interconnections between racism, gender and class has been less than productive. They are best construed as historically contingent and context-specific relationships (Brah 1996: 110).

The authors in this collection also illustrate that in relation to their experiences and their feminist aims, and despite the power relations inherent in social class differences, there are connections to be made between classes as well as within them. We need more debates such as these if we are to enhance our knowledge and develop productive ways of breaking the taboo on discussing classed behaviour.

We have known for some time how class can be a unifying category across other divisions. Working-class women of different ethnicities and cultures, for example, have found many points of connection around class despite differences in their experience of and relationship to racism (Zmroczek & Mahony 1996a). Black, South Asian and white women from middle-class backgrounds may be similarly linked by their experiences of class despite being divided by racism or cultural difference. We would argue that there is a need for further research and analysis in these and related areas.

In conclusion

Class needs to be regarded as a key concept in any attempt to understand women's lives. We have suggested that the search for an all-embracing account of what class is and how it works is futile – it is neither stable nor unitary and new experiences of its impacts and implications are increasingly apparent in the global context of the late 1990s. This is not to deny that class oppression and discrimination exist – quite the reverse. It is to suggest that there are more important issues at stake than quests for definition – that is, those of political engagement and commitment to change. In this book it is our intention to contribute to such projects by reflecting critically on the personal/political experience of class.

In an introduction such as this we might now be expected to follow the academic convention of first summarizing the chapters to come and then highlighting the major themes emerging from them. We shall do neither. The book contains a diverse and thought-provoking range of experiences, theories and politics. We would not want to destroy the richness of these by summarizing them. Neither do we want to draw out what is important for us in each chapter or highlight what new insights each contributor has given us. As two white women academics of working-class origin, living and working in late 1990s England, there seems to be no good reason why our responses should be privileged over those of the reader who may be positioned very differently.[3] For this reason and on this occasion we have decided not to accept the bonuses of analysis and synthesis which come with the job of editing a collection. We recognize, of course, that we have had a considerable influence on this volume – we have structured it through our initial "prompts", accepted papers, edited them and finally decided the order in which they would appear.

For this volume, decisions about ordering have been particularly difficult and indicative of the nature of the book. Each chapter contains a network of issues and as such could stand alongside a number of other chapters, depending on one's decisions about which themes should be prioritized. Our belief in the importance of all the themes and our reluctance to privilege one over another led us to try a utilitarian mode of ordering – alphabetically. This, however, produced an incoherent whole. A number of readers and reviewers have also engaged with this problem and suggested alternative ways of sequencing the chapters. Each suggestion has been different. Finally, we settled on the present order by conceptualizing a stream of themes which, in running along together much of the time, create a series of currents and cross-currents. We would like to suggest to teachers intending to use this book in the classroom that one way of encouraging students to engage with the text is to set them an editorial task, i.e. to ask students to re-order the chapters according to their own conceptual framework. We fully expect that a number of different versions will emerge and that this will provoke some lively discussion!

Finally, we would like to thank the authors in this collection. They have responded magnificently to the brief which has required them to delve deeply into a difficult and personal subject. For some this was a new experience, for others, a new endeavour in relation to this subject. They have responded to our requests, been patient with our delays and understanding about the problems inherent in editing an international volume. We have learned a great deal from them for, by teaching us that we know less than we thought, they have enabled us to understand more.

Notes

1. For detailed and informative new insights into how class works in the English school system see Reay (1998).
2. See Skeggs (1997) on the retreat from including class in academic theory and practice (including by some feminists).
3. We would welcome responses from readers on this point. Chris can be contacted on email at c.zmroczek@roehampton.ac.uk.

References

Bertaux, Daniel and Thompson, Paul 1997. *Pathways to Social Class: A Qualitative Approach to Social Mobility.* Oxford: Clarendon Press.

Brah, Avtar 1996. *Cartographies of Diaspora.* London: Routledge.

Giles, Judy 1995. *Women, Identity and Private Life in Britain 1900–50.* Basingstoke: Macmillan.

Hey, Valerie 1997. Northern accent and southern comfort, in Mahony, P. and Zmroczek, C. (eds) (1997b), pp. 140–51.

Lean, G. and Ball, G. 1996. UK Most Unequal Country in the West, *Independent on Sunday*, 21 July.

Mahony, Pat 1998. Girls will be Girls and Boys will be First, in Elwood, J., Epstein, D., Hey, V. and Maw, J. (eds) *Failing Boys? Issues in Gender and Achievement*. Buckingham: Open University Press (forthcoming).

Mahony, Pat and Zmroczek, Christine 1997a. Why Class Matters. See Mahony, P. and Zmroczek, C. (eds) (1997b), pp. 1–7.

Mahony, Pat and Zmroczek, Christine (eds) 1997b. *Class Matters: "Working-Class" Women's Perspectives on Social Class*. London: Taylor & Francis.

Pakulski, Jan and Waters, Malcolm 1996. *The Death of Class*. London: Sage.

Reay, Diane 1998. *Class Work: Mothers' Involvement in their Children's Primary Schooling*. London: UCL Press.

Reynolds, Tracey 1997. Class Matters, "Race" Matters, Gender Matters. See Mahony P. and Zmroczek, C. (eds) (1997b), pp. 8–17.

Skeggs, Beverley 1997. *Formations of Class and Gender*. London: Sage.

Zmroczek, Christine and Mahony, Pat 1996a. Lives beyond the text, in Bell, D. and Klein, R. (eds) *Radically Speaking: Feminism Reclaimed*. Melbourne: Spinifex and London: Zed Press.

Zmroczek, Christine and Mahony, Pat 1996b. Women's Studies and Working Class Women, in Ang-Lygate, M., Corrin, C. and Henry, M. (eds) *Desperately Seeking Sisterhood: Still Challenging and Building*. London: Taylor & Francis.

CHAPTER ONE

What does it mean to be a middle-class woman in Botswana?

Changu Mannathoko

This chapter will explore the relationship between social class and gender within the context of my experiences as a black woman, mother, feminist, Catholic, professional middle-class, university lecturer and member of a minority ethnic group in Botswana. The relationship between gender and social class is significant as a basis for uniting or dividing women. I am a citizen of Botswana, a country situated in Southern Africa. Botswana is a former British colony, which was known as Bechuanaland Protectorate when it was under British rule from 1885 to 1965. Botswana's neighbours are Zimbabwe, Zambia, Namibia and South Africa. The country has enjoyed 30 years of stable and peaceful democratic rule. The population of Botswana is 1,334,000. There are more women than men in the country because men make up 48 per cent of the population whereas women are 52 per cent. Moreover, the country has a large dependent population because 43.6 per cent of the population is within the 0–14 age group (Botswana Government 1996a).

The unravelling of my situation as a middle-class woman will be done through the investigation of how my experiences can contribute to the understanding of the interaction between gender and social class. The fundamental issues will be discussed by addressing the following questions: (a) Who am I? (b) What are the historical and educational underpinnings of my class position? (c) What are the opportunities and barriers presented by my class position? and (d) How has feminism affected my understanding of social class and how should the feminist debate around social class develop?

Who am I?

I am a professional middle-class woman who works as a senior lecturer in the Department of Educational Foundations at the University of Botswana. As a senior lecturer, I am a white-collar worker whose work is mainly organized around the specific bodies of expert knowledge connected to university research, teaching, professional and community service. This expert knowledge is exclusively owned by the university, the state, UN organizations and donor agencies. The knowledge is certified by the university, the state and internationally recognized institutions and nation states in the North. I only earn an income when working, unlike a ruling-class person who receives a flow of income generated by others. At the same time I am a woman with several identities and multiple responsibilities in both the private and public spheres (Mannothoko 1992). These multiple responsibilities are intertwined with my several identities as a black woman who is a citizen of an independent African state, professional middle-class, a single parent, and member of two ethnic groups.

I was brought up by professional middle-class parents. I have three sisters and I am the first child in the family. My parents were educated during the colonial period (1940s) and were some of the few Batswana who were qualified primary school teachers in the 1950s. In the 1960s both my parents upgraded their qualifications and my father obtained a law degree from a university in the United Kingdom. My mother's responsibilities as a mother and wife did not provide her with the opportunity to further her studies as much as she would have liked. Time and again she gave first priority to the family needs instead of her own. However, her management abilities shone through and from 1968 to 1992 she participated in politics and became a councillor. In the early 1970s she became the second woman mayor of the capital city, Gaborone. She was elected to this position for three terms in succession. My father was a high-level civil servant from 1966 to 1979. Immediately after independence he was appointed the first Botswana ambassador to Zambia and then he became a permanent secretary in several government ministries. He retired from government in 1979 and joined BP (Botswana) as the managing director till he retired in 1991. He now spends most of his time at his cattle ranch. I was therefore brought up by busy professional parents in an environment where it is common practice for both parents to work in the public sphere. I grew up very much aware of the multiple roles my mother had to perform in both the private and public spheres. In the private sphere my mother's duties were eased by domestic workers who were employed to take care of us and the household chores. It was common practice for people of my parents' status to employ domestic workers.

My parents come from different ethnic groups and met in a Catholic boarding mission school when they were secondary school students in the 1940s. My mother is from the majority ethnic group (the Tswana) and her language, "Setswana", is the national language of Botswana. As a national language, Setswana is the medium of instruction in schools and is used in the national mass media. In contrast, my father is from a minority ethnic group and his language, "Ikalanga", is not taught in schools or used in the mass media. When my parents married in 1952, marriages between the two ethnic groups were unusual and my father's ethnic group was looked down upon by the Tswana ethnic group. It was education which brought my parents together and contributed to the erosion of the ethnic borders. Both my parents' ethnic groups have patrilineal lineages and as per tradition I have taken on my father's lineage. However, since my mother is a Motswana, I grew up speaking Setswana at home. I came to speak Ikalanga in 1962–63 when my sister and I lived with my paternal uncle in my father's home village when our parents were being educated in the UK. In the village we were exposed to Ikalanga both in the home and at school. By the time we rejoined our parents in 1964 we spoke Ikalanga fluently. My first language is Setswana, second language English and the third language Ikalanga. I am least fluent in the last because once back with my parents, I was never taught it at school and at home I either spoke Setswana or English. English is the language of the professional middle class in the country and is the medium of communication and instruction in the family, schools, tertiary education and the workplace. The state has selected English and Setswana as the two official languages in the country. English is the medium of instruction from Standard 4 in primary schools right up to tertiary level. This gives middle-class children an academic edge in schools because English is spoken in everyday life in the home.

At the time of writing I am a single parent with a 16-year-old son whom I am bringing up with the invaluable assistance of my parents and my extended family. The father of my son is a Zimbabwe citizen whom I met in Botswana during the Zimbabwe liberation struggle. He was a political activist who was sent to Botswana by the ZANU PF as one of their representatives. We were engaged to get married when we planned to have our son. Ironically, though it was the Zimbabwe liberation struggle which brought us together, the end of the liberation struggle in 1980 tolled the end of the relationship. The father of my son returned to Zimbabwe where he found a well-paid job and bought a high-cost house in a former white middle-class suburb. We began to drift apart because he became absorbed in making his way in the newly independent Zimbabwe while I remained absorbed in the intellectual pursuits of teaching, further studies, work in Non-Governmental Organizations (NGOs), research, writing and caring for our son. We amicably parted ways in 1982. What keeps us in touch is our mutual commitment to our child.

The historical and educational underpinnings of my class position

There are gender-based historical and educational underpinnings to my situation as a middle-class woman. These gender-based hierarchies, ideologies and power relations underpinning my situation have historical roots in the pre-colonial Botswana nation states and British colonial rule. The dominant gender ideology in pre-colonial Botswana states was patriarchal, largely serving male interests. The ideology regulated the productive and personal relationships between men and women at all levels of labour production. In that way men's political, economic and social domination were perpetuated. However, the sharp division of labour that pertains in today's society was not prevalent then. Women and men's work did not rigidly conform to Western ideas of the private–public sphere divide. Women had the primary responsibility for agricultural production and the harshness of the climate made them also engage in food gathering to supplement the family diet. The role of parenting was not restricted to the biological mother; older women and younger children participated in childrearing enabling the biological mothers to undertake other duties (Mafela 1993).

The dominant masculine ideology underwent important structural transformations because of the advent of Christianity and colonialism with major consequences for traditional patriarchy, governance, education and economic self-sufficiency. The Christian missionaries brought to Botswana, Victorian-based ideas of gender reflecting the Western woman's role in nineteenth-century industrial Europe. In these European societies women's domesticity was crucial to the creation of a particular moral order which catered for the requirements of discipline and social order.

Western education in Botswana came with the advent of Christianity, and missionary education primarily concentrated on teaching the Bible and elements of literacy. Around the 1860s, Christianity became the state religion of several prominent Tswana states (Parsons 1984). Therefore, the first schools built in the country were the initiatives of local communities and Christian missionaries.

Girls' education was not always accepted among the Batswana; the acceptance was gradually moderated by pre-capitalist patriarchal economic and cultural understandings and practices of women's work. This accounts for why girls continued to be used in agricultural and household activities during the colonial era, and testifies to the submergence of Western patriarchal hegemony under the needs and interests of the Tswana traditional patriarchs. These contradictions were very evident because of Western domestic education and training policies and practices spread by Christianity, and indirectly supporting colonialism. This domestic education theme was opposed by males across the whole spectrum of Tswana society because it worked contrary to their interests and threatened their power base. The results were tensions, factions as well as opposition from the men.

Among the Tswana commoners, young men and boys from lower classes continued to herd cattle instead of attending school. The acceleration of labour migration to South African mines further bonded San/Basarwa/Bushmen labour to cattle herding to release adult male Tswana people for the mines (Parsons 1984). The missionary form of women and men's education was gender specific and aimed at changing the role of Tswana women in line with missionaries "civilizing" and religious objectives. Mission schools were co-educational but the formal and hidden curricula domesticated women and prepared men for work in the public sphere (Mafela 1993). The selective tradition was at work in this regard because the dynamism of the prevailing political economy ensured that women's education did not remain concerned with domestic work alone; instead it became academic as well.

It is important to keep note of the historical and educational changes in the situation of women in Botswana because the transformations help explain the gender order I live and work in as a middle-class woman. The modernization drive is another important historical change which contributed to changed gender relations and the emergence of the middle-class as we know it today.

Modernization and the migrant labour system

During the nineteenth century, modernization in the region of Southern Africa was concentrated in South Africa. The modernization of South Africa accelerated in the late nineteenth century with the discovery of diamonds and gold in that country. The impact on traditional Southern Africa communities was profound (Schapera 1938; Mogwe 1991). The modernization drive changed gender relations because it led to the migrant labour system and the emergence of the phenomenon of the single female headed family.

By the 1920s large numbers of men from colonial states in Southern Africa (including Botswana, Lesotho, Swaziland, Malawi, Mozambique and Zimbabwe), migrated to South Africa to work in the mines as migrant labourers. Botswana had already begun to understand that mining stimulated modernization, leading to economic development. The traditional family system gradually began to disintegrate as peasant women learnt to cope without their menfolk. In other words, at Independence all Botswana men and women had practical experience of how the rapid modernization of South Africa was crippling their communities socially and economically. Therefore, when diamonds were discovered in Botswana in 1968, the whole nation understood that the mining boom heralded modernity and therefore development for their respective communities. True enough, the state did not disappoint them because the massive construction of new mining towns, rural roads and schools mushroomed all over the country, confirming to the Botswana that modernity is linked to development. There is a need to address the critical problem of the contrary relations between modernization and gender relations.

Many married women learnt to bring up their children without their husbands. In turn, the contradictions between modern and traditional family life resulted in the emergence of the "single mothers" phenomenon. A trend emerged of single-parent families within which children were brought up by the "single mother" together with her family.

I am one of the single middle-class women who are at the head of a family. These single parent families are currently the norm and in the urban areas we the unmarried single mothers are bringing up our children without the direct participation of the extended family system, instead we depend on women domestic workers to care for our children while we are out working in the public sphere. The single mother phenomenon cuts across all social classes nationwide; it is no longer the preserve of peasant women. The majority of us single mothers have never been married, and only a minority are divorcees. Traditional Botswana values do not approve of children being born outside marriage, however, modernity has led to the disintegration of these family values. Consequently, the single mother phenomenon has transformed traditional values in a variety of ways:

- Throughout the country there are visible groups of women like me who are in control of their own households without male support. Many professional middle-class women like myself are single mothers who are financially and socially independent.
- Throughout the country there are children who are growing up without parenting from either the mother or the father. Most of us single mothers rely on the men on the maternal side of the family to provide the male role models. My father and uncles play a major role in this regard.

Little is known about the psychological and social implications of the increasing number of children being brought up by single women because no sociological research has been done in this regard (Mannathoko 1995). But this situation forms an important background to understanding my situation as a single middle-class woman teaching in Botswana's only university.

After 1945, the changes in the budding capitalist political economy were transforming the aspirations of men and women. Men's migration to South African mines changed the character of the communal family and many women in the rural areas began to adjust to living by themselves. They began to work in both the private and public spheres. Increasing employment opportunities provided women with the chance to work away from the homestead, in the public sphere. However, in the education arena the overwhelming majority of teachers educated were men. At independence (1966) most teachers in schools from primary level onwards were men. The historical dimensions of the migrant labour system to South Africa have changed the power dynamics between men and women regardless of social class. Furthermore, these changes have led to the legitimation of the single-parent family, in which the parent is a woman. Western educated men dominated in other spheres of employment during in the colonial period including in the civil service as clerks and interpreters. When Botswana became independent, several of the male teachers moved into positions in government as members of parliament, government ministers, district commissioners, ambassadors and top-level government administrators.

The social stratification system

By 1970 there was a slow but determined emergence of a capitalist based social class. By 1990 there were six distinctive social classes in Botswana society, namely: the ruling class, traditional patriarchs, middle class, working class, peasant class and the under class.

Historically, in pre-colonial Botswana, it was the cultures, politics and economics of the *traditional patriarchs* which dominated in the diverse nation states and chiefdoms. These traditional patriarchs were the male kings, chiefs and headmen who were the official representatives of these nation states. More significantly, these traditional patriarchs survived colonialism and have significant power and authority in today's Botswana rural areas, where 44.3 per cent of the population resides (Botswana Government 1996a). Traditional patriarchs still prevail in current Botswana society as chiefs and are viewed as the custodians of traditional cultures, politics and values that are passed on from generation to generation. Officially, the traditional patriarchs are the representatives of the state in rural areas and are paid by the state to rule their communities. However, in contrast to the pre-colonial period, their authority and power have been curtailed and they govern on behalf of the state.

Both within and outside the Botswana state, it is the values and cultures of the *ruling class* which dominate, its members drawn from the peasant, middle and working class strata of society. However, since the 1980s, the intensification of class formation with distinctive features of capital accumulation, such as investment in property development (estates) and stock markets is consolidating the power of the middle class as a ruling elite and marginalizing the working and peasant classes, distancing them from the relations of ruling. Notwithstanding, the ruling class is composed of the political elite (cabinet ministers, parliamentarians); the highest level professional elite within state ministries, namely permanent secretaries, and boards of directors and executive managers of parastatal corporations and lastly the board of directors and executive managers of Debswana Diamond Mining Corporation. I have adopted Connell et al.'s (1982) definition of ruling class, because it aptly incorporates the social class and patriarchal aspects of the social group.

Individuals holding the above key positions within the state and private sector belong to the ruling class because their practices are within the framework of an extended network of people doing similar work. The result of their patterns of activities is the reinforcing of a generic system of relations of power and privilege in the above institutions. Within the state and the society at large the ruling class controls power and authority. Together with Connell, I have also adopted Haralambos with Heald's (1980) definition of the middle class and working class. Often the middle class and working class are further classified into occupational categories.

What distinguishes the ruling class from the *middle class* is that the latter are not as directly involved in the directing and organizing of other people's work as the former. We, the middle class, are white-collar workers whose work is mainly organized around specific bodies of expert knowledge, exclusively owned by a particular group, and certified by the state and/or internationally recognized institutions and nation states in the North. The middle class do not receive a flow of income generated by others; and only earn an income when working (Connell et al. 1982). Therefore as a social class we are a fragmented social stratum because it is composed of diverse occupational groups.

The *lower middle class* (routine white-collar workers) is mainly composed of clerks, secretaries and sales staff. This group accounts for the majority of the female white-collar labour force in Botswana. For instance, 66 per cent of clerks are women (Botswana Government 1991a). The lower middle class's market advantages over the working class are that their jobs are more secure; they work shorter hours; and they have longer holidays.

The *working class* is made up of blue-collar workers who do not have the wherewithall to acquire a large share of what they produce, neither through ownership of capital, nor through power nor authority in organizations. This class consists of three social groups: skilled manual workers; semi-skilled manual workers; and unskilled manual workers. They share common interests through political party membership, unions and self-help and neighbourhood networks.

The *peasant class* is characterized by small-scale agricultural production and relative political isolation from the urban working classes. Historically, subsistence farming is their main means of livelihood; produce from arable and livestock farming is primarily for home consumption because selling occurs only on those occasions when there is a surplus. The peasant class may be differentiated into rich, middling and poor peasants.

The *underclass* is in fact a very ambiguous social category. Of all those persons whose context for making a livelihood is the real content of abject poverty, they exist in the most extreme conditions of deprivation and destitution, such as landlessness, lack of basic skills of production, unemployment and alienation.

Certain subcategories are thrown up by this primarily six-part classification of Botswana society. In terms of the market situation, the professionals can be divided into higher and lower professionals. The *higher professionals* incorporate judges, lawyers, chief education officers, deputy permanent secretaries, principals of colleges, headteachers of schools, planners, engineers, architects, doctors, university lecturers and accountants. The *lower professionals* include teachers, nurses, college lecturers, social workers, librarians and education officers.

As Connell et al. (1982) explain, the middle class's interests are unstable, whereas the interests of the ruling class, working class and peasantry are stable. The middle class do not have defined sets of cultural institutions committed to the expression and defence of their basic shared interests. The gender-based social class contradictions also permeate the economy. The economic boom of the 1980s has not been matched by socio-economic development for the majority of women, children, workers, peasants and minority groups. The wide economic gap between the few in the wealthy ruling class and high professional middle class on the one hand, and the poor majority on the other, is threatening the country's democratic principles of social justice, unity and self-reliance. Poverty affects more than 60 per cent of all households in Botswana (Botswana Government 1996b).

What, I think, underpins the country's unjust economic policies is the capitalist, free-market policies coupled with a weak manufacturing base, and dependency on international capital. The state's income policies espouse a free market philosophy to stimulate individual initiative, but do not directly tackle the impact of the capitalist policies on the poor majority.

The policies do not protect the most disadvantaged sections of society, including low-income women and the unemployed. The policies do not provide minimum wages for domestic and agricultural workers because the state argues that it would be impossible to enforce them. Cash crop farming and cattle ranching are dominated and owned by men from the ruling elite, professional middle class and traditional patriarchs. Cattle are an asset in a society which makes stock farming highly lucrative. There is a skewed distribution of cattle wealth. In the rural areas men own a higher percentage of the cattle than the women; in the mid-1980s, 83 per cent of the herds having over 150 cattle were owned by men, while women owned only 17 per cent of the same size herds (Botswana Government and UNICEF 1989).

The capitalist income policies inevitably widen income disparities between social groups, regions, women and men which is contrary to the state's published democratic principles of social justice, equality, development and self-reliance. There is conflict and struggle inherent in the above social class and gender inequities. For instance, since 1989 the salaries and benefits of professionals in both the public service and business sector have escalated while the state is refusing to make reasonable increases in the incomes of manual workers. In 1984, 31 per cent of women between the ages of 15 and 34 years were unemployed compared with 19 per cent of men (Botswana Government 1991b).

It is a complex task to allocate myself as a woman to a social class. I based the allocation on some measure of my occupation as a senior lecturer in the university. The middle class is a fragmented social stratum which is why it is difficult to classify women within it. The social dualities and dichotomies which differentiate between males and females further complicate the unpacking of the internal dynamics within the middle class. Middle-class women and men experience this class differently as masculinity and femininity impact on the different ways they experience social class. To illustrate, the gatekeepers in all the policy-making bodies in government, parliament and business are predominantly men. In the teaching profession where I belong, teaching and lecturing have hierarchical and bureaucratic career and promotional structures. This traditional structure is evident in the dominance of men in the management of education institutions such as schools and the Ministry of Education (Botswana Government 1993).

In all the teacher education institutions (TEIs) the gatekeepers are overwhelmingly male, including in primary level training institutions. The policy-making bodies and administrative positions in all the colleges are occupied almost exclusively by men. Only one of the eight colleges has a female principal. As can be seen from Table 1.1, the same pattern of underrepresentation of women is reflected in almost all key positions and in the decision-making bodies. Table 1.1 clearly illustrate middle-class women's difficulties in achieving career progress and middle-class men's relative ease of promotion in the hierarchical and linear TEIs' career structures. In other words, women lecturers hit a glass ceiling when they arrive halfway up the lecturing career ladder.

Table 1.1 Teacher education policy-making bodies

Board or committee	Number		
	Male	Female	Total
National Council on Teacher Education (NTTC)	12	3	15
Colleges Advisory Board	15	5	20
Principals of colleges	7	1	8
Dean, Faculty of Education	1	0	1
Permanent Secretary, Ministry of Education	1	0	1
Chief Education Officers, Ministry of Education	3	2	5
Board of Affiliated Colleges	10	5	15

Source: Adapted from 1994 National Council on Teacher Education Records.

Opportunities and barriers presented by my class position

The opportunities and barriers presented by my class position will be analyzed through a discussion of: the commonalities shared by women regardless of social class; how my professional middle-class privileges inform social behaviour; and the unjust relationship between myself as a professional middle-class woman and the working-class domestic worker in my employ.

Botswana women share commonalities with regard to the patriarchal culture and laws which make all women subordinate to men irrespective of social class. Laws such as the Marriage Act and Citizenship Act impact negatively on all women. The Marriage Act treats women as either children or idiots. Within the Act marital power gives men the authority and power to control women and make decisions on their behalf. In turn, the Citizenship Act of 1982 gave citizenship to people born in Botswana and to children born from the marriage of a local male citizen to a foreign woman. The Act held that a female citizen of Botswana married to a foreigner could not pass her citizenship to her children born after her marriage. The Act was opposed by some citizens especially women's organizations such as Emang Basadi and Women and Law of Southern Africa (WLSA). Unity Dow, a middle-class woman lawyer decided to take the government to court because the Act discriminated against her children (Dow 1995). The High Court ruled in her favour but the state appealed to the Court of Appeal against the decision of the High Court. The Appeal court ruled in favour of Unity Dow. In 1995 parliament passed a new law known as the Citizenship Amendment Act of 1995. This amendment of the Act has redressed an injustice which affected married women of all classes. Resistance to oppressive patriarchal laws unite women across class borders. Women in this instance are united by their common experiences of gender stratification rather than divided by social class.

My status as a middle-class woman gives me access to power and opportunities which a peasant or working-class woman has no access to. My education, qualifications, occupation and networks open doors for me which are never opened for women of lower classes. To highlight this relationship between gender and social class I will discuss the contradictions linked to the relationship between me and my domestic worker.

It is common practice in Botswana and the rest of Southern Africa for ruling-class, middle-class and working-class women to employ women domestic servants as I do, to take care of children and household chores. Together with employing domestic servants, we the professional middle class send our children to day care centres, because we assume that day care centres care for children better and believe in the advantages connected to children's early exposure to schooling.

The woman I employ as a domestic worker has been working for me for the last 11 years. She is a single woman who has never married and has three children. She is from a peasant background, her parents being subsistence farmers who have difficulty in feeding all their children. Her schooling was curtailed because she had to assist her parents to provide for the younger siblings and she became pregnant before she had learnt literacy skills. She has played a critical role in the upbringing of my son. I encouraged her interest in educating herself and she enrolled for literacy classes which she terminated when I was in the UK doing my PhD because of illness and difficulties in adjusting to her new job as a cleaner at the university. When I returned from the UK in 1995, she continued her job as a cleaner while working for me as a part-time domestic worker. She is now continuing with her functional literacy classes. Her meagre income not only feeds her children but also her elderly parents.

Women domestic workers like the woman I employ are from the peasant and working classes. They leave their own children with their extended families in the rural areas, and try to earn a living working for urban ruling-class, middle-class and working-class households (Boyd and Mugabe 1989; Letsie 1992). Clearly, these traditional close-knit family networks serve a vital purpose in freeing peasant and working-class women from confinement to the private sphere. At the same time, there is a growing number of both married and single mothers from middle-class and working-class families employed away from their extended families and therefore depending on domestic servants to look after children while they work in the public sphere.

Professional middle-class women's family responsibilities are eased by the availability of cheap women domestic workers who take care of our children and housekeeping while we are out in the public workplace. Similar patterns pertain in countries of the South such as Pakistan, South Africa and Zimbabwe where domestic workers free professional women for work in the public sphere. Domestic help is still widely available in Pakistan and thus academic women are, to a large extent, relieved of the burdens of the "second shift" faced by their sisters in many countries (Malik and Hussain 1994: 138).

This matter of the employment of women domestic workers (unskilled manual workers) to ease the workload of ruling-class and middle-class women, displays the complexities and lines of oppression that interface between gender and social class. It confirms the point made by feminists, that there are power based differences to the conceptualization of women, mediated by social divisions such as social class and ethnicity.

Feminism and my understanding of social class

I am committed to the feminist vision of liberating all women regardless of social class, ethnicity or "race" from oppression by men. At the same time I find feminism a liberating influence for me because it challenges me to address the difficult and complex problem of how to liberate divided women. Feminism assists me in being sensitive to the tensions and contradictions between social class and gender. Feminist theories of difference and oppression assisted me to unpack the patriarchal bases of the barriers against me as woman while at the same time its theories have provided me with the wherewithal to empower myself in both the private and public spheres. My conceptualization of the liberation of women is grounded in the principle of empowerment. Empowerment has several dimensions which I find useful for application in a variety of arenas including: my personal life, academic duties as a university senior lecturer, and my feminist and activist work in non-governmental organizations (NGOs).

My personal life

Feminism and empowerment have assisted me to be more confident in myself and have enabled me to be secure in my single state. I acknowledge that higher education, a comfortable professional middle-class lifestyle and the support of my parents have made it easier for me to accept that I have opted out of marriage. I have no objection to having a relationship with a like-minded man, but I have no desire for the relationship to end in marriage (Bhebe and Mosha 1996). I value my independent lifestyle. This jealous guarding of my independence is also reflected in my refusal to share a house with the man I go out with. To me sharing a house is uncomfortably like marriage and would compel me to compromise my lifestyle. I am not alone in opting out of marriage because recent research in the country shows that education is making women opt out of marriage (Davies and Gunawardena 1992; Mannathoko 1995). It is the norm for single women to have children, but these women would rather not marry. Moreover, research in schools informs us that young men perceive marriages as important for them to progress in life. To men marriage stabilizes their lives and assists them to develop their careers. In contrast, women perceive marriage as limiting their freedom and compromising their careers.

University senior lecturer

Feminist theories and feminism are invaluable to me in my work as a senior lecturer. In my teaching and research feminist theories provide me with the prime perspectives I require to understand gender injustices in society. These gender injustices are many of the enduring contradictions inherent in relationships between males and females living, working and learning in Botswana society. My theorizing of the gendered politics and cultures of the institutions I live and work in aptly assist me to understand and unpack the hierarchical and bureaucratic character of the state and education institutions.

For example, in workshops for women students, teachers and educational managers, discourse theory assists me to facilitate those who wish to learn to empower themselves. I educate and train girls and women by encouraging them to give voice to their common and differing needs. The empowerment process includes educating girls and women to speak out and powerfully give voice to their ways of knowing. This is done through gender analysis of male and female discourses and discussion of how language is a tool in the control of power within social institutions.

Feminism has made me learn that the acquiring and changing of attitudes is mainly an emotional learning process which cannot be transferred from cognitive learning processes such as rational transfer of information. What quality education and training must deal with is the need for female and male students, teachers and education managers to learn how to confront their own personal knowledge and understand how the gender stereotypes within this personal knowledge are at the core of their resistance to the reform of gender relations. The reform of gender relations represents the innovative public knowledge which threatens the power of the dominant masculine ideology. For me this a major discovery because in my teacher education courses and in-service education I spend time facilitating the students to focus on the tensions between personal knowledge and public knowledge and to acknowledge their own gender stereotypes and biases. They then move on to train their students also to break down the barriers between personal knowledge and public knowledge. My PhD thesis focused on the relationship between gender, ideology and the state in teacher education. As a consequence the majority of the graduate students I supervise are doing research projects or dissertations on women's studies or gender issues. My undergraduate courses also integrate gender issues, especially in the research projects.

Non-Governmental Organizations (NGOs)

Since high school I have been involved in activist work in NGOs. This is largely due to the influence of my mother who has always been involved in women's NGOs. However, it was only in 1988 that I began to look at the NGOs I was involved with from a feminist perspective. The reason is that I became a feminist in 1988 when I began to develop interest in feminist research and joined hands with women's NGOs which were actively opposing the 1984 Citizenship Act which made women second-class citizens.

I began to integrate women's issues and gender analysis into the NGOs I was chairing, namely the Association of Botswana Tertiary Lecturers (ABOTEL), Botswana Educational Research Association (BERA), Mmegi Publishing Trust, Mmegi Publishing House, Educational Research Network in Eastern and Southern Africa (ERNESA). In the research associations we began to conduct workshops on gender research and encouraged members to undertake women's studies research and gender research. I encouraged the management boards to elect more women on to the boards.

Conclusion

Gender and class are intertwined structures because gender is incorporated into the meaning of social class. My life as a middle-class woman is structured by a complex combination of gender and class. This simultaneously inspires and troubles me as a member of the feminist movement in Southern Africa.

References

Bhebe, B. and Mosha, A.C. 1996. *The concept of women remaining single and its economic consequences: a case study, Gaborone City*. Gaborone, University of Botswana.

Botswana Government 1991a. *National Census Report*. Gaborone: Government Printer.

Botswana Government 1991b. *Labour Force Survey*. Central Statistics Office. Gaborone: Government Printer.

Botswana Government 1993. *Report of the National Commission on Education*. Gaborone: Government Printer.

Botswana Government 1996a. *Women and Men in Botswana, Facts and Figures*. Gaborone: Central Statistics Office.

Botswana Government 1996b. *Poverty Alleviation Study*. Gaborone: Botswana Institute of Development Policy Analysis (BIDPA).

Botswana Government and UNICEF 1989. *Status of Women and Children in Botswana*. Gaborone: UNICEF.

Boyd, D. and Mugabe, M. 1989. *An Evaluation of the Situation of Domestic Workers in Botswana*. Gaborone: National Institute of Research and Documentation, University of Botswana.

Connell, R.W., Ashenden, D.J., Kessler, G.W. and Dowset, G.W. 1982. *Making the Difference: Schools, Families and Social Division*. Sydney: Allen & Unwin.

Davies, L. and Gunawardena, C. 1992. *Women and Men in Educational Management: An International Inquiry*. Paris: International Institute of Educational Planning, UNESCO.

Dow, U. 1995. *The Citizenship Case*. Gaborone: Lentswe la Lesedi.

Haralambos, M. with Heald, R.M. 1980. *Sociology: Themes and Perspectives*. London: Bell & Hyman.

Letsie, L. 1992. *An Investigation of Appropriate Methodology for Research into Gender Issues – The Case of Domestic Workers in Botswana*. Unpublished MEd Dissertation, Gaborone, University of Botswana.

Mafela, L. 1993. *Competing Gender Ideologies in Education in Bechuanaland Protectorate, c.1880–c.1945*. PhD dissertation, Chicago, Northwestern University.

Malik, L. and Hussain, N. 1994. Women in higher education in Pakistan: separate but equal? in Stiver-Lie, S., Malik, L. and Harris, D. (eds) *The Gender Gap in Higher Education*. London: Kogan Page.

Mannathoko, C.E. 1992. Feminist theories and the study of gender issues in Southern Africa, in Meena, R. (ed.) *Gender in Southern Africa: Conceptual and Theoretical Issues*. Harare: SAPES Books.

Mannathoko, C.E. 1995. *Gender, ideology and the state in Botswana's teacher education*. Unpublished PhD thesis. Birmingham, UK: University of Birmingham.

Mogwe, G. 1991. *Experiences of Batswana women during the Second World War*. History essay submitted in partial fulfilment of the requirements for the BA Degree, Gaborone, University of Botswana.

Parsons, Q.N. 1984. Education and development in pre-colonial Botswana to 1965, in Crowder, M. (ed.) *Education for Development: Proceedings of a Symposium*. Gaborone: Botswana Society and Macmillan, pp. 21–45.

Schapera, I. 1938. *A History of Tswana Law and Custom*. London: Cassell.

CHAPTER TWO

The "new Hebrew's" new woman: growing up Israeli and middle-class

Ronit Lentin

Each morning at seven, six days a week, Father would set out, in his van, clad in his long khaki shorts and knee-high khaki socks, to his small electrics factory in Haifa bay. He would return, smelling of metal – Father worked with his hands – at around four, have his mid-day meal and take a nap for an hour. This was quiet time – we children had to be silent. We also had to be silent between two and four, the traditional *Schlaf Stunde* in which Mother, and our neighbours, immigrants from *Mitteleuropa* (central Europe – Czechoslovakia, Germany, Austria and, like us, Bukovina), all rested. When Father rose, there was afternoon coffee and cake. Occasionally, Mother's women friends, and their children, would join us for strudel or cheese *buchtels*, my very favourites.

Father invented the first Hebrew washing machine. He called it, in his poetic style, *Kal Li* (It's Easy for Me). A more advanced model was called *Kal Li Me'od* (It's Very Easy for Me). He did not have the necessary capital to develop an automatic model. The big boys imported Italian models, and his Hebrew washing machine became but a memory. He continued working in his factory, making motors, generators and other electrical components. When he and his partner fell on hard times, mostly because of the partner's bad management, they did other things to make ends meet, and borrowed money from family members, money they were not always able to repay.

Father spent his spare time painting and fishing. He was a competent painter – many of his canvases hang on my walls – but painting was merely a hobby, although in later years he was toying with the idea of trying to sell his oils and watercolours. He taught me about art, took me with him to painting classes, and told me the plots of the operas he listened to on the radio. He took me to the Israel Philharmonic concerts to hear Glenn Gould, Arthur Rubinstein, Gina Bachauer, Leonard Bernstein. When Beethoven's Fifth piano concerto was broadcast, he used to wave his hands, saying that in this previous incarnation he must have been a conductor's baton. Our house was always filled with books, art, music and friends, with whom we went on many hikes throughout Israel.

Mother was always reading, usually in English, a language she had studied with a private tutor in her northern Romanian home. She is a keen linguist and recently added Spanish to German, her mother tongue, Hebrew, Romanian, Yiddish, English and French. She always seemed busy, cooking, baking, gardening, reading, visiting, going to the theatre, apart from doing all the housework. I grew up with the belief that she, like her women friends, some of whom ran private kindergartens or made clothes at home, was a working woman. When I discovered that between 1954 and 1989, the proportion of Israeli women aged 15 and over in the civilian labour force grew from 21 per cent to only 40 per cent (Izraeli 1991: 168), I was astounded; Mother and her friends all seemed so busy, so articulate, so able. I know now that Mother would have made a successful public administrator – she has been and is still involved in running, on a voluntary basis, the Haifa branch of Akim, the Israeli Association for people with learning difficulties. But Father refused to allow her to pursue an independent career, or work outside the home. When things became difficult, she worked for him, keeping the firm's books. When he died, she continued until the business wound down. At the age of 63, she opened a second-hand bookshop, using her love and knowledge of books to delight her faithful customers and earn a modest income.

When Father met her, Mother was working as a radar controller for the British RAF, in Haifa, where she moved in order to get away from her parents in Tel Aviv. Grandmother believed that a woman who worked for a living was not much better than a prostitute. A relatively new immigrant – she had fled Czernowitz with her parents and brother in 1940, on the last week it was possible to do so – Mother was criticized by Father's less recent immigrant friends for wearing lipstick. She did not fit in with their image of the tough pioneering women, many of whom began life in Israel as members of a labour group or a kibbutz. Although she came from Bukovina, and although her mother tongue was German, she had trouble convincing his German and Czech friends that she wasn't Romanian. Romanian Jews were low in the socio-ethnic hierarchy. When asked where our parents came from (a question often asked in order to establish one's place in the Israeli hierarchy), we mumbled, embarrassed, something about Bukovina, which was "not really Romania".

When Mother's parents fled Czernowitz, they left all their family's wealth – land, houses, banks, sawmills, hotels – behind. All they could take with them was one single hamper and some Sterling, which Grandmother hid in her silk stockings. In Tel Aviv they settled in a two-roomed rented apartment, in which Grandmother lived out her life. My gentle Grandfather, who did not manage to re-establish his timber business in Israel, because of broken promises by political and business associates, died, so they say, of a broken heart, a broken dream.

I often wonder if Father also died, at 62, of a sudden coronary, of a broken dream, a disappointment. He had had heart troubles before. And depression. But my parents never spoke about it. Nor did they mention their growing financial problems. After all, we were upstanding people, and they believed there was little point in upsetting us children. Or so Mother said in later years.

In *From Class to Nation*, David Ben Gurion, the pre-state political leader and Israel's first Prime Minister, argues that the class of the Hebrew worker in the land of Israel is fundamentally national, and that the nationality of the Jewish employer has essential class elements (Ben Gurion 1933: 316). This conflation of class and nationality led to a situation where social class is rarely seriously debated outside of national considerations in the Israeli context. Carmi and Rosenfeld link the emergence of Israeli militaristic nationalism in the wake of Israel's military victories, to social stratification. They argue that one consequence of Israeli militaristic nationalism was the emergence of a new bureaucratic elite which assumed economic, political and military powers and increased its share of income from 17 to 20 per cent of the national cake. The "old" middle class – business people, landowners, importers, industrialists and top civil servants – was augmented by a "new" middle class – contractors, suppliers and professionals – who worked for the Ministry of Defence and for the defence industry and, together with top defence civil servants and army officers, dominated the Israeli economy and politics (Carmi and Rosenfeld 1993: 300–3).

According to Sammy Smooha (1993), who studies class and ethnic divisions in Israeli society, Israel is a middle-class society. Analyzing Israeli class divisions using economic and occupational criteria, Smooha states that in a society where most of the population is not Western (but originating from Eastern Europe and the Middle East), and where two-thirds of the labour force are engaged in service industries and three-quarters have nine years of schooling or more, 14 per cent of the Israeli population live below the poverty line. Working-class people are engaged mostly in manufacturing and low-status services. The middle class, the largest stratum, is engaged mostly in clerical, sales, services and technical occupations. Average Israelis "tend to work hard in order to maintain a western life style, own an apartment in a decent neighbourhood, raise two to three children, are dedicated to the education of their children and to their own material welfare . . . [despite] lower wages and higher taxes and prices in comparison with the West" (Smooha 1993: 175). The upper middle class includes professionals, managers and small employers and the elite comprises the upper echelons of the economy, the bureaucracy, the professions, arts and culture, politics and the army.

According to Smooha's definition, mine was an upper middle-class family, although I was not aware of it until after 1967 when, as a member of a Trotskyite group, I was jokingly denounced as the daughter of a capitalist. Jokingly, because only one of our members could be deemed working class – we were all children of the Israeli bourgeoisie.

Despite my parents' financial pressures, we had a car long before anyone else did: Father needed it to travel to work, an hour's drive each way. We had a telephone before many of our friends. We owned our own house, a four-bedroomed red-roofed villa with a flower and fruit garden, Mother's pride and joy. We seemed to lack nothing, yet, when we children wanted anything our parents could not afford, we were reminded that "money did not grow on trees". From an early age we were encouraged to take summer jobs and earn our pocket money. Again, despite financial pressures, my parents sent their three children to the best private school money could buy. The Reali School in Haifa was well known for its Prussian discipline and its high academic standards.

I know now how central the school was in shaping my middle-class and national consciousness. Excellence was drummed into us, European culture, history and languages were very well taught, as were Jewish history and Hebrew literature. Pupils' civic duties were stressed, and we were also given strict para-military training, complete with hikes and training camps. However, it was not until a 1992 school reunion that I understood the class divisions hidden under the school's emblem which we wore in a blue triangle on our school uniform and which exhorted us to be "Modest at all times". Haifa is built on three levels, downtown (*hadar haCarmel*), half way up the mountain, and Mount Carmel itself. Father and Mother, as soon as the business allowed, moved from their *hadar haCarmel* apartment to a house on Mount Carmel. We were Carmelites, the upper crust, even if our parents were sometimes in financial difficulties. In the small hours of the morning of that school reunion, when the *hadar* kids settled down in a circle, I questioned my exclusion and was told that we, the Carmel kids, had money. In their perception, we were the upper and they the lower middle class.

Memories began flooding back. Of Mother speaking of people who lacked "*Kinderstube*", or breeding, or of "common" people who "did not know how to behave". She prided herself on knowing which cutlery to use, how to pronounce foreign words, how to dress classically, without ostentation. She would exhort us not to raise our voices, not to speak with our mouths full, or leave food on our plates (although that may have been due to the legacy of the Shoah, and the hunger her relatives had suffered in Transnistria, the south Ukraine camp to which most of Bukovina's Jews were exiled during the war). When I was jealous about a school friend's mother serving shop biscuits, while we "had" to eat Mother's beautiful home-baked cakes and biscuits, she shook her head, murmuring something about my *nouveau riche* friends. I remembered Mother and Father speaking contemptuously about people in whose homes there were no books, no pictures; people who spent their evenings playing cards, instead of reading books, or listening to classical music on the wireless.

Social class was clearly not only about material possessions. It was about "class", about "taste", about knowledge, education, discernment. Social class was, however, about ethnic affiliation. We were Ashkenazis,[1] although we never used the term. Ironically, "some of our best friends" (we were unaware of the antisemitic overtones of such comments) were Sephardis, whose families had lived in Palestine for generations. We were definitely not Mizrahis, those newly arrived immigrants from Arab and North African countries, although Mother

28

would be the first to talk about the "wonderful Moroccans" she knew. In our school there were few Sephardis, and no Mizrahis at all. If I brought home a non-Ashkenazi boyfriend, his credentials had to be carefully vetted, and his shortcomings were attributed to his "lowly" ethnic origins, which had clear class connotations.

Smooha (1993) links class and ethnic inequalities. Ashkenazi Israelis have a clear educational advantage over Mizrahi Israelis, which does not improve for second generation Mizrahis. The educational gap is most acute in third level education where Ashkenazis have a four to one lead over Mizrahis. The educational gap translates into an occupational gap. In 1991 Ashkenazis born outside Israel were twice as likely as Mizrahis to work in the three top occupational categories (professional, managerial and technical). Second-generation Israeli-born Mizrahis had an even lower representation: 21 per cent in comparison with 50 per cent for Israeli-born Ashkenazis. In 1991 the Mizrahi per capita income was 70 per cent of that of the Ashkenazi per capita income. The result is an ethnically informed class stratification, with Mizrahis making up the majority of poor and working-class Israelis, Ashkenazis having a slight advantage over Mizrahis in the middle class and a distinct advantage in the upper middle class. Smooha lists the privileging of the national-military agenda, ethnic discrimination and the weaknesses of the Mizrahi population as reasons for this ethnically informed stratification (Smooha 1993: 178–8).

Class and gender constructions must be viewed in specific cultural contexts. One cannot write about Israel in isolation from the Israeli–Arab conflict, nor can one avoid contextualizing it in the analysis of Israel as a settler-colonial, masculine-military society. Zionism, while deeply rooted in ancient Judaism, sought to re-imagine an ancient religious community as a new political cultural construct. The resulting Zionist "imagined community" (Anderson 1983) was the masculine, fighting, active antithesis of the Jewish diaspora, allegedly passive, cowardly, and therefore "feminized" by contrast. This construction is evident in the writings of Zionist ideologues. Zionism, according to Ben Gurion, was not about conquering the ancient land of the Jews, but about constructing a "new Hebrew". It was a "revolution and rebellion against Jewish tradition" (Ben Gurion 1933: 308–9), a transformation of the national character itself (Avineri 1980: 228).

The resultant construct, *HaIvri hahadash* (literally "new Hebrew man"), was not only conceived as "a new Jewish person who will resemble, physically and psychically, his tall and strong (European) neighbours" (Shapira 1992: 33). He (the construction was always grammatically and conceptually male) was also decidedly Ashkenazi. My generation was constructed in the image of the Russian and Polish Jewish immigrants who, so we were told, "drained the marshes and paved the roads" in the pioneering days of the Jewish colonization of Palestine–Erez Israel. They, and we, were transformed, apparently unproblematically, from a class of small Eastern European township petit bourgeois shopkeepers, to a nation of earthy pioneers building the land and defending it against the Palestinian "enemy". However, with the arrival of the survivors of the Nazi Shoah (Holocaust), another very definite division was constructed between the masculine Israeli-born *Sabras*,[2] who took up arms in defence of their new–old land, and those feminized diaspora Jews who, allegedly, had gone passively, "like sheep to the slaughter", to their death in the gas chambers (Lentin 1996a).

While Zionism centres on the discursive construction of the "new Hebrew man", the very definition of Judaism is matrilineal – you are a Jew if your mother is. This, however, does not result in a powerful position for women in Israeli society. My generation grew up on myths of gender equality which originated in pre-state images of women pioneers, allegedly working alongside their men as equal partners. The reality was more sobering: although partners to the wish to construct a "new Hebrew" man, women pioneers worked together with their menfolk on the political level, but at the same time struggled against patriarchal Judaism and gender discrimination (Malkin 1913). Immigrating to Erez Israel–Palestine and leaving their families and communities was much harder for young pioneering women than for men. Women members of pre-state labour groups, mostly daughters of middle-class families in Eastern Europe who rebelled against their parents' bourgeois lifestyle, worked mostly in the kitchen or the laundry; they were often not paid wages in the early Jewish cooperative settlements while men were. By 1925, most Erez Israeli women were unemployed, even when there was plenty of work, according to *Yishuv*[3] historian Ada Maimon (1955). Young *Yishuv* women worked as cooks, laundresses, seamstresses, secretaries, domestics – anything, anywhere (Hazelton 1978: 16).

The trajectory from diaspora Jew to new Hebrew was a masculine process. But women too aspired to become new Hebrews, new Hebrew women, who would express their identity and femininity in order to acquire a place in society. They searched for new images. Were these to be based on the Russian revolutionary woman? The European peasant woman? The Palestinian peasant woman? Or the new Hebrew man? Such new images could not remain merely personal, they necessitated a transformation of society and its relation to women (Bernstein 1993: 88–9). Izraeli argues that despite a political commitment to the full participation of women in public life, the mere existence of a powerful, and separate, women's organization helped perpetuate the myth of equality and discouraged the emergence of alternative definitions around which Zionist women could organize (Izraeli 1981: 113–14). Ultimately, and despite the disappointment and frustration about their marginality, pre-state Zionist women prioritized the "national good" over feminism (Hazelton 1978; Bijaoui-Fogel 1992; Bernstein 1993).

Images of gender equality clashed with the political alliance between the Zionist labour leadership (which governed Israel, uninterrupted, between 1948 and 1977) and the Jewish Orthodox parties, fundamentally opposed to gender equality. Ironically, images of gender equality were strengthened by the conscription of women into the Israeli Defence Forces (IDF), one of the only armies to conscript women. The equity position, which calls for women to serve in the military in order to gain better access to positions of power, has been rejected by

Simona Sharoni, who argues that "sexism and militarism have been incorporated into the collective identities of Israeli men and women" (Sharoni 1992: 448). Indeed, equality in the IDF is notional, not real. Constructing women as mothers, in the spirit of religious Judaism, the IDF exempts married women and mothers (and women whose religious beliefs, or the religious beliefs of their fathers, preclude them from serving) from military service. The IDF's women's corps is named *Chen*, an acronym for women's corps, but literally meaning "charm", denoting women's function in the IDF, "adding charm and grace which makes [the IDF] also a medium for humanitarian and social activities" (Yuval Davis 1982: 17). Working within Jewish parameters, women – who hold only 60 per cent of IDF positions, mostly administrative and auxiliary – were never allowed to participate in battle (Bloom 1991: 135). Although only 15 per cent of the Israeli army goes to battle, women participate in the image of the IDF as a fighting army by freeing men to fight (Niv 1989: 34–5).

Sharoni (1992: 457) argues that the social construction of Israeli manhood has its roots in the Shoah and the re-assertion of masculinity through the establishment of a Jewish state. Israel's self portrayal as a "nation under siege" made "national security" a top priority, offering Israeli men a privileged status and resulted in the legitimation of national, ethnic and gender inequalities.

I, and my generation, the first generation to be born before or immediately after the establishment of the State of Israel in 1948, grew up against a backdrop of discourses of gender equality and the absence of any public discourse about class, together with discourses of prioritizing "national security" and the clear distinction between "us" – the young, isolated Israeli state struggling for its life after the Shoah, and "them" – our Arab enemies, allegedly anxious to drive us all into the sea. Although neither class nor gender was mentioned as a classifying category in the early years of the state, gender and class inequalities did underpin our view of the world.

In what I now understand as our enclosed middle-class Ashkenazi world, fathers were breadwinners and mothers homemakers. We were aware neither of the segregation of Israeli women within the labour market nor of the concentration of Mizrahi women workers at the bottom of the female labour market, while those Ashkenazi women who worked outside the home were concentrated in professional and scientific jobs (Bernstein 1991: 195). We were aware, however, without paying it much conscious attention, of the fact that most of our homemaking mothers employed Mizrahi, Palestinian or new immigrant women to clean their houses. To this day, the participation of Israeli women in the labour market is facilitated by employing Mizrahi and new immigrant women (mostly from the former Soviet Union) in housework and childcare. Thus middle-class Israeli womanhood constructed careers on the backs of its working-class sisters.

We were also certain, in our protected, childish manner, that housework was women's work. I remember mocking the father of a school friend, who was spotted in an apron, washing dishes or cleaning the floor. My own father, until his last few years, would not be seen dead cooking or clearing the table. Mother, however, must have been aware of the gender inequality, without saying much: both my brothers were assigned as many household chores as I was, and now do their share of housework diligently and lovingly. Needless to say, these inequalities helped to shape my feminism (and my mother's present-day feminism).

When married Israeli women, Ashkenazi or Mizrahi, are employed outside the home, their income is less than a third of the family income (Buber Agassi 1991: 209). Israeli women's lesser access to economic resources, their inferior economic power, is both a cause and effect of their limited political power. The traditional, Orthodox religious public, which considers sharply divided gender roles and the centrality of males in religious and public life as God-given, is another block to women's political power. According to Judith Buber Agassi, a large part of the Israeli public

> supports the – supposedly modern – 'super-woman' ideal of the perfect wife and mother (of three children at least), who is solely responsible for household and childcare (and is grateful to her husband for 'giving her a hand'); at the same time she is also a 'secondary breadwinner,' and always ready to undertake voluntary work. This idea is a formidable obstacle in the Israeli woman's access to power (Buber Agassi 1991: 209–10).

Had she worked outside the home, Mother would have been such a "super woman". Her middle-class Ashkenazi upbringing prevented her, however, from effectively resisting Father's refusal to allow her to exploit her considerable talents and work, say, in a public administration job, which she would have done very well, judging by her present success as voluntary worker. She allowed her family responsibilities to remain her sole fulfilment until later in life. Hers too can be seen as a disappointed existence.

Recently, the Israeli academy has begun to analyze Israel as a settler-colonial society and the Israeli–Arab conflict as the major factor in Israeli social formation (e.g., Ram 1993; Ehrlich 1993; Kimmerling 1993). Israeli feminism, which has moved from analyzing the status of Israeli women to analyzing Israel itself as a military-masculine society (Ram 1993; Shadmi 1992), has largely stopped short of class analysis. However, ethnicity and nationality interlink, as I have demonstrated, in connecting gender and class analysis in the construction of Israel's "new Hebrews" and their "new women". As a daughter of that "first generation to redemption", supposedly a "different race" to that of the despised Jewish diaspora (according to novelist Yehudit Handel, in Orna Ben Dor's film *Cloud Burst*; Ben Dor and Kaplanski 1988), making sense of being Israeli must include the interrelation of gender, class and ethnicity.

Our family's middle-class aspirations, which included access to the best education, classical music, art, culture and the "right" comportment, must also have meant a degree of disappointment in the dream of Zion where, we were told, equality (at least between Jews) would replace our humiliation among the gentiles.

The "new Hebrew man" – purely Ashkenazi – whom the Zionist ideologues wished to construct in Israel, argues Israeli playwright Shmuel Hasfari, did not turn out that well. This model has now been superseded, at least numerically, by Mizrahi Israelis, many of whom are as middle class as their Ashkenazi counterparts. According to Hasfari,

> the Ashkenazis' beloved homeland, Poland, turned its back on them. Europe gave its Jews emancipation, but the twentieth century betrayed them. And these people needed enormous inner strengths in order to digest the trauma and trust anything new (cited in Hitron 1996: 24).

When I was growing up, the terms "middle class" or "Ashkenazi" were not articulated. Differences between Romanian, Russian, Polish, German or Czech Israeli Jews, and the implicit "us" versus "them" (those pitied, but despised, new immigrants from Arab countries) seemed more relevant. And all these differences paled in the shadow of another, more real division, the "us" (Israelis) versus "them" (the Arab enemies). The social group, "middle class" and "Ashkenazi", like all dominant classes and ethnicities, did not regard itself as classed or ethnic at all. We were the universal category, the dominant majority, we were "it". Gender or gender inequalities were terms no one used in those heady early years of the Israeli state. In situations where national security is perceived as the highest value, gender differentiations tend to be ignored. None of my girl friends questioned our conscription, for instance. The fact that I did not serve in the army, because of asthma, marked my difference in a society which values conformity above all else. Until feminist analyses of Israel as a military-masculine society (e.g., Shadmi 1992; Sharoni 1992), we did not question the prioritization of former army officers for top positions in Israeli politics or business, or Israeli men's aggressive attitude to women (cf. Lentin 1996b).

Growing up Israeli, Ashkenazi and middle class has given me a keen sense of justice. There was a short period, during the 1960s with their discourse of revolution and rebellion, when it was shameful to admit to being "middle class". I now know that my class and ethnic identities have given me, via family, school and social environment, a legacy of learning, literature, art, culture, languages; and a link to a mythical "Europe" plus a rootedness in the more arid, more urgent Middle East. My national identity, which at first mobilized me unquestioningly to the Israeli national cause, was transformed, after the 1967 war, to a commitment to working, together with Palestinian women, towards Palestinian self-determination and a just peace between our two nations.

The question as to whether my feminism affected my understanding of class needs to be linked, in the specific Israeli context, to the effect my feminism had on understanding Israeli society as a settler-colonial, military-masculine society. Theorizing, as a feminist, national inequalities between Palestinians and Israelis (in relation to the territories Israel occupied in the 1967 war, but also between Israel's Jewish and Palestinian citizens), must be interlinked to theorizing class

33

and gender inequalities. Ironically, I believe that it is my mid-European, middle-class upbringing, which premised a strong sense of justice and a strong desire for equality, that informs both my feminism and my class consciousness. Far from seeing my class, my ethnicity or my nationality as givens, as "it", feminism has forced me to locate myself and claim my class, ethnicity, and nationality, proudly.

Notes

1. *Ashkenaz* means Germany in Hebrew and the term Ashkenazis refers to European (and American) Jews. *Sepharad* means Spain in Hebrew and the term Sephardis refers to Jews who originate from the Iberian Peninsula, many of whom lived in Erez Israel (the land of Israel) for several generations, unlike the Ashkenazis, most of whom began arriving in the 1880s. *Mizrach* means Orient in Hebrew and the term Mizrahis refers to Jews originating from Arab and North African countries.
2. *Sabra*, the name of a desert cactus fruit, prickly on the outside, but sweet tasting, is the name given to Jewish Israeli-born men and women. Ironically, it is also the name given to locally-born Palestinian (cf Khalifa 1978).
3. The pre-state Jewish settlement in Palestine.

References

Anderson, Benedict 1983. *Imagined Communities: Reflections on the Origins and Spread of Nationalism.* London: Verso.

Avineri, Shlomo 1980. *Hara'ayon Nazioni Ligvanav (Varieties of Zionist Thought).* Tel Aviv: Am Oved.

Ben Dor, Orna and Kaplanski, Daphna 1988. *Shever Anan (Cloud Burst).* 60 min, 16 mm. film directed by Ben Dor and produced by Kaplanski for Israel Television.

Ben Gurion, David 1933. *Mima'amad Le'am (From Class to Nation).* Tel Aviv: Davar.

Bernstein, Deborah S. 1991. Oriental and Ashkenazi women in the labour market. See Swirski, Barbara and Safir, Marilyn P. (eds) (1991), pp. 192–6.

Bernstein, Deborah S. 1993. *"Bein haisha-ha-adam uvein eshet habayit": isha umishpacha betsibur hapo'alim hayehudi ha'ironi bitkufat hayishuv* ("Between the woman as person and housewife": woman and family in the Jewish urban worker population during the Yishuv period). See Ram, Uri (ed.) (1993), pp. 83–103.

Bijaoui-Fogel, Sylvia 1992. From revolution to motherhood: the case of women in the kibbutz 1910–1948, in Bernstein, Deborah S. (ed.) *Pioneers and Homemakers.* Albany, New York: SUNY Press.

Bloom, Anne R. 1991. Women in the defence forces. See Swirski, Barbara and Safir, Marilyn P. (eds) (1991), pp. 128–37.

Buber Agassi, Judith 1991. How much political power do Israeli women have? See Swirski, Barbara and Safir, Marilyn P. (eds) (1991), pp. 203–12.

Carmi, Shulamit and Rosenfeld, Henry 1993. *Hacalcala hamedinit shel haleumiut hamilitaristit beIsrael* (The emergence of militaristic nationalism in Israel). See Ram, Uri (ed.) (1993), pp. 275–327.

Ehrlich, Avishai 1993. *Hevra bemilchama: hasichsuch haleumi vehamivne hahevrati* (A society at war: the national conflict and the social structure). See Ram, Uri (ed.) (1993), pp. 253–74.

Hazelton, Lesely 1978. *Tsela Adam: Haisha Bahevra HaIsraelit (Israeli Women: The Reality Behind the Myth)*. Jerusalem: Idanim.

Hitron, Hagai 1996. *Ha'ashkenazim hadefukim vehaturki hakatan* (The messed-up Ashkenazis and the little Turk). *Ha'aretz Magazine*, 25 October, p. 24.

Izraeli, Dafna N. 1981. The Zionist women's movement in Palestine, 1911–1927: a sociological analysis. *Signs*, 7/1, pp. 87–114.

Izraeli, Dafna N. 1991. Women and work: from collective to career. See Swirski, Barbara and Safir, Marilyn P. (eds) (1991), pp. 165–76.

Khalifa, Sahar 1978. *Hatsabar (The Sabra)*. (Hebrew translation by Salman Maslaha). Jerusalem: Galileo.

Kimmerling, Baruch 1993. *Yachasei medina-hevra beIsrael* (State-society relations in Israel). See Ram, Uri (ed.) (1993), pp. 328–50.

Lentin, Ronit 1996a. *Reoccupying the Territories of Silence: A Feminist Auto/biographical Exploration of the Gendered Relations between Israel and the Shoah*. Unpublished PhD dissertation, Trinity College, Dublin.

Lentin, Ronit 1996b. A *Yiddishe mame* desperately seeking a *mame loshn*: the feminisation of stigma in the relations between Israelis and Holocaust survivors. *Women's Studies International Forum*, 19(1/2), pp. 87–97.

Maimon, Ada 1955. *Hamishim Shneot Tnu'at Hapoalot (Fifty Years to the Women's Workers Movement)*. Tel Aviv: Ayanot.

Malkin, Sara 1913. *Hapoelet BaKinneret (The Woman Labourer in the Lake of Galilee)*, Hapoel Hatsair.

Niv, Kobi 1989. *Le'at, le'at, aval batuach, hevanti* (Slowly, slowly, but surely, I understood). *Politica*, 27: pp. 34–5.

Ram, Uri (ed.) 1993. *Hahevra HaIsraelit: Hebetim Bikorti'im (Israeli Society: Critical Perspectives)*. Tel Aviv: Breirot Publishers.

Ram, Uri 1993. *Hahevra umada hahevra: sociologia mimsadit vesociologia bikortit beIsrael* (Society and social science: establishment sociology and critical sociology in Israel). See Ram, U. (ed.) 1993.

Shadmi, Erella 1992. Women, Palestinians, Zionism: a personal view. *News from Within*, 8(10–11): pp. 13–16.

Shapira, Anita 1992. *Herev Hayona: Hazionut Vehaco'ach 1881–1948 (Land and Power)*. Tel Aviv: Am Oved.

Sharoni, Simona 1992. Every woman is an occupied territory: the politics of militarism and sexism and the Israeli–Palestinian conflict. *Journal of Gender Studies*, 4: pp. 447–62.

Smooha, Sammy 1993. *Shesa'im ma'amadi'im, adati'im uleumi'im vedemocratia beIsrael* (Class, ethnic and national cleavages and democracy in Israel). See Ram, Uri (ed.) (1993), pp. 172–202.

Swirski, Barbara and Safir, Marilyn P. (eds) 1991. *Calling the Equality Bluff: Women in Israel*. New York: Pergamon Press.

Yuval Davis, Nira 1982. *Israeli Women and Men: Division Behind the Unity*. London: Change International Reports: Women and Society.

CHAPTER THREE

Who am I? A journey across class and identity[1]

Gaby Weiner

They live it and I see it and I hear it. They repeat it and I hear it and I
see it, sometimes then always I understand it, sometimes then always
there is a completed history of each one by it, sometime then I will tell
the completed history of each one by it, sometime then I will tell the
completed history of each one as by repeating it I come to know it.
Every one always is repeating the whole of them (Stein 1925: 267).

I accepted the invitation to contribute to this book in the expectation that writing
about my life's experiences would be challenging, instructive, even pleasurable.
It has been all of these, but I did not expect it to be quite so difficult. What
follows, therefore, is tentative and exploratory due both to the nature of autobiography and to the fact that a life's story cannot be completed until the life is
over, and perhaps not even then. I have been troubled also by possible accusa-
tions of self-indulgence and self-centredness, despite Steedman's claim that
autobiography can question central cultural narratives and provide disruption
and counterpoint (Steedman 1986) – something I would want to do as a feminist
writer. And disclosure of personal details is likely to render myself vulnerable to
the critical gaze of friends, colleagues and strangers – another thing to be wary of.

So in this contribution, I address the concerns I and others have about
the nature and task of academic autobiography, later on threading in some of the
narratives and themes of my life.

Shaping Identity

At one time, a person's adult identity was thought to emerge through the adolescent turmoil of the body and by the resolution of future career and life uncer-
tainties. Identity was, in Erikson's words, "a sense of psychological well-being . . .

a feeling of being at home in one's body, a sense of 'knowing where one is going', and an inner recognition from those who count" (Erikson 1959). These were the prevalent ideas of my childhood and adolescence, interpreted through my teachers in school and through the schoolgirls' comics, teenage and, later, women's magazines that I read, as I struggled to pursue the twin goals of femininity and achievement in 1950s and 1960s Britain.

Today's ideas about identity place less emphasis on personal development and more on the nature of consciousness and conception of personhood, not only as experienced or remembered, but as recounted (Anderson 1991).

So, for many people, to talk of influences such as social class on individual consciousness and identity, is difficult. Social class analysis has been much more amenable to the meta-narrative, to the distant story of the great struggle between classes and the "polarized notion of antagonistic class relations: slave-masters exploit slaves, lords exploit serfs, capitalists exploit workers" (Wright 1997: xxvii). However, as Wright also points out, many people do not appear to fit neatly into this polarized image, because, like identity, the ways in which social class is experienced and absorbed today, for some at least, appear not to be as fixed as perhaps they once were. Also the conventional harnessing of class identity to the male head of household, and its consequent negation of women's status, has rendered many class analyses highly problematic.

Further, as Mahony and Zmroczek (1997) point out, class is not just an economic position. "Class experience is deeply rooted, retained and carried through life rather than left behind (or below)", as individuals find themselves in a different social class from that into which they were born (ibid.: 4). So individuals may well move across social class divisions (either materially, or consciously, or both) several times during a lifetime as earning and consumption patterns change.

Identities, moreover, will be shaped by a range of other factors: for example, my identity seems most to have been shaped by the fact that I was born a girl, and because my parents were relatively poor, were refugees, Jews and "foreigners" in postwar and post-imperial London. Growing up in a working-class district in North London in the 1950s, I was also moulded by the victory narratives of the postwar period and, perhaps more beneficially, by the British welfare state. However, my family seemed to be positioned "out on the borderlines", as Steedman put it, "for which the central interpretative devices of the culture don't quite work" (Steedman 1986: 9). In postwar Britain, it felt that I could be neither properly feminine, nor properly British, nor properly Jewish, nor properly working class. Other people (see, e.g., Heron 1985; Acker 1994) have felt this confusion of identity, but it was not recognized in the educational texts of the 1950s when I was growing up, neither is it particularly well articulated today.

The theoretical frameworks of poststructuralism and postmodernism, with their emphasis on fluidity and recognition of the fragmented subject, have enabled me to grapple with such fractured concepts of personhood, fusing with feminism to aid exploration of the complexities that constitute women's lives.

Madeleine Grumet shows more acutely than most how feminism has been aware of and tried to address complexities of identity:

> Holding political theory in one hand and the humiliation of not fitting into last year's bathing suit in another, feminists understand that knowing and being are not identical . . . This doubling of knowing and being keeps us ambivalent . . . and healthy and sick, and valiant (Grumet 1990: 338).

Many early class analyses found it difficult to incorporate such intricacies (e.g., Glass 1954; Jackson and Marsden 1962; Marwick 1980) and more recent shifts in class loyalties and composition caused by emergent ethnicities arising from mobilities of postwar populations (for example, from the Indian subcontinent), and from new technologies have added further challenges.

What follows, then, is an attempt to come to grips with the complexities of personhood by interrogating a specific site of class and gender identity formation – that of myself.

Autobiography as evidence

Why do people write autobiography? Media stars and politicians often write about themselves for money, or to keep their names prominent in the public eye. An autobiography may appear as part of the output of a writing career or as a history of significant events linked together by a life-story. In the main, autobiography is a genre of the successful or quasi-successful, although there have been some produced by "ordinary people" (Weisser 1996).

For women, as I found when writing this chapter, autobiographical writing is highly problematic: requiring a focus on the self which is antithetical to conventional femininity that requires a focus on others. Consequently, women autobiographers feel compelled to defend their concentration on self. Nineteenth-century female autobiographers, for example, frequently claimed that they were writing for unselfish reasons – for other women or for the common good – so as not to portray themselves as overly ambitious or career-oriented. They tended to minimize what they saw as the selfish impulses which had thrust them into full and stimulating careers and strove to convince readers that their professional acclaim was, initially at least, fortuitous and unsought (Sanders 1986, 1989).

Do the same problems exercise women autobiographers today? Why have I felt such discomfort at writing autobiographically? What can be drawn from autobiographical writing which moves beyond assuaging curiosity about the famous? Smith and Watson (1996: 3) argue that such is the popular power of the auto/biographical narrative that "if we are not telling our stories, we are consuming other people's lives". How, then, can relatively distant and specific origins and childhood experiences such as my own be of relevance or importance to present-day readers? Moreover, what is the relationship between personal values, self-identity and auto-narrative? If autobiographical accounts are "both highly personal and highly political", as Griffiths (1995) suggests, how should autobiography be read and understood? Certainly not, it seems, as the truth.

But autobiographical accounts are seductive precisely because they promise authenticity through first-hand stories of people and events, threaded through with narrative. Smith and Watson warn that autobiography has attracted a number of potent and dangerous myths: that there is only one story to tell; that the story is coherent; that the author is articulate and the story articulable; and that "the narrative lies waiting to be spoken" (Smith & Watson 1996: 9).

Perhaps because of the myths surrounding autobiographies, most people read them for fun. However, it is important that they are seen as specific versions of the "truth" and as conscious selections of remembered events, written for particular purposes, the interpretation of which may be questioned and challenged on the grounds of meaning and representation as well as accuracy (Weiner 1994). Readers of tabloid newspaper auto/biography, ironically, are more likely to be conscious of this (because of the more obvious blurring of truth and fiction) than readers of more scholarly work in academically reputable journals and volumes.

There is also the problem of voice and narrative form. Autobiographies may embrace a number of techniques. They usually have a strong narrative structure but because they rely on recall and reconstruction, there is a blurring of the boundaries between truth and fiction:

> Autobiography is much more like fictional reconstruction, loosely based on life-history events. So when I'm investigating my past, all the personal memories I have to work from are hints, glimpses, snatched conversations, shreds of unreliable information that have been reworked in the light of present/past dialogue . . . , and the changing cultural codes and images which I feel both part of and increasingly outside (Jackson 1990: 5).

Other approaches identify and deconstruct critical moments or incidents which mark "a significant turning-point or change in the life of a person" (Tripp 1994: 24). These might include examples from childhood, adolescence or adulthood. Remembered moments in my life range from my childhood terror – when on my daily way home from primary school, a group of boys thought it amusing to try to grab my school beret, to early marriage days where magazines exhorted me to put on a touch of lipstick before I saw my husband at the breakfast table, to my guilt as a young mother, engendered by a newspaper poll which purported to show that the most important characteristic of a good mother was "always being there", to the regular and gratuitous comments, it seemed, about the quaintness of my accent, name, personality or background. No doubt most of us can recall instances when a number of factors have coalesced to produce moments of illumination or devastation.

I have fused these two main approaches in order to address what I see as the main influences on my life's experiences. I try to show how autobiography is a way of elucidating not only the complex interplay between the psychological and the social, but how individuals are or are not able to manipulate their positioning within the variety of discourses of which they are part, and which may or may not subordinate them. It also provides a discursive space for exploration of self and identity, historically and culturally, which has proved difficult to incorporate in other academic, more objectivist, discourses.

Conscious of the difficulties with the genre, however, I try not to present my life as a victory or master narrative, though clearly I have power over and a vested interest in the specific construction that is placed here on my life's actions. Also the intention is to offer an insight into how social phenomena interact with identity and subjectivity, rather than use the opportunity for self-therapy or introspection.

The conclusion of this preamble is that, though autobiography should be read critically and in the knowledge that "narrators take up models of identity that are currently available" (Smith and Watson 1996: 9), what follows needs also to be read as but one of "my" stories.

An autobiographical snapshot

I was born in May 1944 in Welwyn Garden City, England, the only child of an Austrian bookkeeper mother and a Polish, Communist, Yiddish-speaking, sometime actor father. My mother had escaped from Vienna in 1938 to join relatives in London and my father, who had been a migrant worker (coal-miner) in Belgium, had likewise fled to England, having been separated from his wife and children at the beginning of the war. My mother and father never married.

I was brought up by my mother and her two sisters when my father, an early victim of Cold War paranoia, was deported back to Belgium and reunited with his surviving family a year or so after the end of the Second World War. My knowledge of my father's side of the family is consequently weak, though I was able to meet him at irregular intervals over the years. My remaining family were mostly agnostics and atheists. Yet, I was encouraged to affirm my Jewishness, because of the phenomenon of the Holocaust which had caused the deaths in concentration camps of the Jewish people including my maternal grandmother, and uncles and aunts – even if the events and details were withheld from me. My memory is of a stable, secure and affectionate, if slightly eccentric, childhood, spent within an extended family of female relatives and my mother's friends in north London. I attended the local primary school, and was one of only a handful to pass the "scholarship" (later known as the eleven-plus) to a local single-sex grammar school.

I met my prospective husband (a draughtsman, later a fully qualified civil engineer) at the local youth branch of the Labour Party, married at 18, had my first child just over a year later, and my second 18 months after the first. I returned to education to train as a primary teacher when my youngest child was two and a half years old. I went to college then because my mother, who had recently retired, suggested that I should. She noted my dissatisfaction with mid-1960s models of motherhood and wifedom, and also, perhaps, that I had not fulfilled the academic potential promised throughout my schooling. She thus offered to take responsibility for childcare when the hours at the nursery class which my children attended fell short of those required for my college course. I chose to go into teaching principally because it would fit in with my children's daily and yearly school timetable, and subsequently became a primary teacher, before taking a full-time master's degree, and then moving into research, and eventually into higher education. I currently work in the education department of a London university, south of the river, and am now divorced.

The stances that I have taken over the years were, it seems, the consequence of a number of factors including my childhood feeling of "otherness" in being the only identified Jew in my small Islington primary school and in having parents and relatives who spoke with foreign accents; the passionate belief of members of my family in the necessity of developing a socialist politics of democracy and social justice; my mother's total commitment to the best possible future for me; and feminism which was "in the air" throughout my twenties when I became first a mother and then a teacher.

I was fortunate to reap the benefits of the newly constituted, British postwar welfare state; for example, I received free medical treatment when I became seriously ill with pneumonia at the age of six, qualified to attend the local, single-sex grammar school at the age of eleven, and gained free nursery places for my two children while I trained to be a primary teacher at a time of teacher shortage in the early 1970s.

Feminism became the predominant influence of my adult life, if only because at various periods it has seemed more focused and less ambivalent than other forms of "progressive" politics. I was only on the fringes of the emerging Women's Liberation Movement in London in the early 1970s, though I keenly followed press reports of the activities of American feminists and Civil Rights campaigners. The appearance of their publications combined with the politically progressive values of my childhood to provide me with a then fresh, particularly 1960s political consciousness concerning equality and change which is still with me. I pursued this political agenda throughout my undergraduate and postgraduate studies, and in my later writing. I reserved particular criticism for forms of progressive politics which ignored or downplayed gender inequalities such as 1950s and 1960s class perspectives on education (e.g. Glass 1954; Halsey et al. 1961; Bernstein 1964; Jackson & Marsden 1962) which seemed not to address "my" origins relating to gender, ethnicity, or refugee background.

I have also seen various shifts in my personal and professional circumstances, not only on the basis of age, family status and career, but in the various ways that my past and my present positionings have come together, sometimes in unsettling ways.

The importance of an education

Ainley (1993) suggests that despite the radicalism of the postwar Labour administration of 1945–51, the British class system remained largely intact. In the case of education, a tripartite secondary system (grammar, central/technical, secondary-modern) was advanced, mirroring the three traditional divisions of male labour (brain, non-manual, manual). In practice, state secondary schooling became bipartite because most of the planned, central/technical schools failed to materialize. Tripartism was produced, nevertheless, through the combination of private and public schooling viz. private (called "public", and latterly, "independent") schools for the gentry and the upper middle class, grammar schools for the "middling" classes and secondary moderns for working-class children.

By the 1950s and 1960s inequalities in the social distribution of educational opportunity became the main target of a generation of British social scientists (e.g. Glass 1954; Halsey 1957). They convinced the 1960s' Labour administration that grammar schools were attracting a disproportionately high number of children from middle-class homes and therefore disadvantaging working-class children. As a consequence, the neighbourhood comprehensive school was adopted as the most effective model of educational equality, even if under the slogan "grammar schools for all". Despite these shifts towards more egalitarian schooling, however, the early 1960s saw class barriers reconstituted in higher education with the proportion of working-class children entering universities actually decreasing (Ainley 1993).

Post Second World War attitudes towards women were also conservative. It was assumed that women would return from employment in the field and factory to their "natural" roles in the family (Dean 1991); hence women's work (paid or unpaid) was excluded from contemporary debates about labour force shifts and patterns. Thus, while the creation of the British welfare state was premised on a concern to redistribute social privilege and benefits more equally, assumptions concerning women firmly positioned them in the home.

> For the sake of rebuilding the war-stricken nation, women's primary role was defined in British social policy as that of homemaker and childrearer. The Beveridge Report (1942) relied on the reassertion of traditional sex roles (Coppock et al. 1995: 12).

Thus the structure of the welfare state and, indeed, the school day, assumed that women worked primarily in the home and were dependent economically on their husbands' wage. What this meant in terms of education was that in the 1950s, 1960s and into the 1970s, equality issues were viewed wholly in terms of social class. Implicitly, ideas about the naturalness of gender differences were maintained and reproduced through schooling, emphasized, for example, by the widespread incorporation within teacher training of Bowlby's theories of maternal deprivation and Parson's functionalist perspectives on distinctive sex roles (Bowlby 1953; Parsons 1952).

How did these larger patterns affect my family and myself? It is difficult to say, as precisely where my family stood in the social order when I was a child and my later positioning as an adult, have proved difficult to fix, though feminism has taught me that many of my experiences have been gendered, and therefore familiar to some, perhaps many, other women.

Education was seen as vitally important to members of my family, in order I suspect, to ensure their toe-hold in their country of adoption. With little to show from her childhood and 20 years or so working life in Vienna as a skilled office worker, my mother was always hugely aware of the relative privilege in Britain, of access to free medicine and free education, security in old age (although she lived only until her mid-sixties) and freedom from persecution.

I was encouraged to do well in primary school, and my achievement of the scholarship to grammar school was a moment of celebration for the entire family which saw upward mobility through education as the main route to prosperity and respectability. Significantly, my selection of secondary school did not include a neighbouring new, purpose-built comprehensive although several of my friends made it their first choice. On gaining my grammar school place, it was expected that I would go to university – even though I would be the first family member to do so. But as a fairly rebellious adolescent, attention to my studies plummeted as my interest switched to the dynamic left politics of north London in the late 1950s and early 1960s, particularly to the emergent anti-nuclear movement. Instead of going to university, I joined the radical politics of the early 1960s – and got married. Interestingly, there was little opposition to my early marriage from my family, principally because my husband-to-be had a reasonable job as a draughtsman, was Jewish, was suitably politically affiliated, and because he would relieve my mother of the responsibility of her troublesome daughter. Also, marriage was still perceived as the most beneficial career prospect for women, and indicative of the elusive achievement of femininity.

I felt relatively comfortable among my peers in school, at college (attended mainly by mature students) and as a teacher, with, I suppose, my adult identity approved of and confirmed (in Erikson's terms). I neither mixed with nor was particularly knowledgeable about social groupings other than my own until I went to university to pursue postgraduate studies. However, while studying for my master's degree in the mid-1970s and then later as a researcher, I realized that I was beginning to knock on the door of a different class, members of which spoke with refined accents, had access to higher status knowledge and had the power of patronage. I was compelled to remake myself, to construct a new identity in order to gain entry into this new and enticing world of academia.

I was not then and have never been entirely successful in this since comments on accent and my apparently unconventional and "direct" manner have remained a regular occurrence in my professional life. While attributed to the personal and often artlessly proffered, these comments are shaped by what Bourdieu and Passeron call the "class ethnocentrism" of universities and research institutions, which assume the equitableness and justice of the "natural language of human intelligence" (Bourdieu & Passeron 1994: 8). Yet, such ethnocentrism merely confirms cultural privilege, through the use of specific linguistic codes and procedures which are elusive and impenetrable to outsiders. If some manage to overcome their seeming inappropriateness of birth and/or culture of origin, others do not, seeing themselves as perpetually "outside the norm" as one black, female academic recently put it (Powney & Weiner 1992). Class ethnocentrism seemed less pervasive in the newer British universities where I spent much of the 1990s, or perhaps I became more immune to its effects. Occasionally, however, I meet colleagues from my early research days who somehow, in voice or tone, bring back my outsider memories of inadequacy and discomfort, and remind me of my inevitable failure to make their particular grade.

Becoming British: citizenship and identity

Born at the end of the war with my childhood shaped by immediate postwar features such as food rationing, bomb craters, and free medicine and education, I was delighted as a child to be part of the victory narrative of postwar Britain and took immense pride as did most of my friends, in the fact that Britain had some jurisdiction over a quarter of the globe. The war stories and romantic fiction of popular books, magazines and films were eagerly consumed and absorbed into my growing consciousness of femininity and of being British. My mother's admiration of Winston Churchill as a war leader never faded, despite her criticism of his postwar politics. The near proximity of the war had little impact – the tales of the Battle of Britain were as distant, exotic and exciting as the Wars of the Roses or the Norman Conquest.

Neither had I any sense of the disruption that fascism and war had brought to my family, or to the British nation. It is only in recent years, as I have deliberately sought out accounts of what it was like to live during the war and to live through the genocide of the Jews in Europe, that the horror of the Holocaust has taken on personal meaning. I now know that I was born out of disruption and despair, a positive sign to my parents' generation that there could be a future. And the future was to be had by looking forward and not looking back. Along with many of the generation of Second World War refugees and Holocaust survivors, members of my family remained silent about their wartime sufferings, not wishing, I suppose, to put additional burdens on their children or "infect" them with any form of victim culture.

Later on, as already mentioned, I was also closely involved in the British social and political movements of the 1960s and 1970s, and was deeply disappointed by the regressively chauvinist and Little Englander stances of the Thatcher and Major administrations of the 1980s and 1990s. Ironically, British government mono-cultural and anti-European stances of recent decades have brought sharply into relief and drawn attention to my Middle-European roots and culture: for example, emphases on the teaching of Christianity incorporated in the British national curriculum in the late 1980s made me, for the first time for many years, acutely aware of my Jewish origins.

Thus, though I am a British citizen, and was educated and have spent all my working life steeped in British culture, much of British culture seems closed or alien to me. It still often feels as though I am a long-term visitor rather than a fully fledged and accepted British citizen.

I am a British citizen by dint of birth but my mother was not. Despite a number of applications, she was never granted British citizenship during her 30-year stay, presumably because of my father's political activities in the early 1940s. She was thus never able to vote, nervous that my youthful political activities would threaten not my right to citizenship but her right to remain in Britain, and frequently fearful of deportation.

So I remain affected by my past, aware of the historical and cultural specificity of my family background and experience, and how it has shaped my identity, but also of the way it connects to the present. Even though the events of the Holocaust are but a half-century away, it seems unforgivable to me that, today, similar human tragedies continue, often underestimated and unrecognized. We still seem unable to anticipate or acknowledge potential tyrannies or threats to citizenship. For example, Pearson noted the insufficient attention paid to the "immanent and immediate growth of xenophobia and racism" at a conference on Women and Citizenship in Europe in 1991.

> We did indeed recognise the ways in which 'Fortress Europe' would exclude from citizenship minorities and immigrants; we were not suf-ficiently aware of the implications of the resurgence of right-wing and fascist parties in Western Europe, of the extent of anti-immigrant and anti-semitic ideologies within the new Germany and in the former Soviet Union (Pearson 1992: 7–8).

Religion and ethnicity

Perhaps because my family's values were shaped by their culture as Jews, by their treatment as Jews, but also by their politics and agnosticism/atheism, Judaism for me has not been a religious commitment but a discourse that I have picked up and bought into at various times in my life.

I have sometimes used being Jewish to provide me with an identity that being British cannot offer, and as a platform for reaffirmation of my "grand narrative" commitment to the struggles against injustice. I have used it also to establish specific informal networks of power/knowledge where others have seemed con-sciously or unconsciously, to exclude me, and have taken pride in the intel-lectual achievements of Jewish individuals and groups, particularly of Jewish feminists (from Emma Goldman to Golda Meir).

More recently, I have found myself wanting to know more about the Holocaust, and how it was possible that six million people came to be murdered, sharing only their religious beliefs and/or origins. How did it, could it happen? The questions that I was not able to put to my mother and her generation have re-emerged. Others, such as Thomas Keneally whose book *Schindler's Ark* was made into the film *Schindler's List* (directed by Stephen Spielberg) have also posed these questions in different ways (see also, e.g., Dawidowicz 1976, 1990; Muller 1979; Poliakov 1985; Bauman 1989). It seems that I can never "not be Jewish" because of the Holocaust crimes against the Jews which continue to shock and haunt me.

I have, however, not embraced the Jewish religion because of what I see as its patriarchy and misogyny; for example, in linking menstruation with impurity, separating men and women for religious rituals, and excluding women from aspects of biblical study and scholarship (Henry & Taitz 1983). I have also been critical of Israeli government policy over a prolonged period of time, from the point when I violently disagreed with my mother about our position on the Six-Day War in 1967. Moreover, I have found that the British Judaism is not exempt from prejudice. I was prevented from marrying in an Orthodox (British mainstream) synagogue because of my illegitimacy, though I was eventually allowed to marry in a Liberal synagogue. Other discordant tones within the British Jewish community were detected by me as a child. For example, invited by similarly educationally upwardly mobile English relatives each year to join in the delights of Passover ritual and ceremony, I was always aware of the need to be grateful for being allowed to participate, and of my mother's and my positioning at the edge of the Jewish family and outside British Judaism.

My story to date

One reader of an earlier draft of this chapter noted that what I have written thus far provides an analysis of the inputs into my life but neglects the outcomes. To discuss or prioritize one or more "outcomes" as particularly influential, however, would be misleading, as my life's journey is not yet played out, and my perceptions and understandings may well change. What I can say is that I have learnt from both experiencing and reflecting on my life, to apply analytic frameworks to personal experience – to see the personal as political. I try to locate my life's experiences, particularly at a professional level, in the political rather than the personal domain. This has enabled me to deconstruct incidents and happenings and to learn from them, rather than being cast down by apparent defeats, slights and injustices.

The outsider status of my family has made me, I suggest, more analytical of the forms of prejudices and bigotry that are evident in every-day and in academic life, and more able to locate specific oppressive discourses of class, gender, race and ethnicity, and religion. My background has also provided me with the capacity to be adaptable and flexible when confronted with new challenges and changing circumstances – in an uncertain world, I have retained the refugee outlook of making the best of life while I can.

Reflections

Earlier in this chapter, I claimed that my aim in writing this piece was to come to grips with the complexities of personhood by interrogating myself as a specific site of class and gender identity formation. It is for others to decide if I have been successful in this endeavour.

However, what has emerged, I suggest, is the perception that identity needs to be viewed both as a struggle within each of us in coming to terms with our past, present and future, and in its fragmented form, as a means by which we may (or may not) engage in the range of cultural and political strategies available to us. Also, that by reflecting on an individual life, we can see that "we ourselves are shaped by the past, but from our vantage point we are continually reshaping the past which shapes us" (Hill 1974: 284).

In respect of the larger questions around the nature and impact of class, ethnicity, gender at the level of experience, the picture is more opaque. What can be gained from my story is that macro-patterns help to explain certain experiences, yet not others. Class perspectives illuminate why I gained a grammar school place, and why I felt uncomfortable at university. Gender perspectives offer explanations for my early marriage and why I took up school teaching. But for me, being Jewish and not being British, being an illegitimate child of refugees, being the only child of an exceptional mother, have also been important and irreducible influences.

Thus while class and gender may be viewed as distinct elements – observable and analyzable at the macro-level – how we experience each social fracturing is rather more difficult to evoke. How each of us puts together the range of fracturings and subjectivities that constitute our lived experience is yet more complex but ultimately more rewarding. Nevertheless, I suggest, it is important that we continue with these forms of inquiry because they provide windows on the social world which are missing from other research approaches. In order to do so, we also need to draw on the widest possible range of data gathering methodologies (including auto/biography) and analytical frameworks (including social class and feminism) available to us.

Note

1. I have had a lot of help with this chapter. In particular, I would like to thank for their comments and advice: Stephen Ball, Miriam David, Anne Gold, David Hamilton, Ulla Johansson, Pat Mahony and Chris Zmroczek.

References

Acker, S. 1994. *Gendered Education*. Buckingham: Open University Press.

Ainley, P. 1993. *Class and Skill: Divisions of Knowledge and Labour*. London: Cassell.

Anderson, B. 1991. *Imagined Communities*. London: Verso.

Bauman, Z. 1989. *Modernity and the Holocaust*. Cambridge: Polity Press.

Bernstein, B. 1964. Social Class, Speech Systems and Psychotherapy. *Sociology*, 15 (1): 54–64.

Bourdieu, P. and Passeron, J.-C. 1994. Introduction: Language and Relationship to Language in the Teaching Situation, in Bourdieu, P., Passeron, J.-C., St Martin, M. *Academic Discourse*. Cambridge: Polity Press.

Bowlby, J. 1953. *Child Care and the Growth of Love*. Harmondsworth: Penguin.

Coppock, V., Haydon D. and Richter I. 1995. *The Illusions of Post-Feminism: New Women, Old Myths*, London: Tavistock.

Dawidowicz, L. 1976. *A Holocaust Reader*. New York: Bantam Books.

Dawidowicz, L. 1990. *The War Against the Jews 1933–45*. London: Penguin Books.

Dean, D. 1991. Education for moral improvement, domesticity and social cohesion: expectations and fears of the Labour Government. *Oxford Review of Education*, 17(3), 269–85.

Erikson E.H. 1959. Identity and the life cycle. *Psychological Issues*, 1, 1.

Glass, D. (ed.) 1954. *Social Mobility in Britain*. London: Routledge.

Griffiths, M. 1995. *Feminisms and the Self: The Web of Identity*. London: Routledge.

Grumet, M. 1990. Show and tell: a response to the value issue in alternative paradigms of inquiry, in Guba, E.G. (ed.) *The Paradigm Dialog*. Newbury Park, California: Sage.

Halsey, A.H. 1957. *Social Class and Educational Opportunity*. London: Heinemann.

Halsey, A.H., Floud, J. and Anderson, J. (eds) 1961. *Education, Economy and Society*. New York: Free Press.

Henry, S. and Taitz, E. 1983, *Written Out of History: Our Jewish Foremothers*. New York: Biblio Press.

Heron, L. (ed.) 1985. *Truth, Dare or Promise: Girls Growing Up in the Fifties*. London: Virago.

Hill, C. 1974. *Change and Continuity in the Seventeenth Century*. London: Weidenfeld & Nicolson.

Jackson, B. and Marsden, D. 1962. *Education and the Working Class*. London: Routledge.

Jackson, D. 1990, *Unmasking Masculinity: a Critical Autobiography*. London: Unwin Hyman.

Keneally, T. 1982. *Schindler's Ark*. London: Hodder & Stoughton.

Mahony, P. & Zmroczek, C. 1997. Why Class Matters, in Mahony, P. & Zmroczek, C. (eds) *Class Matters: 'Working-Class' Women's Perspectives on Social Class*. London: Taylor & Francis.

Marwick, A. 1980. *Class, Image and Reality in Britain and in the USA since 1930*. London: Collins.

Muller, F. 1979. *Eyewitness Auschwitz*. New York: Stein & Day.

Parsons, T. 1952. *The Social System*. London: Tavistock.

Pearson, R. 1992. Looking both ways: extending the debate on women and citizenship in Europe, in Ward, A., Gregory, J. and Yuval-Davis, N. (eds), *Women and Citizenship in Europe*. Stoke-on-Trent, UK: Trentham Books.

Poliakov, L. 1985. *The History of Anti-Semitism*, 3 vols. London: Oxford University Press.

Powney, J. and Weiner, G. 1992. *'Outside of the Norm': Equity and Management in Educational Institutions*. London: South Bank University.

Sanders, V. 1986. "Absolutely an act of duty" choice of profession in autobiographies of Victorian women, *Prose Studies*, 9(3), 54–70.

Sanders, V. 1989. *The Private Lives of Victorian Women: Autobiography in the Nineteenth Century*. Hertfordshire, UK: Harvester Wheatsheaf.

Smith, S. and Watson, J. 1996. Introduction, in Smith, S. & Watson, J. (eds) *Getting a Life: Everyday Uses of Autobiography*. Minneapolis: University of Minnesota Press.

Steedman, C. 1986. *Landscape of a New Woman*. London: Virago (reprinted in Blair M., Holland J., Sheldon S. (eds) 1995. *Identity and Diversity: Gender and the Experience of Education*. Clevedon, UK: Multilingual Matters.

Stein, G. 1925. The making of Americans, in Stein G., *Selected Writings of Gertrude Stein*. New York: Random House.

Tripp, D. 1994. *Critical Incidents in Teaching*. London: Routledge.

Weiner, G. 1994. *Feminisms and Education: an Introduction*. Buckingham: Open University Press.

Weisser, S.O. 1996. "What kind of life have I got?": gender and the life story of an "ordinary" woman, in Smith, S. and Watson, J. (eds) (1996), pp. 249–70.

Wright, E.O. 1997. *Class Counts: Comparative Studies in Class Analysis*. Cambridge: Cambridge University Press.

CHAPTER FOUR

Class, attainment and sexuality in late twentieth-century Britain

Valerie Walkerdine, Helen Lucey and June Melody

Introduction

During his term of office, John Major, the Conservative British prime minister, announced that Britain was now a classless society. The irony of this statement may have been less apparent to some in the boom economy of the 1980s, but became a cruel joke in the face of the 1990s bust. In this chapter, we will discuss aspects of the lives of a group of young women who grew up through that turbulent period of British history. They took part in a research project, which began when 30 of the girls were four and eight of them were six years old. The group of 30 girls was part of a research project when they were four, undertaken by Tizard and Hughes at the Thomas Coram Research Unit, University of London. This project, written up as *Young Children Learning* (Tizard & Hughes 1984), aimed to explore language at home and at school. The researchers observed 15 working-class and 15 middle-class mother and daughter pairs, recording their conversations at home and the girls in the nursery school. While the authors kindly allowed us access to both the sample and the transcripts of the recordings, we found we were at total odds with their interpretation of the relation of class and gender in the data. We therefore reworked the data to examine arguments about class and gendered socialization and the regulation of working- and middle-class mothering practices. We then followed up the same girls at aged ten, including additionally a small case-study of girls from one infants' school in London. More recently, we received funding to follow the same girls up to research their transition to womanhood.[1] For this project, on which we draw for this chapter, the young women (aged 21 and 16 in 1993), and their families were interviewed and the young women made video diaries of their lives. The majority of the young women were white, though there was one

Afro-Caribbean, one Asian and one mixed race young woman in the overall sample. A subsidiary sample of six black and Asian 21-year-old young women was added to the original sample. We have discussed the girls' early years and their primary schooling at length in earlier publications (Walkerdine & Lucey 1989; Walkerdine 1989, 1998). Our aim here is to explore some of the ways in which class differences are present for these young women in relation to their educational success, career trajectory and experiences of sexuality and mother-hood. We want to concentrate in particular on the way in which the relations of sexuality and attainment figure differently for the middle- and working-class 21 year olds.

All of us grew up working class in Britain, Valerie in the postwar period in Derby, in the Midlands, and Helen and June in London, as daughters of Irish immigrants, and have struggled in various ways to get an education (Walkerdine 1991). This has had a profound effect upon our research. We have found it impossible to work on issues of gender without taking our own class into account and have had to come to terms with the place of our own subjectivity in the research process. At first, for example, we found that working with data on middle-class child-rearing practices made us feel angry and envious, which we wrote about in ways which were not usually incorporated into a research account (Walkerdine & Lucey 1989). Of course, everybody has their own subjective feelings about the research they work on, and although feminism has empha-sized the importance of one's own subjectivity for research, it is still difficult to step outside the confines of concerns about objectivity to incorporate insights from our own lives into the research. However, while we have learned much along the way from our angry outbursts and painful feelings, there is no doubt that our own class composition is important to research on class as it allows us very different insights from those of middle-class researchers. For us, middle-class practices often appear strange and we question their basis in ways that middle-class researchers may well take for granted. In addition, we deliberately interrogate our own emotional responses to our data and to the families with whom we work. We have found that we can learn a great deal about ourselves and our subjects by understanding the conscious and unconscious processes and fantasies that emerge. Using a method developed from psychoanalytic tech-niques, we can more closely question our own responses to the data. It has been a struggle to present a very different picture of ourselves as working class, as well as the processes of education through which we came to be educated out, to pass for middle class and what that means about our own class status. It has been a struggle too to insist that class is both an issue for feminism and an important topic for research, no matter what John Major or anyone else may say about classlessness. Very little has been written about middle-class schooling or indeed about the middle classes generally. And more than this, the working class is usually defined as the pathological object of a normative and surveillant gaze (Blackman 1996).

Femininity and class

To begin the discussion of this chapter let us talk about femininity as it is intersected by class. While feminism has long been able to cope with difference and diversity among women, "class" often presents a huge stumbling block for contemporary politics in the West. What, however, if "class" as an identity designation is itself lived not simply as an economic relation (to the means of production) but as a complex and contradictory identity? We know that under certain economic conditions of capitalism, class was formed as a major tool of social regulation: "classification" was the means by which governments, certainly from the nineteenth century onwards, made sense of their difficult-to-govern urban populations, as well as the newly emerging bourgeoisie, in its matter of difference from the aristocracy. Radical politics used such designations to link political transformation through revolution with a recognition of class belonging, involving a psychological project requiring a transformation of perception or consciousness (Walkerdine 1996, 1997). "The Working Class" became the repository of fantasies of otherness and promises of transformation, which, for so long have failed to be delivered, until disappointment bred destruction and the cry that there no longer exists any "real" working class (Gorz 1982). But, perhaps there never was, nor any "real" middle class either. As Judith Butler remarks:

> to the extent that we understand identity-claims as rallying points for political mobilisation, they appear to hold out the promise of unity, solidarity, universality. As a corollary then, one might understand the resentment and rancour against identity as signs of dissension and dissatisfaction that follow the failure of that promise to deliver (1990: 188).

She adds, following the work of Zizek, that such identity-claims are "phantasmatic sites, impossible sites, and hence as alternately compelling and disappointing" (ibid.).

It is interesting that for Marx and those who followed, to be working class, while a designation and classification for the forces of surveillance (Foucault 1979), was, in fact, something to be struggled over. To be working class one had not simply to be poor and exploited, a worker, but to recognize oneself as a member of "the working class", with its historic mission. This has plagued the left ever since because the working class as object of regulation saw only a pathology, something wrong to be corrected (Blackman 1996), whereas the left saw only a failure of consciousness and hence, of political action. Over many years it has caused us great sadness and anger that what Butler calls the cycle of compulsion and disappointment has been visited upon the poor and exploited, upon the working class, because the middle class left in Britain so rarely found the class for itself that they so desperately wanted to see. All this has meant that the issues of subjectivity, how life was lived for those designated and regulated as working class, was never of any interest to the left, and indeed to feminism, and so there is little in terms of an oppositional discourse around these issues.

And where are we now that things have changed so dramatically on the eve of the new century? How might we begin to rethink these issues as intersected by the huge economic changes that are happening in countries such as Britain? We are witnessing the decline of the manufacturing base, the rise of the service sector, the loss of traditional male manual work and the rise of what has been described as the feminization of the economy (Wilkinson 1994). How can we understand classed identities within this changed scenario? How is femininity intersected by class in the present?

Post-industrial societies and the regulation of femininity

What we are witnessing in societies such as Britain, as has been widely reported in the press recently, is a decline in male manual work and the increase of women entering traditionally male professions. Middle-class girls are doing very well at school and working-class boys badly. While this may not be a significant change, what has changed are the discourses through which that gendered and classed attainment is read. Now that working-class boys can no longer easily obtain manual work requiring no or minimal qualifications, girls are being accused of doing too well in school, to account for boys' failure. However, what is patently clear is that the girls who are doing well and the boys who are doing poorly do not come from the same constituency. The girls who succeed are overwhelmingly middle class and the boys who fail are working class. There is a huge class difference in attainment which is reflected in the attainment figures for our project data. Wilkinson (1994) argues that the male workforce is declining while women's participation is increasing, with women accounting for 38 per cent of professional jobs. This latter is forecast as being the highest growth occupational group over the next ten years.

What does this mean for the way in which femininity is lived and regulated at this period? If girls' success at school is understood as a reason for boys' failure and if the labour market is becoming feminized, this will also have a significant impact on the "feminization" of masculinity too. In order, therefore, to understand the production and regulation of classed femininity, it is important to point to the fact that not only has the manufacturing base declined in Britain, alongside that of many other Western countries, but what accompanied it was a decline in trade unionism, brought about in Britain largely through anti-union legislation introduced by Margaret Thatcher's Conservative government. This meant a decline in the practices through which class had traditionally been constituted. What, then, would a classed identity mean with the demise of these practices? Alongside this there is, as we have said earlier, the left's loss of a political object – "the working class". The decline we are discussing (which for sociologists was certainly trumpeted as happening from at least the 1950s, e.g.

Halsey et al. 1988; Gorz 1982) has meant that patterns of consumption were heralded by some as markers of classification, rather than traditional class categories. For example, work in cultural studies in Britain in the 1980s started to talk about the way in which erstwhile working-class people now had more purchasing power, and this work started to use the categories applied by advertising agencies and market research to judge niche markets. While these certainly approximated to the Registrar General's classification of class by occupation, this was a move to classify by patterns of consumption. However, this said, what we are presented with is a set of transformed practices for producing classed subjectivities, all of which contain a great deal of pain and nostalgia. The pain of the economic and political transformations of the 1980s should not be discounted, both for working-class subjects themselves, as well as for the projections of the middle-class left. How, then, do fantasy and fiction blend in the production of classed subjectivities in the present?

In the analysis which follows we want to concentrate on the blending of two forms of analysis: poststructural, using the work of Michel Foucault, and psychoanalytic. By this means we will begin to examine how the events of the 1980s and 1990s have shaped the practices through which girls' subjectivities are constituted. If we begin with their families, this period was one of great change for working- and middle-class families alike. It was the Conservatives' policies which, for example, promoted the idea of a "share-owning democracy', in which the working class could buy both their council homes and shares in recently privatized public utilities. It is thus important to understand Butler's "resentment and rancour against identity", upon which the Conservatives' political strategies were based: in a country haunted by the privileges of class, the attempt to produce a different identity for working-class subjects, one which gave them apparent access to those privileges for so long denied them, was a huge pull. While the middle-class left was demanding the retention of a working class which was the "phantasmatic site" of revolutionary consciousness, the right was pulling these subjects in the opposite direction. It could be argued that the left's fantasy of the working class was the opposite of their own upbringing. Much counter-culture in the 1970s depended upon the rejection by middle-class young people of their "bourgeois" practices. This meant that any arrangement which was not bourgeois was automatically coded as working class. So, for example, living in communes, not adopting petit bourgeois morality, not doing the washing up, were understood as signs of class opposition and class allegiance. In addition, working-class men and women became dangerously attractive sexually as Others for these young people. In these myriad ways, the left constructed an attractive fantasy of what it meant to be working class, which bore little relation to the true practices and modes of regulation through which actual working-class people were, at that time, subjected. Consequently, working-class subjects rarely fulfilled the fantasies projected on to them. It is not difficult to understand, therefore, that such subjects became the target of the left's huge disappointment in their failure to live up to their own dreams for the transformation of their own lives. What Thatcher offered the working class, by contrast, was a different set of dreams, in which they would no longer be the poor and exploited, the butt of middle-class prejudice. If the strategies of social regulation had held up working-class people as pathological to the middle-class norm (see Blackman 1996), then it is not surprising that being associated with extremes (whether of deviance or political position) was not a favoured site of working-class fantasy. Consequently, it is instructive to examine the changes discussed by the working-class parents in our study, in the way that they understand access to work and their own identities.

The fact that class membership is now produced and regulated differently, namely in different economic and political circumstances, with the erosion of the traditional practices through which it was formerly produced, is evident from remarks made by the parents of the young women as well as the young women themselves. As one father remarks:

> Well there's a big difference (between now and the sixties) because when I left school I could walk into a job straight away, and if I didn't like it I could come out of that job and get another one in the afternoon. And I done that quite a few times till I was 21 . . . You could do that then, but now they haven't got a chance.

His wife adds that "You've got to hang on to what you've got.'

It is by the strategy of being "in the middle" that many parents and their daughters now defend themselves against the difficulty of being presented as at either an extreme of individual or social pathology (through being designated poor, unemployed, "rough" or deviant) or of political extremism. So, for example, Dawn describes herself as middle class because "working class to my mind is someone that goes round talking like that'. Along with several others, she mentions that the upper class have a lot of money and are snobs. One of the fathers puts himself "in the middle" because "I think there is an upper class now and between the upper class and the lower class there's a big gap, isn't there?" Another father says, "We don't look at class to be honest . . . Well, everyone likes to say they're middle class, but, I mean, I work for a living so . . . it's a difficult one . . . we're better than some but not so good as others.'

If, as we have argued, being in the middle maps out a position (much like the term "middle-class, blue-collar" in the USA), which is neither poor underclass nor rich upper class and which presents a form of subjectivity which is neither pathological nor extreme, simply in the middle, how do we understand class in this very changed scenario? If class is lived as the power to consume rather than in relation to production, if it is women rather than men who fill the labour market, gaining in the professions, doing the part-time, poorly paid service work demanded by the economy, how is class lived as feminized and how do girls and women live the markers of class and men and boys the markers of classlessness? How does all of this relate to patterns of attainment?

Classed attainment

In our study, the middle-class girls, that is all but one, went to university. Most achieved high grades and went to high-ranking universities. Of the working-class girls, 43 per cent left school at 16 after GCSEs, with 25 per cent going to university (three girls) and none in the straightforward way achieved by the middle-class girls. At 21, 37 per cent of the working-class girls were employed full time, 13 per cent part time and 19 per cent were unemployed. We are here using the terms "working" and "middle class" to designate the young women as they were categorized in the original study at four and at six. Given the discussion above, these designations are clearly problematic. A much longer discussion of this issue appears in Walkerdine, Lucey and Melody (forthcoming), but we use the designations here for short-hand and identification purposes.

Thus, it can be seen that the middle-class girls appear to fulfil the characteristics of Wilkinson's (1994) "Genderquake", that is, they are being fitted to enter the professions previously filled by their fathers and brothers. Their academic success is glittering: most of them do exceptionally well at school and go on to good universities. What we want to do here briefly is to examine how these young women are produced as professional middle class through the regulation of the relation between their intellect and their sexuality and to compare this with the regulation of another group, the small number of working-class young women in the sample who have had babies. In this way, we can explore the opposing ways in which femininity and class is lived.

Creating the bourgeois subject as feminine

Our main argument is that the kind of transformations we are witnessing in the gendered division of labour also require a transformation of gendered class relations. We can use post-structuralism to understand the production of those new subject positions. This necessitates an understanding of the genealogy, the historical production of these figures. To this we can add an analysis of practices through which they are produced in the present and an understanding of the way in which they are held together psychically through fantasy and psychodynamic and unconscious processes. In this chapter we will merely outline the basis of this work.

In our previous work (Walkerdine & Lucey 1989) we made it clear that when the middle-class girls were four years old, there were a number of practices in which the girls and their mothers were positioned as subjects, which were specific to this group. For example, the lack of clear boundaries between work and play, the turning of domestic work into educative play and the importance of rational argument, as a means of empowerment for the young girls themselves. Alongside this was the turning of passionate emotions into nice and nasty feelings, sensible and silly behaviour.

In this chapter we examine the historical production of the bourgeois individual, understanding the family and cultural practices as part of the production of that individual. However, we would not be so foolish as to suggest that these simple practices in any sense were the root cause of the success of the girls, nor, that if these practices were adopted by working-class families, that their daughters would be equally successful at school. Far from it. We think that in each case, educational performance is produced by a complex intersection of the social, cultural and psychic. We want to make it clear that the liberal attempts to ensure educational success for working-class children by importing into their homes practices which work for the middle class are ill-founded and socially and psychologically naive. They assume that these practices can be prised out of the social and cultural milieu that produces them, as well as the psychic defensive organization of which they are a part. What we are talking about here specifically is the making of the bourgeoisie and the fictions upon which it is founded.

It might be argued that we are mistaken to begin to examine and criticize middle-class strategies when, above all, they so patently produce success for their daughters. Why then should we want to take that apart, even criticize it? We wish to argue that the production of that success for middle-class girls is historically specific. We want to show both how it is formed and what it means. There have been so few studies of the middle class, and in the educational literature they are so often regarded as the norm. In order to examine these practices, we had to "make strange" practices that were so often taken for granted. However, because all of us grew up working class, they were to some extent strange to us and this enabled us to have another take on what was going on. Part of this was that we began to ask what success meant and what was the price that was paid for it. Why, we asked, do these girls seem to follow a trajectory that looks a little like a conveyor belt and why must they be kept to that path at all costs, with so much fear that if they fall off they will be in a desert, with no water and visible means of life support? Because there seemed to be something keeping the families on this track at all costs, we began to ask what were the desperate investments, what was it that was being so studiously and relentlessly avoided? It was these questions which led us to produce the account that we provide in this chapter.

Reason and emotion in the production of the post-Enlightenment subject

We argued in *Democracy in the Kitchen* (Walkerdine & Lucey 1989) that rationality in the form of rational argument was a central strategy in the regulation of the middle-class girls, alongside the turning of passionate emotions into feelings. To understand why these particular practices were widespread we need to look not only at the recent history of class, education and psychology, but also at the way in which the rational and the feminine have been understood in the move towards the production of a rationally ordered bourgeois liberal democracy. In an earlier volume (Walkerdine 1989) we argued that

> Our argument in a nutshell, is that ideas about reason and reasoning cannot be understood historically outside considerations of gender. Since the Enlightenment, if not before, the Cartesian concept of reason has been deeply embroiled in attempts to control nature. Rationality was taken as a kind of rebirth of the thinking self, without the intervention of a woman. The rational self was a profoundly masculine one from which woman was excluded, her powers not only inferior but also subservient. The 'thinking' subject was male; the female provided the biological prop both to procreation and to servicing the possibility of 'man'. Philosophical doctrine was transformed into the object of a science in which reason became a capacity invested within the body, and later mind, of man alone (ibid.: 27).

Foucault (1979) calls such developments "fictions which function in truth". They are not essential truths about science or men or women, but because they became enshrined, at least from the nineteenth century, in scientific debates about rationality, science and woman, especially the science of woman, they then came to be understood as matters of fact, statements that could safely be made and empirically supported about women and about reason. It was during the nineteenth century that "human nature" became the object of scientific inquiry and the female body and mind the objects of a deeply patriarchal scientific gaze. Ideas about female nature included a female body suffused (from the hysteria of the womb) with madness, irrationality, whereas the upper- and middle-class white male body was the natural repository of the rational mind: a rationality not only naturally given, but deeply necessary to the civilizing process. Europe with its immense colonial powers produced itself as the natural progenitor of civilization, keeping at bay the hordes of primitive, animal irrationality, be it vested in colonial peoples or the European masses. We wish to argue that the "truth" about rationality embodied a deeply held fantasy of its opposition to the powers of unreason, everything contained within that fantasy from the masses, to colonial peoples, the mad, women etc. Bhabha (1984) conceptualizes this well when he writes of the "fear, phobia and fetish" with which colonial peoples were viewed in the discourses of the colonizer. In other words, our argument is that not only is reasoning held to be a supreme and important power for the production and maintenance of a particular form of government, but that this form holds within it deep fears about otherness, the price to be paid for the loss of reason, the fall off the edge of the bourgeoisie.

Foucault argued that alongside the rise in human and social sciences there was a change in power and government, in which population management became a central and strategic mode of government (Henriques et al. 1984). This ties in with what sociologists have described as the rise of the "new middle class', that is a professional class, whose members are central to the management and government of a liberal democracy in which power operates not through coercion but by autonomy, free will, choice. Thus, it can be seen that as well as the middle class as owners of capital, the professions become an important source of power. Professionals, of course, must have a strong and clear grasp of reason, above all else in order for them to take their place as the governors of those Others.

In all of this it is difficult to understand how women, who became the subject of scientific observation, should become the bearers of rationality. We argued previously (Walkerdine 1989) that typically girls and the feminine were understood as antithetical to the playful, masculine child of reason, yet also necessary in order to provide the essential feminine caring context in which rational development can occur. This is precisely what the mothers of these middle-class girls do: they provide the basis for rational argument, and they do more than this, they make emotions safe. Emotions can be understood as part of the irrational, the dreaded animal passions. It follows, therefore, that the bourgeoisie has to tame these in some way. We suggest that this is just what these mothers do.

What has happened in the last 20 years has created the possibility of making the feminine rational or the rational feminine, which has allowed these girls to become rational subjects, taking the place in the professions once occupied by men. To understand this we would need to look not only at the changes in the labour market but also at the effects of second wave feminism. However, as we shall see, the entry of the middle-class girls into masculine norms of rational academic excellence comes at a price. It is not achieved easily at all and indeed is produced out of the very suppression of aspects of femininity and sexuality.

The production of the subject is not easily achieved, but is a struggle both in terms of regulation and in terms of the psychic and unconscious processes needed to produce the subject.

The production of excellence

We want to show how the story of rationality as natural and normal, the new middle class as given through the destiny of their intelligence, is produced by a great deal of work, some of it social and cultural, some of it psychic, defensive. As we have seen, the majority of middle-class girls in our sample do extremely well at school and go on to "good" universities and prepare to enter the professions (most of them do not wish to go into business).

Let us examine how, precisely, this is produced. We have already documented some of the work that went into preparing the four year olds. According to Tizard and Hughes (1984) nursery school staff paid far more attention to the language styles of the middle-class girls, thus reinforcing what had already gone on in the home. At age ten, the middle-class girls' performance already so far outstripped that of the working-class sample that the performance of the top working-class girl was worse than the lowest achiever attending a middle class school. In addition, a quarter of the middle-class families had already taken their daughters out of state schools at age 10 and put them into private preparatory schools (with the majority of them being in private schools from the age of eleven). Such schools were all single-sex and in these schools, behaviour which was split along gender lines in the state school (e.g. boys taking the place of playful rationality, girls working hard) was organized quite differently. Here, girls took all of those places, which meant that the top-performing girls behaved and were treated far more like the boys in the state schools. In addition to this, excellence was simply the expected norm. Nobody was supposed to do poorly and girls were expected to work as hard as it took to produce excellence. Anything else was simply considered to be failure.

When we began the work on this phase of the research, we had a hard time figuring this out. After all, we were used to understanding excellent performance as exceptional, to be praised and congratulated. Yet what we were met with was something quite other. Exceptional performance was treated as quite ordinary, as something expected, unworthy of comment. Indeed, this was summed up by Sam's mother who, on hearing that her daughter had got ten GCSE's (nine with an A grade and one with a C), made only one comment according to Sam, "Pity about the C.' We felt dumbfounded. After all, what we were far more used to hearing was the elaborate praise accorded to the working-class girls over performance that was far inferior and which would have been the object of ridicule or shame in middle-class households. We began to ask why it should have been the case that only the highest performance would do. This was brought home to us with the case of two sisters. Anna, one of our sample, was described as brilliant. The parents went on to describe her younger sister, Natasha, whom the interviewer (June Melody) had never met. In the course of the conversation, June gained the strong impression that Natasha had a severe educational problem, might even have special educational needs. Her mother after all mentioned the possibility of brain damage during her birth. In fact, it later became clear that Natasha was not only a gifted violinist, but she had also gained three A levels: one A and two Bs. These grades would certainly have been sufficient to get her a place in a university, but she was considered to be struggling academically and was directed towards hotel management. Yet such grades would have been proudly displayed in working-class homes. How does it come to be the case that the parents show such distress at anything other than excellence? What function does excellence serve and how is it achieved? More than this, we can see that in fact the identities of Anna and Natasha as brilliant and stupid, are fictions, fantasies constructed in the complex dynamics of the family. Natasha is the one who isn't Anna, isn't brilliant, is a problem. So here, "failure" is constituted dynamically.

Clever but feminine

Of course, academic excellence is what so completely ensures the production and reproduction of the new middle class. It gets the girls places in the right universities and makes sure that they do well there, getting the right jobs afterwards. Only excellence, in these straitened times of the 1990s, will act as enough of an insurance: after all graduate unemployment is very high and competition fierce. Yet these girls, who indeed are so spectacularly successful, seem to exist on a conveyer belt going through a desert, in which no deviation from the path can be contemplated. The road to be trodden by these young women is successful certainly, but straight and circumscribed indeed. To attain this goal, they have to play a balancing act in relation to cleverness and femininity, to manage that intersection and the contradictions which it brings. To our eyes, many of them at first glance appear to have everything: they are brainy, successful and extremely good looking: a post feminist's dream indeed.

Yet, they struggle hard to achieve this double success and not all of them have been successful in finding employment. There are several examples of girls' anxiety around trying to be clever and feminine, sometimes pushed to extremes, such as Julia, the middle-class girl who pulled her hair out, but who did not see herself as being allowed to do anything other than do well and go to a good university. In fact, despite her quite extreme emotional problems, she achieved ten grade A GCSEs, two grade As and one B at A level, and went on to Oxford, feeling that she was not allowed to fail. Her mother said that the staff at her expensive private school simply did not pay much attention to her emotional problems, caring more that she should achieve the highest academic standards.

Being feminine cannot be allowed to interfere with academic success: indeed nothing can. This is illustrated graphically by the difference in working-class and middle-class attitudes to pregnancy and motherhood (see Melody et al. 1996). While working-class parents do not like their daughters becoming pregnant they often come round and will accept a baby in the household, if that is what the girl wants. But the middle-class girls and their parents simply cannot contemplate a baby. Several girls mention that their having a baby would "kill" one of their parents.

So birth is equated not with the beginning of life, with something new, but with the end of it, with dying. Nothing, but nothing is allowed to get in the way of the ambition. Indeed, anybody who has a problem with achieving success is immediately presented with any number of costly therapeutics to allay the problem and produce the hoped-for success, as with the example of Julia, quoted above. For her parents as well as for herself, her high grades were not exceptional, indeed could even be interpreted as failure, since many of her classmates got three As. While her parents felt that they had not pressured her, her interview makes it crystal clear that she felt extremely pushed to high performance (which was simply the norm) and that this anxiety manifested itself as both hair pulling and anorexia, about which the school took little notice. The time of her school success is the very time at which Julia hates the available images of herself:

> . . . all the pictures of myself there I absolutely hate at that time, I just really look so awful, and that one [looking at photos of herself] I sort of seem quite happy but – like I mean quite sort of smiling and – but I think I felt really drained after.

We can see from the above examples that the production of the middle-class girl as the rational bourgeois subject requires a huge investment. The right kind of schooling has to be provided, in which she will usually be made to feel that exceptional performance is merely normal, not noteworthy, that this performance is never enough. She may also be made to feel that femininity is also to be struggled over, sometimes renouncing sexuality, because the onset of womanhood is too painful when pitted against the extraordinary academic efforts the girl has to make. So, it is not difficult to understand that the anxiety displayed by so many of these girls at ten has escalated. Some cope with it, but others do not and various professionals have to be brought in to help so that the girl can be kept on track. Sometimes, as with Julia, she is kept on track even though she is clearly extremely disturbed. What, one may ask, would she actually have to do to herself to be allowed to get off the conveyer belt? Certainly anorexia and pulling all her hair out have not been enough for anybody to allow her the luxury of letting go.

What is this huge psychic and economic investment, then, which goes into making these young women bourgeois individuals? Why must they succeed at all costs? Why is their emotional state at all times subsumed to rationality, to excellence, to brilliance? We suggest that the huge investment in success covers over the terror of its opposite. That what is defended against here is the fear of falling off the edge of middle-class life and culture, of falling off the edge of rationality and into the darkness of those held to be in the pit of unreason, the dark forces of the masses, and the equally dark forces of their own passionate desires so easily projected on to the "great unwashed". If nobody can let rationality go there must be some powerful emotions at work and it is so easy to locate them in all of those feared as Others who appear to threaten civilization. After all, if the working class is rapidly splintering and changing, with part of it becoming the non-working underclass, with the middle class containing a defence against falling off the edge, these young women's impossible rebellion must carry all those defences – they cannot be allowed to be seen to fail. It does seem as if their only trajectory is to become both very clever and very beautiful. So, as Butler (1990) argues, gender can be seen as a masquerade, now realized by the "I can have everything girls". Yet this heady normality, the utopian success, hides the opposite, the defences against failure, the terrible defence against the impossibility which this supergirl identity represents.

The working class women as single mothers

Let us look at those Others, the working-class young women who have babies. How and what does this tell us about the different modes of regulation in the two groups? These are the young women, who for the middle class girls, have fallen off the edge. Out of our sample of 21 year olds, 21 per cent of the middle class and 31 per cent of the working class become pregnant. While these figures clearly differ, demonstrating not a difference in the amount of sexual activity (according to the interviews at least) but the results of that sexual activity, a bigger difference lies in the results of those pregnancies. None of the middle-class girls decided to keep their pregnancy, whereas in the working class sample, 6 per cent had a termination, 6 per cent had a miscarriage and 19 per cent had a baby. If, therefore, the middle-class girls are expected to regulate their sexuality and fertility in favour of academic attainment, it is not because they have less sex or start it later, but in terms of the results of their sexual activity. No middle-class girl serious about her attainment would be able to be allowed to consider getting pregnant. As one young woman put it, "It's just something I've never thought about. I've never contemplated having a child . . . I think it'd kill my mother." This makes teenage motherhood an entirely working-class affair. What, therefore, allows the working-class girls to have babies and how does this relate to changes in femininity?

In order to understand this in detail we would need to explore the genealogy of the single mother, which we have no space to do here. Suffice it to say that recent Conservative governments have made a great deal of "young ladies who get pregnant just to jump the housing list" (Peter Lilley 1992, quoted in the *Guardian*, 5 September 1995). Again, however, we need to understand the relation of this to the current practices and emotional, psychic relations through which the girls' subjectivity is constituted. In this chapter we concentrate on the latter two issues (though for a more detailed discussion see Melody et al. 1996).

Although some working-class girls were relatively successful in education (in that they achieved above the norm) none achieved the kind of sparkling success of the middle-class sample. What is significant, therefore, is that going on to higher education does not represent for these girls a maintenance of bourgeois identity, in which they take the place of male family members. Far from it: for these young women to move to higher education is to move into a strange, hostile and often frightening world (Walkerdine 1996). To become the embodiment of the bourgeois subject for them is not the maintenance of anything but a significant transformation. It is in this light that we might begin to understand how motherhood functions differently for these girls than for their middle-class counterparts. What is it that allows them to contemplate not only pregnancy and motherhood, but also to be supported by their parents in a way quite foreign to the middle-class families?

> Like my Mum and Nan said like we will help you through it. If they hadn't said that I think I would actually have put her up for adoption . . . I would have done it, but like now I would have regretted it so much.

It would be easy, at one level, to put forward as an explanation the fact that many working-class girls do not have a career or even job prospects, making motherhood a realistic choice as their "job". But we think that the situation is more complex than this. In our sample at least, all of the young mothers did well at school. All but one achieved at least five GCSEs, grades A to C and one achieved four grade As. All but one had been set for A levels and some for university. They were, then, precisely those working-class girls who were faced with the possibility of transformation into the bourgeois subject. But, as we have indicated, such a step for these girls could be quite frightening in its unfamiliarity. At one level having a baby kept the girl at home with her family, preventing the loss of home and family. We could therefore view motherhood as a complex attempt to maintain present status in the face of overwhelming change and loss. The psychoanalytic aspects of this situation are important but beyond the scope of this chapter (but see Walkerdine et al. forthcoming). Yet several of the young mothers expressed the desire to continue with their education and were trying to find ways of combining childcare with getting a degree, something which was not easy to contemplate, not least because of lack of money.

Conclusion

Both of these groups of young women present us with a class organization which is different from their mothers' generation. The middle-class girls want to have a career first and then motherhood later while the working-class mothers want to integrate having a baby with a later career. Yet, discursively and in terms of fantasy, these two groups are poles apart. One group is positioned as the scrounging female underclass and the other the superwoman. In that sense they are each others Other. Both are highly though differently regulated, producing different subject effects. The middle-class girls are self-regulating and norms of regulation come down more heavily on the working-class girls who become the object of a more obvious surveillant gaze.

From the position in which we stand, it is sometimes as hard to be detached from our envy of the young middle-class women as it was when they were four and could choose any dessert they wanted. It is still hard for us to see their regulation as painful and as harsh as that of the working-class girls. To understand this, we need to examine the specificity of our own education out of the working class, educated to enter a class of which we have always felt on the margins. But more than this, we were also brought up to be "respectable" girls, who did not bring our families into disrepute by getting pregnant early or out of wedlock. From this position it is easy to operate as though the middle-class girls have everything that we have ever wanted. But actually, the working-class families' acceptance of the consequences of their daughters' sexuality and the recognition by these young women that they do not have to marry the father of their child nor consider that because they are young mothers they can never have an education, is a huge step forward and for two of us without children, that also is a source of envy and longing. Femininity and class meet and link together in important but different ways for the two groups and while those differences are intersected by privilege, they are no less the object of regulation.

Things have changed certainly for this new generation, but the very trumpeting of female success that we see often around us does ignore the central class dimensions of what is happening and the way in which the work on women and class is never about one class only. Sad to say, though, middle-class women's engagement with the classed aspects of their own subjectivity is difficult to reach.

Of course, the difficult other side of the complex feminization of class is the position of working- and middle-class men, as we outlined in the introduction. Certainly, men are notably absent in this picture of single-minded career women and single mothers. While, therefore, we are presenting the beginnings of an attempt to examine the transformation of class in relation to gender at the end of the twentieth century, we need to make it clear that while class is transforming, differences between the classes remain as stark as ever, if differently embodied. This makes the dream of classlessness a fantasy indeed. The disappearance of class from a radical political agenda should not signal that class has gone away as an issue, but that its transformation requires urgent attention so that we might give the study and politics of inequality the attention it so desperately deserves.

Note

1. This research was supported by the Economic and Social Research Council of Great Britain.

References

Bhabha, H. 1984. The Other question: the stereotype and colonial discourse, *Screen*, 24, 18–36.

Blackman, L. 1996. The dangerous classes: retelling the psychiatric story. *Feminism and Psychology*, 6(3), 361–80.

Butler, J. 1990. Gender trouble, feminist theory and psychoanalytic discourse, in Nicholson, L. (ed.) *Feminism/Postmodernism*. New York: Routledge.

Foucault, M. 1979. *Discipline and Punish*. Harmondsworth: Penguin.

Gorz, A. 1982. *Farewell to the Working Class*. London: Pluto Press.

Halsey, A.H. et al. 1988. *Origins and Destinations: Family, Class and Education in Modern Britain*. Oxford: Clarendon Press.

Henriques, J. et al. 1984. *Changing the Subject: Psychology, Social Regulation and Subjectivity*. Oxford: Methuen (republished 1998, London: Routledge).

Melody, J., Lucey, H. and Walkerdine, V. 1996. *Motherhood, Class and Sexuality*, Working Papers for Project 4/21.

Tizard, B. and Hughes, M. 1984. *Young Children Learning*. London: Fontana.

Walkerdine, V. 1989. *Counting Girls Out*. London: Virago (republished Brighton: Falmer Press, 1998).

Walkerdine, V. 1991. *Schoolgirl Fictions*. London: Verso.

Walkerdine, V. 1996. Subject to change without notice: psychology, post-modernity and the popular, in Thrift, N. (ed.) *Mapping the Subject*. Routledge: London.

Walkerdine, V. 1997. *Daddy's Girl: Young Girls and Popular Culture*, London: Macmillan and Cambridge, Mass.: Harvard University Press.

Walkerdine, V. and Lucey, H. 1989. *Democracy in the kitchen: Regulating Mothers and Socialising Daughters*. London: Virago.

Walkerdine, V., Lucey, H. and Melody, J. (in press) *Growing up Girl: Gender and Class in the 21st Century*, London: Macmillan.

Wilkinson, J. 1994. *Generations of the Genderquake*. London: Institute for Public Policy Research.

CHAPTER FIVE

Women in and after a "classless" society

Hana Havelková

The confusions and debates persist in Czech society about whether the egalitarian experiment of the "real" socialist regimes was thoroughly wrong or whether it contained some positive aspects. My chapter is intended to make a contribution to the search for a non-simplified view of this theoretical and practical question. The attempt in my country to introduce gender equality by force provides a good example of a whole set of paradoxes which stem from the totalitarian system within which they originated. I will focus on some of these paradoxes, which formed and continue to form the framework of our lives.

Class revolution: source of paradoxes

It needs to be clear at the outset that "class" for us was and still is defined in classical Marxist terms to indicate the relationship of the exploiter and the exploited to the means of production. To this day we tend not to use it outside that framework, preferring instead such terms as "differentiation", "status" and "social strata" to denote forms of inequality which in the UK would be regarded as markers of class difference.

The initial socialist project was aimed at achieving a classless society, or levelling up social differences. Three categories of inequalities were to be targeted – between workers and intelligentsia, between town and country and between men and women. In all the three categories the project was operationalized through the following main methods: the initial act of "the expropriation of the rich" (involving confiscation of wealth and property) and through this the "expropriation of men" (Wagnerova 1996); its follow-up in the form of an extremely anti-meritocratic redistribution system in which everybody was a state employee with approximately the same salary and social provision; through ideological rhetoric; and through affirmative action which supported people who had been disadvantaged under the former system.

69

In my view, the totalitarian manner in which the differences were "eliminated" was significant in two ways. On one hand, the result was more radical than it could ever have been in a democratic country and to some extent even internalized by the population. This in turn helped to justify the totalitarian nature of the system, to large groups of the population, including the idealistic young intelligentsia. On the other hand, because of the overall paternalistic nature of the system, the social status of a person was not a matter of individual achievement, but bestowed from above. It was not based on any personal merit like knowledge, efficiency or effectivity, but was entirely dependent on the status the state ascribed to the objective position you were working in. Since status was universally determined by the "father" (the state or party), citizens were placed (in all but name), in the position of children, perceiving even small status differences very sharply and enviously. As a result, the ideology of overall social equality, permanently supported by official propaganda, led to feelings of injustice in almost every profession especially in relation to salary. In the case of women, this paradox can be demonstrated by the fact that on the one hand women's social or public status undoubtedly increased because of communist policies. On the other hand the policies were not really liberating for women as individuals, subject as they were to the same system of status determination as the men. Women from former socialist countries often express their feelings about this in such contradictory statements as "We are too emancipated," and "The emancipation did not bring anything to women; it has not really liberated us."

The second paradox is that the totalitarian practices both enabled radical processes aimed at social equality to be implemented and on the other hand they blocked it. First, spontaneous development within the target groups was halted both directly and indirectly. Directly, any gatherings and social movements were banned by law; indirectly, social problems were officially declared "solved" and the population partly believed it and partly knew that nothing else could be done from below. For women it meant, among other things, that the spontaneously developing women's movement was stopped totally. The women's movement had had a long history in this country and before the communist takeover comprised over 60 various women's organizations mostly organized under the umbrella of the so-called Council of the Czechoslovak Women (Garver 1986). The Communist Party replaced this rich feminist scene by one single official women's organization called The Union of Czech Women, which was directly subordinated to the party and was to spread party ideology among women. Indirectly, any activity from below was paralysed because women were strongly supported and protected by the state so, theoretically, they had no reason to complain. Yet they knew that something was wrong with this kind of emancipation, but there were no real mechanisms or contexts for discussion (gatherings were not allowed) which would have made it possible for them actively to change things. For it was the very principle of the totalitarian regime that all social arrangements were imposed from above. Secondly, the party–state arrangements often contradicted each other: for example, a woman who benefited from socialist policies by attaining the highest level of education was disbarred by the same policies from using and enjoying it in the same way that a career woman in Western countries might, because her social status as a member of the intelligentsia was subject to restrictions from above.

Despite massive redistribution of social goods, the regime generated new differences between, for example, the professionals and the workers, and also cultural differences. My third claim (and another paradox), then, is that the new differences on the one hand partly reversed the old ones. The factory and agricultural workers were mostly better paid than the vast majority of the intelligentsia. They were also ideologically praised as the ones who really "work". On the other hand, in the realm of gender, the regime tended to reproduce traditional sex roles, not officially, but in an unspoken and subtle way. That is why the "class struggle", which after the first phase was continued in a softer and more sophisticated way, still overshadowed gender tensions, which were even more "foggy". The paternalistic and unequal state policy against the professions led to solidarities between men and women within the professions rather than to solidarity between women across them. The same held true for the new hierarchy based on party membership. Women often used their maternal duties as an excuse to avoid party membership, a strategy not available to men (Havelková 1993a) with the result that there were far fewer female party members than male ones. In this sense women had more freedom than men to escape collaboration with the communists and if it meant that women were excluded from top management positions, it was a small price to pay for that freedom, so women did not interpret it as a direct discrimination. It was regarded as the result of a thoroughly distorted political system.

Though women's opportunities in the new regime were enhanced, as time went on the labour market and the status structure became gradually segregated. It became segregated horizontally with women entering areas of the labour market that were not favoured by the paternalist system and therefore progressively abandoned by men, which led to an extreme feminization of the school and health systems. It also became segregated vertically because women occupied lower positions in relation to men even in the feminized sectors. Yet due to "specific" factors such as party membership, this gender segregation has not as yet been sufficiently recognized by the public as a gender problem.

This situation could have been fostered by another. Because of the dominance of social class in the official propaganda and explicit attempts at social engineering, women in my country might have perceived as more important the changes in positions between women themselves rather than those between men and women. And here we have a fourth paradox: on the one hand an unprecedented homogenization of women's "fate" in Czech society was brought about (this led to a unified family model as I explore below); on the other hand, a new women's elite grew up (though in a status-inconsistent way of high prestige/low income), so that the differences between the group of educated women and the women workers (who were low prestige/low income) were very visible.

Advancement

The communist takeover in Czechoslovakia took place in February 1948 (called "victorious February"). I was born one year later and so lived all my life, till the "velvet revolution" of 1989, in a society which was declaring itself as "classless".[1] The ground was fertile for such a takeover in Czechoslovakia.[2] It has been amply documented that among the socialist countries, Czechoslovakia was the most egalitarian one (Machonin 1992, 1996). Or, to put it another way, it was in this country where the socialist project was realized in the most thoroughgoing way. Moreover, according to many observers, the egalitarianism in this country was also internalized to a greater extent than in others.[3]

With respect to the advancement of women, one can even say that communist policies not only did not contradict some pre-communist trends, but even supported them (Havelková 1995). For example, the progressive family law which was prepared by the group of pre-communist women lawyers was taken up and included into the communist legislation without any changes. This law, which came into force in 1950, excluded any reference to the man as the "head of family" which was quite unique in Europe at that time. Also the employment rate of Czech women was traditionally quite high and so, in the Czech case, women were not suddenly put into work by the communist regime. The figures show that in 1938 women made up 36.5 per cent of the total labour force, in 1953, 40.3 per cent, in 1963, 44.9 per cent (Busheikin & Marikova 1995). Similar trends can be noticed in the sphere of education. In 1930 women comprised 25 per cent of the university students (Garver 1986) and coeducational schooling was introduced as early as the initial years of the 1920s. Women's voting rights were included in the first Czechoslovak constitution in 1920.

In the first period of communist rule in the 1950s and 1960s, the social status of women was raised dramatically. This was made possible through the overall social mobility at that time, facilitating women's access to the public sphere. In addition, formal arrangements were introduced to support women's advancement in the public sphere. Yet the initial goal was even more ambitious. In the 1950s, there were attempts to equalize gender relations in the family by removing the boundaries between the public and private space, both ideologically and practically.

In the postwar and above all the post-February Czech culture (i.e. post communist takeover of 25 February 1948), as documented for example by Vladimir Macura's semiotic analysis, the traditional attributes of the home, of woman's role and also of love were attacked, rooted out and derided.

> Usual motifs of home become less frequent: tranquillity, relaxation, order – all these are derided as inferior, banal interests in food and housework, interests showing a lack of political awareness . . . Traditional types of mother-woman in the sense of guardians of the home here suddenly turn out to be an alien and disturbing element . . . the

home becomes acceptable only if it opens itself to the outer world, if the world becomes a part of it and the home itself is turned into a part of the world at large (Macura 1992: 36).

Such attacks were directed against all "activities of closed spaces", including love.

> The challenge was to take love out of the private space of 'house', and to de-eroticize it as much as possible. If the woman is too much a part of the private space of home, she is denounced together with condemnation of home, no matter whether the woman is mother or lover. The woman ideal is now woman as co-fighter and as comrade (Macura 1992: 37–8).

The whole programme of the opening-up of the home had to fail, for it was soon recognized as supporting state control over the individual. So another paradox is that the communist mode of liberation connected with anti-traditionalism at the same time as evoking traditionalism in people as a reaction against official policy. Yet the reconstruction came only after deconstruction; the norms of social behaviour changed (for instance, certain sexist attitudes and prejudices were not politically acceptable), so that the anti-traditional patterns and values came to be combined with the traditional ones. Part of the explanation of why women in The Czech Republic as well as in other former socialist countries stick to their traditional family role is that it was part of their civic resistance.

The most important impact on people's lives resulted from a real opening of public space to women. "Public space" was used to refer mainly to the world of work and education and these were considered to be the main routes to liberation. The general right to work prevented women's involuntary unemployment. It is sometimes wrongly believed that all women had a legal duty to work but this was not true for married women. Unmarried women, on the other hand, had to work, mainly in order to prevent themselves falling into prostitution. Czech women have used the right to work to a great extent. For example, in 1971 women's employment reached 47 per cent of the total workforce. The high value formally placed on work was internalized to a considerable extent, although the need for a double income in the family to maintain a basic standard of living made it almost unavoidable. Also, the idea that society would take over a great part of the housework and childcare was widely accepted. Housework services called "The Liberated Household" were introduced everywhere and many mothers put their small babies in the nurseries. Two decades later, such practices have disappeared.

Another "revolution" was that of women's educational access. The development in the area of education can be called a women's education boom indeed. Already in the late 1960s, the education level of both sexes was equalized in the population under 30 years of age. Among other things, it meant that not only was the number of daughters with higher education eight times greater than that of their mothers, but also much greater than that of their fathers (Wagnerova 1974).

Women's political participation was promoted by means of quotas and by encouraging women, for this, from the ideological point of view, was the most visible demonstration of achieved "equality". So the number of women in the National Assembly increased from 7.1 per cent in 1948–9 to 28.6 per cent in 1976–9. On regional national committees women comprised 31.1 per cent of members. There was also a rule that a vice-president of the National Assembly had to be a woman. In the first communist government, there were two women ministers – for the first and the last time.

Women's reproductive rights were liberalized for the first time in 1958, when the grounds for abortion were broadened to include age, number of children and social factors. Abortion requests were considered by commissions composed of doctors and representatives, and although both their composition and their practices were permanently discussed and criticized, their rate of rejection never exceeded 10 per cent of applications (Wagnerova 1974). Abortions were free of charge and carried out in state hospitals. This relatively liberal policy on abortion was further liberalized in the late 1970s and 1980s, when abortion on demand was introduced up to three months into a pregnancy.

The major systemic changes introduced by the communist regime were more or less finished in the 1950s, as were the resulting dynamic changes in society. Both the social programme and the political system at large started to be critically reconsidered. Because of this and in the context of a more liberal political climate, disciplines such as demography and sociology were re-established again at the end of 1960s, having been condemned and banned after 1948 as "bourgeois quasi-sciences". These disciplines immediately started to pay attention to women's status and to the conflict in women's roles. Unlike 20 years later, that is in the present, when women's issues are mostly silently included in the theorizing about the family, at that time women's issues were theorized as women's issues. Following conventional statistical indicators, one could truly claim that

> the changes have not resulted in true equality in the type of education men and women receive or in the distribution of wages or decision-making roles in the economy. Nor have they led to corresponding changes in women's political participation or roles in the home (Wolchik 1979: 592).

Yet others, such as Alena Wagnerova, starting from her personal experience, observed considerable changes in both gender relationships and women's position, when compared to the West. "As far as the woman's position in society is concerned, my stay in West Germany equalled a journey into the past" (Wagnerova 1974: 7).

The "Prague Spring" saw a brief period of social action and public discussion aimed at solving existing problems. These were stopped by the Soviet invasion in 1968 so that what could have been critically discussed and corrected in the late 1960s and the 1970s persisted for another 20 years. The structural conditions became rigid, the positive, dynamic outward effects were drastically slowed down, and the backlash effects gradually deepened. The shift in people's interest from the public to the private sphere connected with still higher value being placed on the family and this reinforced the role of women in it. The feminization of certain professions (for example, health care services and the textile industry) developed to an extreme extent – for example, by the end of 1980s, women comprised about 86 per cent of the teaching force (Cermakova 1995a). In the period from 1968 to 1989 the Communist Party also introduced measures (accompanied by a strong ideology) such as pro-natal policy and extended maternity leave with financial support which further underpinned people's orientation to the family. At this time the political goal was to encourage people to forget their discontent with the political situation. The public discussions on the social situation of women from the late 1960s were virtually forgotten; social studies focused mainly on the family as a whole.

Classes, genders, professions and individuals

There was a permanent interplay between the Communist Party's policies and the reactions of the population, often somewhat ignored by theorists. At the beginning, the totalitarian character of communist politics was obvious, especially in relation to the methods of liquidating political opponents. Its drastic methods were presented as legitimized by the "people's" or the "general" or the society's (collective) interest rather than by those of individuals. The social role and autonomy of every individual were oppressed and almost absolutely restricted. The concept of private property vanished – only the categories "personal" and "national" property were allowed. Personal property was allowed within legally determined limits but if, for example, a family house exceeded a certain size, it was expropriated for public purposes. Everybody became a state employee and thus economically dependent on the state. The social subjectivity of a person was minimized in all spheres of life (Havelková 1993b). Institutional restrictions were accompanied by normative ones. For instance, the individual had not to stand out, to be too visible, to try to differ from others. Such behaviour would be called "non-collective" and would be condemned through children's upbringing in the kindergartens or at school and in the workplace.

Besides their inclusion in the classes of workers and peasants, women as a group were targeted for special attention and a special care by the state in order to equalize their social position. Yet as individuals they had of course to suppress their identity the same way as the men. Also such alleged achievements as the numbers of women deputies in parliament had in fact almost no impact, for women as well as men were not able to act as political agents but only as puppets (every law was approved by 100 per cent of parliament). They were nominated and then permanently manipulated by the Communist Party. Moreover, women's roles were "prescribed". Alena Heitlinger (1993) draws attention to the fact that women's role was defined as a unity of economic, maternal and political function and she notes that a counterpart to this triple role has never been spelled out for men.

On the other side, men were deprived of their traditional superiority generated by and maintained through greater access to money – both in public and private spheres.

> Nationalization (i.e. expropriation) not only hit capitalists and small and large landowners as such but also at men, striking at the core of their identity and self-awareness, since in taking away their property it also deprived them of an important attribute of their social dominance. The communist transformation of society also took away the importance of whole series of occupations (business, commerce, self-employment) which had until then been traditional domains of male self-realization. Collectivization not only attacked capitalist power but also fundamentally limited the power of men. Together with its consequences it meant that patterns of male behaviour and interaction lost much of their significance as the binding criteria of human behaviour. In terms of goods relationships, the 'price of men' fell. This negative 'redistribution', during which men lost but women did not gain, only partly improved the conditions for women to share in society's resources. In any case, the former economic inequality between men and women was levelled out (Wagnerova 1996: 104).

In this connection, some authors speak of the "feminization" or "emasculinization" of society (Tatur 1992).

By the end of the 1950s, despite all the bad things the communists did, the "egalitarian utopia" still functioned widely as a legitimating framework, even justifying the oppression of the individual. Yet in the 1960s as the signs of the "world of status" started to emerge (especially when directly awarded by the party), the ideological framework began to lose its cogency. The mediating function of the egalitarian policy lost its legitimizing meaning and came more and more to be perceived as part of the state's manipulation. Even the preferred target groups (workers, peasants and women) were not able to act as social subjects: their problems were declared solved, and spontaneous group gatherings were legally forbidden. As a result, the value of equality itself started to be critically reconsidered and its compatibility with the principle of individual freedom was queried. It became clear that at least under given political conditions, the egalitarian programme was connected with distortions (or systemic limitations) of basic liberal goals, which initially many people had believed to be "completed" by the socialist "corrections". Gradually even the idealistic intelligentsia saw that instead of social rights there were social provisions serving the political manipulations of the "liberated". Equalization by means of redistribution was regarded as a direct cause of the destruction of the economy and the quality of life.

A radical and anti-patriarchal programme was doomed to fail when operating within this implicitly feudal/paternalistic political system. In the name of "post-capitalism", i.e. socialism, a pre-capitalist division of power was introduced. In terms of patriarchy, when using Carole Pateman's vocabulary (Pateman 1988), there was an attempt to break down familial patriarchy by radical transformation of the family, yet this attempt was pursued in a paternalistic, precontractual political state system, denying individual autonomy. Men as well as women were put in the position of children. We can even say that with the absence of civil contract, the "sexual contract" also lost its political meaning.

Women's situation was contradictory. As a group and as objects of the egalitarian programme, women experienced promotion in their social status. As individuals and citizens, they were oppressed in the same way as men, i.e. women were not subordinated to men but to paternalistic power. In this respect, solidarity between the sexes under the communist regime is often mentioned as something specific to Eastern European societies, especially in terms of family solidarity and in terms of shared "humanistic" or "democratic" ideas which stood in opposition to the official line. Yet this solidarity between the sexes has to be regarded, from the cultural point of view, as a myth. Sexist anti-woman jokes never ceased to be liked by men. Another implication is the deterioration in the way the communist power gendered its policy. Although it accomplished some features of the liberal feminist project, it was at the same time tied to the logic of the collective society. The result was that women's identity as women gradually lost its meaning as it gave way to the prioritization of the individual's identity, particularly after 1968. Thus the oppositional insistence on being an individual has militated against the development of a feminist consciousness (Siklova 1993: 34–5).

In addition, new social differentiations (what in the UK might be called "class") intervened in this picture. State power distinguished between "productive" and "non-productive" labour, the latter including education, health care, humanities, but also services. In these areas (traditionally "women's work") the remuneration was worse. Yet even here, the gender basis of this discrimination was not obvious because "choice" of profession was linked to many other factors. Thus as struggles between different social groups re-emerged, they were split into small mutual animosities, which in everyday life overshadowed both the fact that women belonged officially to the target group and the fact that they were victims of job segregations. The perception of women as a non-privileged class was absent.

Homogenization of women's lives

The social equality programme and increased social mobility diminished the differences between women, especially in the first period. The measures which were introduced had various kinds of impact on women's lives. Because the category of "domestic servant" ceased to exist (being classified as typical exploitation), many former career women found life more difficult, as did wealthy women (whose had been expropriated) who were not used to work. But for former servants or women from lower classes, these social changes often meant personal advancement and improvement in their situation, which they often perceived not in terms of comparison with men but with other women.

Although new differences developed in the social structure of the female population (especially in terms of education and prestige), there was a striking uniformity in women's lives (woman's "fate"). This arose to some extent from the general decrease in individual choice but also from the social redistribution of wealth which meant that there were only a few families that could live on one income. Limited life choice had two main aspects – similar models of employment and similar models of marriage. The standard employment model meant that almost all women were employed (including 95 per cent of mothers), almost all in full-time, permanent jobs and that those with career aspirations mostly stopped short of trying to gain top positions. This was because of the surprisingly uniform marital model which meant that career women generally married quite early and had children (only 6 per cent of Czech women are childless) (Castle-Kanerová 1992). The twin demands of work and family meant that they could not manage more than two children. So the number of children became "standardized" too, usually one or two, seldom more than three (17 per cent). Only 7 per cent of women in the population had more than four children whereas today, more than 80 per cent of married women over 30 years of age have at least two children (Cermakova 1995b).

As I have said, the main reason that women had to be in paid employment was as a *direct* consequence of official policy. Men were not able to provide sufficiently for their families because they had been deprived of their traditional role as breadwinners. The reason for the standardized marital model was an *indirect* consequence of official policy and arose from the specific role which family life attained under communism. I consider the standardization of women's or families' lives one of the most fascinating consequences of state socialism. It shows how economic, social and political frameworks can lead to similar "spontaneous" responses from below. It was not directly laid down that the number of children should be limited but it became the response of almost every individual or family in adjusting to external conditions.

The combination of the radical opening-up of the public sphere to women and the simultaneous resurrection of traditional family patterns is another obvious paradox and definitely in striking contrast to the liberation model of the Western feminist movement from the 1970s. Not only was it the cause of the well-known double burden for women in the socialist countries, but it also made the classical problem of woman's double role more serious and more complex. To understand this strange combination fully, we need to understand the distorted character of the public sphere itself, the way that the family operated as a refuge from it and as a compensation for what it failed to offer (e.g. free speech) and the dubious value of a career under the communist regime (Havelková 1993a, 1993b).

Current transformation of Czech society

The transformation process that started after the revolution in 1989 is under-pinned by principles which are entirely different to the communist ones. Individual political freedom and freedom of choice are regarded as superior to all other values. Consequently, a process of "de-egalitarianization" has been going on, visible in conspicuous trends in income differentiation. Since entrepreneurship became legal again, the "new rich", the successful entrepreneurs, have emerged whereas state employees continue to live on their restricted state-regulated incomes. At the same time, the Czech government has been (so far) very careful to maintain social peace by ensuring a safety net of welfare and the "pillow" has been rather soft. Thus again, two seemingly contradictory tendencies can be observed in Czech society with respect to women's situation. For women who already have children, the "socialist" pattern of the double burden is not only reproduced, but even strengthened. So far the low unemployment rate in The Czech Republic[4] has prevented any large-scale pauperization of the population, although groups endangered by poverty exist and will most probably grow in future.

Six years after the transformation started, little evidence existed to suggest a negative impact on women. This in itself is a very important "event". Yet the process is very much in flux, social differentiation (what the reader might identify as the re-emergence of "class") is increasing and unemployment is suspiciously low and cannot be kept so forever, so research evidence is usually accompanied by such qualifiers as "so far" or "as yet". In other words, the present picture of the impact of the transformation on the social status of women is in flux. Nevertheless, the transformation processes were strongly gendered from the very beginning. For example, men eagerly returned to their traditional public and professional positions and are becoming economically and socially stronger than women. For women the situation is more complex. Women more than ever are required to perform two roles. The current context makes more demands both on women's nurturing roles (to cope with the greater psychological pressures on their family members) and on their working activity (to cope with economic hardships in the family). In other words, there is a certain division of roles – men concentrating mainly on public success, women on the well-being of their families. At the same time, women do not leave their public places either.

The legacy of horizontal gender segregation in the labour market has made women's labour irreplaceable. Women comprise 77.8 per cent of health care workers, 71.9 per cent in the banking and insurance industries, 58.6 per cent in services and commerce (Czech Statistical Bureau 1994). Women's role as second breadwinner is so important that today they perceive their job outside the family as their "duty" as do their husbands and their communities. Thus, after 1989, not only did they not leave their jobs, but they took additional ones. Over-employment and resulting exhaustion is becoming a problem. In 1995, 45 per cent of the total labour force continues to be women. Moreover, a "continuous employment model" is typical for Czech women, who

> during their productive years combine work and family and continue to work even when they have children, or only with very short interruptions. Such high degree of work activity is exceptional among western European women (Cermakova 1995a: 8).

The recent liberalization of the economy and society also brought new opportunities for women. It is estimated that about 10 per cent have improved their professional and social status since 1989 (Cermakova 1995a). As a result, the difference in average income between men and women, which during the whole communist era was around 25 per cent, has decreased from the mid 1990s to about 21 per cent. It is very important to note that there is potential for even greater advancement in women's economic status, for there are about 74 per cent of women in highly qualified and prestigious professions (doctors, university professors, etc.), who come under the state wage regulation. In other words, women are again indirectly discriminated against. Earlier the so-called "non-productive" sphere (the professions) were worse off, now it is state sector employees. I must add that the inherited state provisions as well as the network of kindergartens (only slightly reduced) makes this enormous amount of economic activity still possible.

So although at first glance the new situation has had more visible impact on the biographies of men, the impact on the lives of women is less spectacular, but no less serious. Women pay for the public social peace by inter- or intrapersonal conflicts, which can already be traced in recent demographic trends, showing both an increase in divorce (almost every second marriage in Prague) and a dramatic population decline (a sudden change in young women's marital strategy). There are also initial signs of an impact of their extensive economic activity on women's health, yet women who already have children do not (as before), have much choice. Newly married women, on the other hand, are having their first child about four years later than they did before 1989. It would seem that the former uniform model of "women's fate" is beginning to disappear. The influence of age and education on economic status tends to be even greater among the female than among the male population (Machonin 1996).

At the moment, in terms of current trends concerning developments in the social status of women, the jury is out on whether women will keep, improve or lose their present status. Perhaps we can predict an increasing gap between qualified women who so far have tended to diminish their status in relation to the men with the same qualifications, whereas women with few qualifications are way below their male counterparts. In other words, differences between the sexes are, as always, intersected by differences in social stratification.

Personal experience

I have tried to give as fair an analysis as possible of "women in a 'classless' society". In truth I hated totalitarianism with its censorship of public discussion and its sense of everything being in decline. I shall now give a brief personal account of what the experience was like for me and for my family.

My mother was one of 11 children and the family was poor. She was 22 years old when the communists took over. Her father worked on the railways and co-founded the local Communist Party in the 1920s. The events of 1948 meant something positive to this family. There was a sense of being equal to the mesdames they used to serve and, later, socialism made it possible for my mother to become a teacher because distance education gave her access to higher education. On the other hand my aunt, who had a gift for mathematics, could not progress due to the lack of a meritocracy (perhaps her lack of cultural capital meant she did not even try) and successful people (for example doctors) still came from the bourgeois families whose expectations were high.

My father came from a rich farming family who exploited others. He was 27 when the communists took over. The hatred between my two grandfathers was mutual and they nearly killed each other at my parents' wedding. When the rich farmers' property was expropriated, my father's elder brother, who had inherited the farm, refused to join the collective. This meant that he had to deliver a certain amount of produce to the state. He worked all summer to try to meet his targets and because he failed, had to spend all winter in jail. After four years of this he could not hold out any longer and joined the collective.

My father studied economics. His ambition had been to become a financial adviser to small businesses but of course this was not allowed. However, such was his self-confidence that he became a director of a milk factory which was a good position for a young person. My father always maintained that the economy was being badly run and would collapse, and he was right. The mistake had been to "industrialize" a country which was already industrialized. It had a great deal of light industry and craftsmanship but when the socialists introduced subsidized heavy industry all this was destroyed.

Throughout my childhood my parents did not contradict the official view that "the new system is beautiful". I found out later that they did not tell me how they really felt because they did not want me to have to deal with conflicting messages at home and at school. As I grew older I hated the regime – the control, the lack of freedom and the arrogance of the bureaucrats.

I did well at school. Girls were regarded as more disciplined than boys and because we were the best students, the teachers liked us. I was the best student in my group at university and I went on to do a PhD. Again I was well supported in my studies and my career progressed without any obstacles – until I refused to join the Communist Party in the early 1970s after the Soviet invasion. At that point my career stopped. I was not allowed to finish my PhD and there was a danger that I would be fired so I followed the example of a number of other women – I got pregnant and spent two years at home. When I returned my PhD had expired and so I was transferred into a research job. Again the question of joining the party was raised and again I got pregnant. When I returned I felt for the first time that I was not a fully valued employee, not because I was a woman but because I was a mother. For the first time I experienced discrimination (evidence of which was that my salary stopped increasing). Even though my own career had been stopped because of my refusal to join the party, I regarded this as one of the distortions of the system, not as discrimination against me.

Since 1989 many new opportunities have arisen for me. I was offered a new job and began dealing with women's issues. In this I have encountered no resistance, quite the opposite, my bosses have always supported me in my feminist work. I began to travel and to gain a real sense of having a new life. Under communism I felt I was sitting in the corner: I was only allowed to work on issues to do with methodology and other philosophers' work whereas now I am addressing real problems of democracy and women's issues. I really like work and that creates a new problem which is quite widespread. I and my husband have not been on holiday for eight years. We always went on holiday under communism but now there are so many opportunities, so many things to do that we cannot find the time. We were not allowed to publish before and now we cannot stop. Like children, we are having to learn from the beginning to have a more balanced life. Learning to say "No" to more and more work is what we are dealing with today.

Notes

1. The regime never declared itself as "communist", but as a society marching towards a Communism. It lasted from 1948 to 1968. In 1960, after accomplishing the major social reforms, The Czechoslovak Republic was renamed The Czechoslovak Socialist Republic. The Prague Spring in 1968, which lasted from January till August, marked an attempt to liberalize the system by making it more meritocratic. August 1968 saw the Soviet invasion which halted the attempt to find a third way between socialism and capitalism.

2. The usual explanations point to the rather egalitarian, petit bourgeois character of the Czech society in the nineteenth century, to its democratic traditions, particularly to the inter-war democratic Czechoslovakia, as well as to a strong social democratic and later also communist left and well-organized working class. The first expropriations of the biggest enterprises started immediately after the Second World War and there were strong socialist tendencies within the democratic regime. As a result Czechoslovakia was the only country where the Communist Party came to power in a parliamentary way.

3. The reader should be careful: my reflections, based on the Czech case, can on the one hand mediate a relatively "pure" experience of social equality, yet on the other hand my explanations could be misleading. In the Soviet Union, for example, despite its having the longest history of communism, the sense of traditional social hierarchy remained common both in the social structure and in people's minds.

4. The unemployment rate was currently running at 0 per cent in Prague and around 3 per cent in the rest of the country (Czech Statistical Bureau 1996).

   Since this chapter was written, the unemployment rate has increased dramatically, particularly between 1997 and 1999, and is still rising. At this point, spring 1999, it still averages below 10 per cent in the Czech Republic but is expected to increase considerably by the year 2000. This was a scenario the author anticipated but one that postdates the particular phase of societal transformation which is described above.

References

Busheikin, L. & Marikova, H. 1995. The changing lives of Czech women – what the statistics say, in Busheikin, L. and Kolczak, A. (eds) *Altos and Sopranos: A Pocket Handbook of Women's Organizations*. Prague: Prague Gender Studies Centre.

Castle-Kanerová, M. 1992. Social policy in Czechoslovakia, in Deacon, B. (ed.) *The New Eastern Europe: Social Policy Past, Present and Future*. London: Sage.

Cermakova, M. 1995a. Women in the Czech society: continuity or change, in Cermakova, M. (ed.) *Women, Work and Society*. Prague: Sociologicky ustav AV CR.

Cermakova, M. 1995b. The current Czech family model, in Havelková, H. (ed.) *Is There a Central European Model of Marriage and Family?* Prague: Divadelni ustav.

Czech Statistical Bureau 1994. *The Statistical Yearbook of the Czech Republic '94*. Prague: Cesky statisticky urad.

Czech Statistical Bureau 1996. *The Statistical Yearbook of the Czech Republic '96*. Prague: Cesky statisticky urad.

Garver, B.M. 1986. Women in the First Czechoslovak Republic, in Wolchik, S. and Meyer, A. (eds) *Women, State, and Party in Eastern Europe*. Durham, North Carolina: Duke University Press.

Havelková, H. 1993a. "Patriarchy" in Czech Society, *Hypatia*, 8(4), 89–96.

Havelková, H . 1993b. A few pre-feminist thoughts, in Funk, N. and Mueller, M. (eds) *Gender Politics and Post-Communism: Reflections from Eastern Europe and the Former Soviet Union*. New York/London: Routledge, Chapman & Hall, Inc.

Havelková, H. 1995. Die liberale Geschichte der Frauenfrage in den tschechischen Ländern, in Havelková, H. (ed.) *Gibt es ein mitteleuropäisches Ehe- und Familienmodell?* Prague: Divadelni ustav.

Heitlinger, A. 1993. The impact of the transition from communism on the status of women in the Czech and Slovak Republics, in Funk, N. and Mueller, M. (eds) *Gender Politics and Post-Communism: Reflections from Eastern Europe and the Former Soviet Union*. New York/London: Routledge, Chapman & Hall, Inc.

Machonin, P. 1992. Political and economic transition or social transformation, *Sisyphus*, 8, 129–33.

Machonin, P. 1996. Modernisation and social transformation in the Czech Republic, *Czech Sociological Review*, 4, 171–86.

Macura, V. 1992. *Stastny vek. Symboly, emblemy a myty 1948–89* (The Happy Age. Symbols, Emblems and Myths 1948–89). Prague: Prazska imaginace (only in Czech).

Pateman, C. 1988. *The Sexual Contract.* Cambridge: Polity Press.

Siklova, J. 1993. Are women in Central and Eastern Europe conservative?, in Funk, N. and Mueller, M. (eds) *Gender Politics and Post-Communism: Reflections from Eastern Europe and the Former Soviet Union.* New York/London: Routledge, Chapman & Hall, Inc.

Tatur, M. 1992. Why is there no women's movement in Eastern Europe?, in Lewis, P.G. (ed.) *Democracy and Civil Society in Eastern Europe. Selected papers from the Fourth World Congress for Soviet and East European Studies.* Basingstoke: Macmillan.

Wagnerova, A. 1974. *Frau im Sozialismus: Beispiel CSSR.* Hamburg: Campus Verlag.

Wagnerova, A. 1996. Emancipation and ownership, *Czech Sociological Review,* 4(1), 101–8.

Wolchik, S.L. 1979. The status of women in a socialist order: Czechoslovakia, 1948–1978, *American Quarterly of Soviet and East European Studies,* 38(4), 583–602.

CHAPTER SIX

Class, gender and ethnicity: snapshots of a mixed heritage

Christine Zmroczek

I am a working-class English girl, a white British academic, part of the Polish intelligentsia[1] and descendant of the *szlachta* (nobility). The purpose of this chapter is to explore what this collage of experience can contribute to debates about social class.

Qualitative understandings of social class have been and continue to be neglected in favour of quantitative analyses. There has been a heavy dependence on generalizations derived from statistical evidence and little literature which helps us to begin to theorize more realistically about class in people's lived experiences.[2] Statistics are, of course, very valuable, but can never give a full picture – they are not intended to do so. Feminist sociologists in particular have argued for mixed methods (see, e.g., Oakley 1974; Cavendish 1982; Westwood 1984; Brannen 1992) and the value of experience, life history, oral history and autobiography for theorizing about class is beginning to be recognized, albeit slowly.

In this chapter I present some aspects of my own process of conscious realization of class, gender and ethnicity to illustrate how they interact politically and are interdependent. In other words, I explore how, in the process of understanding gender, I came to understand class and how deepening my understanding of class has led me to reflect more thoughtfully on questions of ethnicity. I discuss the complexities of class and particularly the transgenerational and transnational implications implicit in examining class formation. I draw attention to the importance of family as a key site of class transmission, reproduction, agency and structure. I use my own experiences structured through those of my family in different generations, different countries and different class locations to examine some of the ways in which class works.

Family stories

My mother was born in 1920s London into a working-class family which had begun to aspire to lower middle-class status. The family did not fit into traditional stereotypes of working-class people defined around (male) trade union membership and certain types of manual work – but these definitions did not even then and do not now fit many working-class families and households. My grandfather was a window dresser and later a tea salesman. He had been unable to fulfil his ambition to attend an art school as his wage was needed when his father was killed in an accident at work. My grandmother trained in secretarial work before her marriage and indeed kept her marriage secret for a year so as not to lose her job.[3]

My grandmother was brought up by her maternal grandmother, who had been a lady's maid and who trained her to be a "lady". This left my grandmother with some unfortunate mismatches between her expectations and reality. She had few of the skills associated with working-class housekeeping. She was a slapdash and careless cook, hated housework and running a household, and was not good at managing the meagre budget. My mother seems to have taken over most of the responsibility for running the household at an early age when, during the Second World War, the family moved from London to escape the bombing. My grandmother, much to her delight, resumed office work and my mother never returned to school. This background, however, later left my mother out of place among the older generation of working-class women who were our neighbours during my childhood. Their notions of respectability were not hers. She resented being told when it was proper to hang out her washing (not on Sundays) and thought it ridiculous to scrub the front pavement like the woman opposite. She stood out as young, inexperienced, not local and rather spiky and proud with of course a strange foreign husband and an unpronounceable name. The example of her lack of conformity has, I am sure, fuelled mine.

My father was Polish. The Second World War brought him eventually to England where, as the family story goes, he and my mother met and fell in love at first sight. They sustained this romance for over 40 years until his death, despite the considerable differences between them of language, country, culture and class.

My father's background on his mother's side was the *szlachta* – the Polish nobility. The *szlachta* as a class were in demise from the eighteenth century. The culture of impoverished but proud nobility, however, was to be revived at various times, as part of the struggle for Polish independence and nationhood (Davies 1986, 1996). What remained of the estates of my father's maternal family had been drunk and gambled away during my grandmother's childhood in the late nineteenth century. She was sent to a convent to avoid the deprivations this caused at home. It was here, in the first decade of the 1900s, that her older brother brought my grandfather, a fellow officer, to meet her when she was 14, with a view to marriage. Family stories do not tell me if she was given a choice.

They married when she was 16 so that he could provide her with a home, although they did not live together until some two years later when my grand-father considered her old enough to become a mother.

Why was my grandfather willing to marry such a poor girl before he had even met her? He may have been attracted to her status as *szlachta* as even without money or land, her nobility was not in question, or he may have faced the fact that he was unable to make a better marriage. His origins are something of a mystery. The landowner of the estates on which his family worked, no doubt as peasants,[4] had taken a fancy to him and he was educated alongside the master's son as a companion for him. When he was old enough the landowner bought him a commission in the army which is how he came to know my grandmother's brother.

My grandmother's status was passed down to her six children despite there being no money to go with it, aside from grandfather's salary as a government official in a small town in the south of Poland. Somewhat surprisingly for the 1920s and 1930s, every member of the family was encouraged to go to university including the four girls who had priority in terms of support and resources. This appears to follow a tradition of the *szlachta*, who as Norman Davies notes had become "the pioneers of the new intelligentsia" (1986: 332) since the nineteenth century.

> The Polish intelligentsia was the social class, or rather the functional group, on which the educational and cultural activities of the nation came to depend. In eastern Europe, the intelligentsia was assumed to be politically disaffected, and it was very often excluded from any form of public service, employment, or expression. For this reason it possessed very different traditions and habits from 'the educated class' of Western societies and from trendy 'intellectuals' in democratic countries who could parade their grievances without fear of arrest or harassment. In origin, it owed a great deal to the declassé nobility, the largest educated element in old Poland . . . Unlike other social classes in nineteenth century Poland, the intelligentsia has to be defined by the function which its members perceived for themselves – to guard, treasure and expand Polish culture (Davies 1986: 266).

In most countries throughout history women are charged with transgenerational transmission of values and culture. In Poland they were highly instrumental in the preservation and development of Polish culture in the eighteenth and nineteenth centuries. They were afforded some measure of equality in the *szlachta*, particularly in regard to property which they could hold in their own right, unlike other European women at the time. During the men's long periods of enforced absence, in the service of the foreign and occupying forces of the eighteenth century partitions, women were charged with educating the children and guarding the family property and national heritage represented in Polish culture (ibid.).

This tradition survived throughout the nineteenth and twentieth centuries in various forms, one being the notion of Matka Polka: the strong, courageous, accepting, feminine, stalwart and patriotic mother figure (Oleksy 1995).

In my family there was a tradition of girls being educated to take up their roles in the intelligentsia and they were supported with any available money. My father had to find his own ways of surviving financially at the University of Cracow with only the most basic of an allowance. He struggled by for two years offering private tuition and doing any other odd jobs he could and was brought food from the homes of his more comfortably situated maternal cousins who lived in Cracow. Then he decided to take up the offer of a place at the prestigious Army Training School. In 1939 as war broke out he was completing his training as an officer in the new Tanks Division.

As children, whenever we could, my sisters and I would try to get Dad to overcome his reluctance to talk about his wartime experiences. They were more exciting to us than any adventure story. After fighting in one of the last engagements of the Polish Army in the first days of the war he was interned in Hungary. He was involved in the escape of many men from the castle where they were imprisoned and only narrowly missed arrest by escaping himself at the last moment during a church service. He made his way, often in great danger, through war-torn and occupied Europe to France where he fought with the reorganized Polish Army. His unit left France by the skin of its teeth along with the British Army as the Nazis took control in June 1940. The Polish Army was incorporated into the British Army for the remaining years of the war. My father's fight for his country, united with the Allied cause, resulted in several medals for bravery, which we played with as children when we found them in his garden shed.[5] He was an officer in the Polish 1st Army Corps attached to the British Army when he and my mother met in 1942. Their dreams of returning to a free Poland after the war were crushed in 1945 by the Yalta agreement between the leaders of the three Allied powers, Churchill, Roosevelt and Stalin, when Poland came under the sphere of influence of the USSR.

In 1947, soon after I was born, my father left the army for civilian life and found himself, much to his surprise, virtually a refugee in a suddenly unfriendly postwar Britain. In common with many other Poles who had served in the Allied forces, my father was not able to return to Poland without risking imprisonment or death (see Sword et al. 1989). He was probably particularly unlucky to have settled in Norfolk where my mother was living with her parents, as it was extremely insular by all accounts. He was unable to find work for some time and was eventually forced to take a job on a building site in order to provide the bare essentials for my mother and I. He was a manual worker, although not a builder, for the rest of his life.

My father was also cut off from any Polish community in Britain as far as I know from that time on. I think now, although it was not something ever talked about, that this may have been related to his fall in status. I can only guess that he made a conscious decision not to dwell in the past nor in hope for a future in

Poland but to accept his life for what it was here and now. I always remember my father as a placid, good tempered and accepting man, seemingly content with what he had, which was little enough in material terms. But too much contact with other Poles could have been both a painful reminder and an embarrassment, as his life now was that of a poor working-class man.

From the time when I was three years old, we lived in a very small and cramped four-roomed terraced house in a working-class city street in Norwich with no electricity, no running hot water, no bathroom and an outside lavatory. We had gas lighting in most rooms but there was no light at all in my bedroom which I later shared with my two sisters. We had a coal fire in the living room for heating, although it was not lit until Mum expected us home from school so as to conserve expensive fuel. In winter the other rooms were breathtakingly cold and the windows regularly iced up on the inside.

As a child this was my normality. Most of the neighbours had electric light, but they too had few other modern conveniences. I did not think much about it, nor about the degree of poverty it demonstrated – it was just the way things were – although I can remember my mother bewailing the awful inconveniences of trying to keep house for a husband and family in these circumstances. And I can remember her standing at the sink doing the washing by hand in every spare moment. I also remember her chronic chilblains and family jokes about how cold her touch always was. When I was 13 our gas lighting was replaced by electricity, which meant my parents had to find more rent for this luxury addition to the house. It also meant that we could have a television, but everything else remained the same until the family moved to a council[6] house in 1969. But by then I had left home to fulfil my ambition to work in London.

Class, gender and ethnicity: gradual recognition

Conscious realization of the place and meaning of the central issues of class, gender and ethnicity is for me a gradual process of continually changing and deepening awareness. I cannot remember when I was not aware of gender differences. The need to submit to becoming a "girl" was deeply ingrained in my childhood but inextricably mixed with class issues (the need to fit in, be quiet, be nice, avoid being called "common") and also with issues of difference relating to ethnicity. I became a feminist in the early 1970s while living in the USA when I realized just how aptly and excitingly feminist theories both explained my uncomfortable awareness of gender inequalities and outright sexism, previously unnamed and unexplained, and provided some hope for change in which I could participate.

As for class, when I was younger it did not seem to matter as everyone I knew was "in the same boat". If I did feel different, I explained it to myself by reference to my ethnicity, although I did not name it as such then but rather as the uniqueness of my family in comparison with those around me. I certainly remember feeling "different" quite often in a number of disparate situations, without knowing why, except that our family was a bit odd and unconventional – and half Polish.

Looking back, I do not think I actually knew anyone who was not working class until I was eleven and won a scholarship to the fee paying Catholic convent high school. At first, naively, I did not notice the differences between me and my classmates, although I did wonder why teachers singled me out to complain about my lack of equipment and uniform. I could not understand how they could possibly keep expecting me to be provided with more and more extras when I knew my mother had wept over the cost of the original list of required items. I was delighted to be invited to so many Christmas parties that first year, and my mother bought me a grown up secondhand party dress from a friend. The first party was a disaster, the dress was quite wrong, I heard the other mothers talking about it, and I did not know how to play the games that all the other girls knew. I went to the other parties, and even quite enjoyed some of them, marvelling at the size of the houses and the luxury of my friends' bedrooms, but I never wore the dress again. I made excuses to my mother because I could not face telling her after she had made such an effort to get me that special dress. What clothes to wear in what situations is still an issue for me – and for many other working-class women (Steedman 1986; Zmroczek & Mahony 1996b; Mahony & Zmroczek 1997a).

Another instance that stands out for me happened after I had begged to be allowed to have school dinners so as to be like most of the rest of my class. My parents were reluctant as it meant yet more money to be found for over-priced food, but they managed somehow. I can still feel the humiliation as the nun presiding over the meal rapped on the table and called out to me to eat properly. I was quite bewildered by this and she required me to stay behind while she demonstrated the niceties of the "proper" way to use a knife and fork when eating peas, with the fork held the wrong way round, in my view. This peculiar habit was certainly not used in our house where much was said about how enjoying your food was more important than how it got to your mouth. So the advice of the nun both humiliated me and made me angry, because it seemed to be a direct criticism of my parents and their manners. I sat there while she made sarcastic remarks about my table manners and quietly determined to get my own back. By the next term I had managed to persuade a number of my classmates that bringing a packed lunch was a much more trendy and interesting thing to do and there was *en masse* defection from school dinners. I remember feeling quite triumphant about it and clearly it marked an important development in my rebellious streak. I still did not, however, really think about such incidents as "classed".

On reflection it would seem that some of these kinds of experience were so painful that I could not place them in my otherwise happy life in a loving family. Also, from an early age I was fiercely protective of my family's right to be different on account of my Polish father. I was proud of him and of being half

Polish myself instead of what I thought of then as boringly English and from dull old Norfolk. My sisters and I were encouraged in this attitude by our mother who would not put up with any nonsense from local people about our name (Zmroczek in 1950s Norwich did cause quite a stir most of the time). I sensed from school that it was somehow "wrong" to be poor and I interpreted this as a slight against my father's strenuous efforts to bring home enough money to support us and my mother's struggles to make ends meet. This made it difficult for me to recognize the class nature of the prejudice I was experiencing.

So I tried to ignore my own experiences of class difference and class inequity, both at school and later in my first job in a bank. In 1964 (before computerization), I began the job as did all new employees, with a year "behind the scenes" on the accounting machines. I wondered why I was not trained to become a cashier at the end of the year like the rest of my cohort. The men in particular were explicitly being groomed for banking careers on what is now known as "the fast track". When the third year began and I was still behind the scenes I went to speak to the under manager, who had shown a friendly interest in me. He was embarrassed by my question and mumbled something about dress codes and my appearance. Although outside I modelled myself on the fashionable 1960s look, the new mini skirts, straight curtains of hair and panda eyes, at work I had made a particular effort to dress conservatively. Hurt and angry, not long after I requested a transfer to a London bank, where I thought I would be more welcome. This turned out not to be the case and I gave the bank my notice a few months after arriving there. Thereafter I embarked on a more adventurous path than a banking career – so perhaps this class snobbery ultimately did me a favour. It could be looked at quite differently though, as class and gender discrimination have been barriers to many other working-class women trying to establish themselves in their chosen fields.

Why did I fail to understand these and countless other early experiences as class based? Class was spoken of in my childhood home in different ways, but usually obliquely. The exception was my grandmother whose sharp, angry and colourful outbursts about the inequalities between rich and poor, and criticisms of Churchill and the Royal Family were often shushed as inappropriate for young ears because of her "bad" language. There was little in the way of class analysis for me to draw on and a lot in the way of class snobbery; families at the top end of the street, for example, were designated as "not very good class" or "common". Others were said to be "nice". My sisters and I were trained to identify and avoid being "common" from an early age, like many other working-class children (D'Cruze 1997).

The ways in which working-class people constantly classify and judge each other as a part of a striving to "better" themselves or maintain their "respectability" have been illuminated in the writings of feminists such as Skeggs (1997) and Giles (1995). Such judgements also anticipate – in an attempt to forestall – the ways in which some middle-class people view those "beneath" them, subjecting them to the minutiae of snobbish and largely irrelevant criticism over dress, speech and manners (see Guymer in this volume). This mirrors the ways in which first-generation migrants are often the first to criticize themselves to avoid the shame, pain, distress and anger of having someone else do it. My father, for example, always referred to himself jokily as "a bloody Pole", anticipating the insult and attempting to turn it away through humour. In doing so he was repeating over and over again throughout his life an early insult commonly directed at Polish people in postwar Britain (Sword 1996).

I have always been secure in the knowledge of all that I have gained by being part of the working classes. I have never wanted not to be working class or to "get away from it" or "escape" as is commonly assumed about working-class people (Steedman 1986; Skeggs 1997). I did not consciously and consistently think of myself as working class until I went to Sussex University in 1977 when I was 30. I was almost immediately confronted by the strange and alienating middle-class culture there. Five years' exposure to feminism in the USA, however, had politicized me and also given me more confidence in my own analyses, so it was as an undergraduate that I began both to identify and to feel angry about the exclusions and invisibilities that I and so many others have experienced through class discrimination. Feminism and class also brought me together with others at university for whom ethnicity and racism were a priority. We were able to build bridges through our shared concerns and experiences of being "othered" which enable us to learn from our differences. Paradoxically, I also began to have doubts about whether I could call myself working class now that I was at university.[7] I took some time to consider this question and I became angry at the absence of meaningful theories to help me with this dilemma. As subsequently became apparent, my dilemma was widely shared (hooks 1984; Tokarcyk & Fay 1993; Zandy 1995; Zmroczek & Mahony 1996b; Mahony & Zmroczek 1997a). My interest in re-theorizing class as part of a politics of commitment to other working-class women who might also be facing some of the same problems began here.

Working-class academic – or not?

So now I am the working-class girl made into academic woman. I am proud to describe myself as an academic although I have very mixed feelings about it. I struggled through a long and rather hard journey as I was a mature returner to education, after many years in a variety of low paid, tedious, often menial and low status jobs and two divorces. I was, and continue to be, beset with many doubts about my ability and right to an academic life similar to those described in some of the few books by and about working-class women academics (hooks 1989; hooks 1994; Mahony & Zmroczek 1997a; Tokarcyk & Fay 1993; Walkerdine 1990). Like many others, I was also bereft, at least until recently, of much of the important knowledge about how to operate in this world. The resonances of these facets of the lives of working-class women in higher education will always be with me. Like many other working-class feminist academics I want to open the way for others, to demystify the processes and practices of higher education. There is no good reason why other working-class women, and men too, should not have the joys of intellectual life if they want them. And without doubt, it does have its joys for most of us, despite the contradictions and problems (see, e.g., Reay 1997; Hey 1997; D'Cruze 1997) and in my experience it is usually better paid than waitressing or bar work!

More specifically I am, as I said at the beginning, a British academic. I work in a British institution in the British system and I work to change some of its worst aspects. I am white. I believe it is important to state this as a way of demonstrating my inevitable bias, my various ignorances of the ways in which racism impinges on the lives of so many people. Many of the insights in my growing awareness of the implications of my own ethnicity have come from friends and colleagues and from women's writing (including those in this volume). In addition, because of the ways I have experienced my own ethnicity, I have sometimes been able to connect with women and men of different ethnicities across the barriers of "white" to gain a deeper understanding.

Another reason I am glad to be an academic is that I have been very much welcomed by women and some men in Polish academic life in recent years. This has meant a lot to me and has presented me with considerable personal challenges. It has given me the courage to think of myself as Polish in different ways. Poland has always been part of my life and part of my memories – as Teleky says, "part of my imagination" (1997: 173). Although I did not actually visit Poland until I was 20 years old, for as long as I can remember, Poland was real in the stories, memories, anecdotes and proverbs told us children by my father. It was real in the excitement of the arrival of a letter from grandmother or my aunts, or once when I was six years old a visit from my uncle and his wife on their way to live in the USA. There were occasional visits from Polish men, former friends and acquaintance of my father, but they were few. As I said earlier, we were not part of a Polish community in exile. We children did not learn Polish at home and we missed out on the lessons of history, patriotism and culture that went with Polish Saturday School for many other British Poles brought up in big cities. It is only now that I have begun seriously to study Polish language and culture. Why did I wait so long? I have always been fiercely proud of my Polish heritage yet it is only more recently that I have felt able to name myself "Polish". I cannot explain why.[8] I am pained by my tardiness but I have taken comfort from Teleky's explanation of his slowness to research the details of his Hungarian ethnicity:

My 'ethnicity' isn't simply an additional way of seeing myself or my world, which would make it external to me, a kind of psychological decoration, a tattoo. It is more intrinsic than that. I can't imagine myself without it. As far back as I can remember, the stories I heard included Hungary, just as fairy tales have forests and castles. Hungary is part of my imagination. Which may explain why it took so long for me to find it – I took it for granted, as if I knew it better than I did, the way one takes a hand, a foot, for granted (Teleky 1997: 173).

My family in Poland, particularly the older generations, have not always been willing to include me as Polish. Not surprisingly I used to feel at my most self-consciously English when I visited in the early days. I remember my grandmother shouting at me in Polish because I could not understand her, yet understanding enough to know that she was saying what kind of a useless girl is this, she can't speak Polish, she can't understand. This resonated with another memory which I had blotted out until recently when my sister Jenny reminded me that my father, usually the most placid of men, had also shouted at me for mispronunciation in early attempts to learn Polish as a teenager. These experiences imprinted themselves deep inside me and contribute to my tongue-tied inability to speak Polish with family members which continues to this today, although I can manage reasonably well in simple every-day encounters with others.

The welcome into Polish academia has also meant that I have had to confront my mixed class heritage. I have been welcomed into the "club" of Polish intelligentsia, albeit as a very ignorant member, on the grounds of my academic status. However, I am aware that with some academic colleagues and friends there is also a shared class heritage of which *szlachta* is a part. I do not want to give the impression that I speak about myself, either in English or in Polish as "noble" or *szlachta*, but it is apparent that class signifiers operate just as subtly in Poland as in Britain, although they are very different. In Britain, it is relatively easy and fairly common practice to ascribe a class to a person with reasonable accuracy on the basis of a few clues. In Poland I do not exactly know how people come to place me as accurately as they do. With colleagues my academic status is what is most obvious as they do not necessarily know about my working-class upbringing. Brief answers to the usual questions about my father, that he served as an officer in the Polish army, seem a further aid or confirmation that places me as part of an elite. This is in almost direct opposition to my English working-class identity which always has potential to place me on the margins of academic life in Britain. I confess here to an "us" and "them" mentality which surfaces quite often in response to class discriminations. I find it hard to digest that in Poland the "us" of which I am part is what I would in England designate as "them". I have to accept the fact that I am part of this elite if I want to be able to call myself Polish. This *is* the Polish part of me, just as much as the working-class English girl and white British academic. It is precisely because I am a mixture of these different parts that I intend this exploration of my autobiography as a contribution to the politics of class, to debates aimed at understanding how class works.

My own observations and conversations tell me that class still matters very much in Poland as in Britain, although there are very different histories in the two countries. In Britain it is possible to trace the development of social class for at least the past two hundred years since industrialization (Thompson 1979). In Poland, there is a very different picture. In the past two hundred years borders have shifted continuously due to attempts by their neighbours to colonize Poles. Prior to 1989 the only period of independence since 1795 was between 1918 and 1939. Industrialization barely took place, according to Morawski (1992), until the period 1949–70, when a largely agricultural economy was turned into one based on industrial production of goods and services. Unlike Britain where "peasant" has long ceased to be a category of analysis or stratification, the largest segment of the Polish population that has been defined at any one time has been, and remains, the peasants (Davies 1986; Fuszara & Grudinska 1994). While the emancipation of serfs was officially accomplished in 1864, the social relations between master/landowner and peasant continued to be marked by feudalism well into the twentieth century. The tradition of subsistence farming on strips of land continued to keep rural life harsh and difficult and for many it remains so even now (Pine 1992; Weclawowicz 1996).

Prior to 1989 there were over 40 years of communist rule in Poland by the so called People's Republic of Poland imposed through and kept in place by the USSR. However, "Sovietisation was never accepted, and was constantly challenged . . ." (Weclawowicz 1996: 10). During this period a major focus of the system was to remove old class and social divisions through the removal of property rights, "officially stated as the fulfilment of egalitarian principles" (Wnuk-Lipinski 1992: 173). In reality, as Wnuk-Lipinski goes on to say, new social formations were put in place which developed new kinds of inequalities, new "classes" in a so-called classless society. Those who served the communist system, the government and officials, known in Polish as the *nomenklatura*,[9] were rewarded with material, cultural and economic benefits. Manual workers were to epitomize the "people's" socialism and be rewarded with as many material benefits as a communist regime could and thought it wise to sustain, while the intelligentsia and middle classes were to be shown their lack of importance in the new scheme of things. But it did not always work out quite that way.[10]

The attempt to obliterate the Polish intelligentsia and the ruling classes of society had begun earlier as part of both Russian and German strategy to gain complete control of Polish territory during the Second World War. Mass killings of officers, teachers, professionals and other potential leaders of society took place from 1940 onwards.[11] The German plan to exterminate the Poles, together with the holocaust of the Jewish people, was carried out with ferocity until the end of the war (Davies 1981, 1986). The Russian "liberators", who invaded Poland as Allies as the war drew to a close, removed by means of deportation, captivity and death those who might otherwise have opposed the new regime, and made it clear to those Poles who might have returned from abroad that similar treatment awaited them (Davies 1981; Sword et al. 1989).

In total six million Polish people died in the Second World War, that is almost one in five of the prewar population. As Davies recounts:

The hand of death did not fall evenly on all sections of the population. It fell most frequently on the youth – on young men and women who fought and resisted, on the trained and educated classes who were selected for elimination by the genocidal planners of the occupying forces and on the brave and active who did not care to serve the tyrants in silence . . . the wartime holocaust also consumed the greater part of the Polish Jewry, almost one half of the total victims . . . depriving [Poland] of cultural variety and human talents which it could ill afford to lose (1986: 100).

But this was not all, as Davies goes on to point out:

By one means or another Poland was further deprived of several million other subjects, who, if not actually killed by the War were separated from their homeland for ever. The political exiles . . . who had formed the core of the ruling elite, and the deportees and slave labourers, Poland's German and Ukrainian minorities . . . [were] expelled . . . and . . . decimated . . . (ibid.: 100–1).

These enormous losses seemed to have inspired new generations with the desire to maintain an intelligentsia at whatever personal cost to the individuals involved. For most people in postwar communist Poland, membership of the intelligentsia did not mean money, or prestigious posts but status. Due to educational reform, there were also to be growing numbers of a so called "technical" intelligentsia, newly qualified educated people drawn from a mixture of social strata, but without the commitment to the *kultura szlachecka* (the old "noble" culture) (Davies 1996). Some of this new kind of intelligentsia – and some of the old – supported the communist regime which they saw as giving them opportunities. Of course this is not unusual, as Long notes: "Many intellectuals have depended for their livelihood upon regimes which they opposed" (1996: 4). However, the majority of the intelligentsia were committed to education in order to reaffirm their status as protectors of Polish culture and independence, therefore demonstrating their lack of support for the communist regime. This was undertaken, literally, at the expense of material benefits. My Polish cousins, born during and soon after the war, chose education, university and professions such as teaching, medicine, science, literature and art with pride, knowing that they would earn far less than factory workers, for example.

From the 1960s to the 1980s as far as I could see on my visits, being poor but educated was a matter of great pride to many of my family and their friends. They derived satisfaction from their deprivations. To have material goods even at "Iron Curtain" levels of abundance marked a person as a member of the Communist Party machinery. Simple Western-type pleasures such as eating out in a restaurant were avoided even when offered by unsuspecting foreign visitors like myself because to do so would have brought unwanted contact with the wrong kinds of people – party members. The lack of money in my family in Britain was viewed through these lenses. We were seen as living in some similar state of genteel and worthy poverty to that of the Polish family.

By the late 1970s many of my Polish family were involved in the efforts of Solidarność to be rid of the oppressive communist system. Solidarność united the different classes of society far more effectively than the imposed one-class society of the Polish People's Republic. Workers and intelligentsia alike, including some of the communist intellectuals, risked their jobs, their well-being, their freedom and at times their lives to strive towards a new Polish society.[12]

The eventual success of the Polish people in regaining their independence in 1989 has meant, among many other important factors, that classes in Polish society are once more being reformulated.[13] Recently I have asked friends, colleagues, and family from a range of age groups – although all from the intelligentsia – to talk with me about class in Poland, both before and after 1989. I have asked them to explain to me how they see class working, what issues there are, whether it is still a relevant concept and what changes they foresee. The responses I get are remarkably similar to those from many middle-class Britons: that it really doesn't matter, that it is no longer an issue, and so on. Some people explain how it could not be an issue in the postwar period as the government decreed equality, and that this means class divisions have faded away. Upon closer questioning it often appears that even these people do not really believe what they are saying.[14]

I have wanted to speak with people from other classes but as yet I have found it hard to break out of the confines of the academic community and intelligentsia. This is clearly much to do with my lack of fluency in Polish, but I have been interested in the response of some people I know to requests for a way to meet other people. They have not really taken me seriously, partly perhaps because they foresee my language difficulties, but also it seems to me because they cannot see why I would want to do it. Putting it another way, I can observe in some people a rather dismissive attitude which appears to me to be decidedly class based. For example I am told stories, quite fondly, of the idiosyncrasies of peasants or mountain people which, when I probe more deeply, frequently end up with remarks such as, "Well, they are different." Often I cannot determine whether there is disdain or only an egalitarian acceptance of difference in such replies. On other occasions, though, I can discern very clearly a distaste and snobbery relating to the habits of peasants or mountain people. This is particularly noticeable from those who have been intimately associated with them and seem to want to ensure that I understand there is a distance between them. In discussing the *szlachta*, Norman Davies also notes a "superiority complex which some Poles display with respect to their more proletarian neighbours" (1986: 333).

Even without fluent Polish, I have become more aware of different ways of speaking in Polish society and different manners to go along with them. I wanted to know how this related to class. I asked about accents, such a defining factor in

Britain, but I am assured that accent is not an issue in Poland since the standard-ization of postwar education. Dialects, however, are still strong and used with pride, as I have observed for example in the Tatra mountain district where a vibrant local culture and language exist (Pine 1992). Nonetheless, it is clear there are elaborate codes of behaviour which I have observed in the academy and in my family circles. In part these may have been constructed subtly to belie the one-class ideology and in part to maintain with some nostalgia some of what is still seen as intrinsic to "Polishness" in terms of manners, traditional hospital-ity and other kinds of public behaviour.

Handkissing is a good example. In my experience it is done by "gentlemen" to "ladies" as a standard if old fashioned gesture. It usually occurs on more formal occasions but also takes place within the family too as a special greeting. I was surprised to have my hand kissed quite recently by one of my most trendy and fashionable young relatives. I have not seen it used by working-class or peasant men except, again, to "ladies" in some situations where an extreme courtesy and perhaps thanks are being displayed so I am not aware if it is widespread in society. As an academic colleague, my hand is rather frequently kissed at formal occasions and with it goes attention to my needs which, as a visitor, can be helpful. I remarked on this to Polish feminist friends at one formal occasion and they raised their eyebrows at me in horror, pointing out that I do not have to live with the consequences of this out-dated chivalry. It expresses itself in Polish society all too often, they assured me, as out-and-out sexism.

Despite the legal and formal notions of equality in "socialist" Poland, women were discriminated against in all areas of public and private life. They were expected cheerfully to bear, in keeping with the culture of Matka Polka, the burden of full-time work, together with virtually the entire responsibility for household, children, husband and other dependents, with very little in the way of consumer goods to alleviate the load (Oleksy 1995; Einhorn 1993). According to many commentators (Bystydzienski 1995; Einhorn 1993; Hoffman 1993; Gontarczyk-Wesola 1997; Watson 1997), there would appear to be even less concern about discrimination against women in "new", post-communist Poland, where loss of formal equality, jobs and human rights such as abortion have taken place. Women are developing strategies to overcome these problems (Nowicka 1997; Zajicek & Casalanti 1995); however, work on developing new analyses of class and gender is yet to be carried out in Poland.

In conclusion

Class, gender and ethnicity have been constant factors in my life, although there were times when I was not as conscious of them as I am now. Since I am composed of multiple identities and subjectivities, the three statements with which I began this chapter are among the hundreds I might make about myself.

I am also composed of my past. I can say I am a working-class girl although now I am a woman, because I will always also be that girl. I will always carry her forward as part of me, whatever changes may occur in my life. I am what I was as well as what I have become. Because of this I have no doubts that I am working class, although I have many middle-class aspects to my life these days, after a university education and jobs in higher education. These parts of my life have piled up on top of one another but have not obliterated each other. The working-class girl may be covered over to some extent, but the original features are still there and her growth and development would not have occurred as they have without access to a middle-class education. Part of my political project around class is to widen access to meaningful education for working-class women.

The processes of thinking more deeply about and confronting new meanings about "being Polish", have had implications for how I think about class. My frequent academic visits to Poland and the friendships and contacts I have made outside my family there have led me to recognize more clearly that I am part of the "intelligentsia". This clash of class backgrounds although rather difficult for someone who has been used to thinking about class from a working-class perspective, is proving to be highly stimulating. The new insights I have gained, although fragmentary and incomplete, are contributing to the intentionally political act of attempting to theorize experience through the use of autobiography and life history. This chapter is about the lived experience of class, witnessed from both sides of a class divide, through being both "us" and "them". It has shown that definitions of class and how to categorize people on the basis of them are constantly changing and culturally and historically specific.

Further, this exploration of my autobiography demonstrates that those of us from mixed class and/or ethnic backgrounds have particular contributions to make towards creating new knowledge about how class operates in the countries and cultures with which we are familiar. Being both internal and external to two or more societies or cultures, and in many cases feeling somewhat estranged or removed from them, may give fresh insights into how they work. It also calls into question again the static nature of some accounts of class, especially those which are too firmly based on one country or one ethnic group or which fail to include women. The understandings of people outside the "norms" in any society are crucial in forging new understandings which contain within them the realities of people's lives. It is vitally important to learn from intimate and subjective knowledge about class, gender and ethnic discriminations so that we can work towards ending them.

Notes

1. "Intelligentsia" is a particularly Polish concept which signifies the importance of keeping alive the idea, language and culture of Polish national life in the nineteenth and twentieth centuries. According to Norman Davies it is defined as "the class of

enlightened persons" (1986: 266) in the Polish Language Dictionary of 1898. In the *Wielki Slownik Polsko-Angielski* (Stanislawski 1982) it is defined as "the intellectuals; white collar workers". See Davies (1986: 266–8 and 394–400) for a detailed discussion of the changing meanings of the term and the importance and composition of the group to which it refers up to the present.

2. See, for example, recently published volumes by Marshall (1997) and Wright (1997) and Thompson's critique of this method in his chapter in Bertaux and Thompson (1997).

3. A marriage bar, that is having to leave employment on marriage, operated both formally as for example in the Civil Service and in teaching and informally among employers until well into the second half of the twentieth century (Beddoes 1989).

4. My father often made jokes about his love of the land, a trait associated with the peasantry, although his father's origins were shrouded in mystery and, as my father recalled, rarely mentioned in his childhood.

5. Dad was always very modest about his wartime exploits. More details of activities of the Polish Army and the rest of the Polish forces can be found in numerous publications (see, e.g. Sword et al. 1989).

6. Local government subsidized.

7. This remains a common problem and was identified by students who answered questionnaires I gave them between 1993 and 1997 as part of a larger study (Zmroczek in progress).

8. Similar dislocations involved in dual or multiple identities have been documented; see Forum Polek 1988; Sword 1996; Temple 1997; D'Cruze 1997; Madhavarau (this volume); De Marco Torgovnick 1994; Herne et al. 1994; Hoffman 1991.

9. Wnuk-Lipinski defines nomenclature as "the mechanism . . . which intervenes most strongly in the promotional processes, particularly for the higher and more strategic positions" (1992: 174). See also Weclawowicz (1996), Chapter 8.

10. For more detailed discussion see Davies (1981), Davies (1986) Weclawowicz (1996) and Clancy et al. (1992).

11. See, for example, J.K. Zawodny, *Death in the Forest: the Story of the Katyn Forest Massacre* (1971).

12. For more details see, among others, Davies (1986), Long (1996), Weclawowicz (1996), Wnuk-Lipinski (1992) and Wiatr (1992).

13. For discussion of this process see, for example, Wnuk-Lipinski (1992), Weclawowicz (1996), Chapter 8.

14. It may also be that I am asking the wrong questions or using the wrong vocabulary. See Havelková (this volume) for discussion of the different ways in which class is viewed and discussed in Czech society.

References

Afshar, Haleh and Maynard, Mary 1994. *The Dynamics of Race and Gender: Some Feminist Interventions*. London: Taylor & Francis.

Beddoes, Dierdre 1989. *Back to Home and Duty: Women between the Wars 1918–1939*. London: Pandora/HarperCollins.

Bertaux, Daniel and Thompson, Paul 1997. *Pathways to Social Class: A Qualitative Approach to Social Mobility*. Oxford: Clarendon Press.

Brah, Avtar 1991. Questions of difference and international feminism, in Aaron, Jane and Walby, Sylvia (eds) *Out of the Margins*. London: Taylor & Francis.

Brah, Avtar 1992. Difference, diversity and differentiation in Donald, J. and Rattansi, A. (eds) *Race, Culture and Difference*, London: Sage.

Brah, Avtar 1996. *Cartographies of Diaspora*. London: Routledge.

Brannen, Julia (ed.) 1992. *Mixing Methods: Qualitative and Quantitative Research*. Aldershot: Sage.

Bystydzienski, Jill M. 1995. Women and families in poland: pressing problems and possible solutions, in Lobodinska, B. (ed.) *Family, Women and Employment in Central-Eastern Europe*. Westport, CT: Greenwood Press.

Cavendish, Ruth 1982. *Women on the Line*. London: Routledge & Kegan Paul.

Clancy, Patrick, Kelly, Mary, Wiatr, Jerzy and Zoltaniecki, Ryszard 1992. *Ireland and Poland: Comparative Perspectives*. Dublin: University College Dublin, Department of Sociology.

Davies, Norman 1981. *God's Playground, Vol. 2*. Oxford: Clarendon Press.

Davies, Norman 1986. *Heart of Europe*. Oxford: Oxford University Press.

Davies, Norman 1996. *Europe*. Oxford: Oxford University Press.

D'Cruze, Shani 1997. 'You're not with your common friends now': race and class evasion in 1960s London, in Mahony, Pat and Zmroczek, Christine (eds) (1997a), pp. 65–77.

De Marco Torgovnick, Marianna 1994. *Crossing Ocean Parkway: Readings by an Italian American Daughter*. Chicago: Chicago University Press.

Einhorn Barbara 1993. *Cinderella Goes to Market: Citizenship, Gender and Women's Movements in East-Central Europe*. London: Verso.

Forum Polek/Polish Women's Forum 1988. *A Women's Anthology in Polish and English*. London: Forum Publication Group.

Franklin, Anita (this volume). Personal reflections from the margins: an interface with race, class, nation and gender.

Fuszara, Malgorzata and Grudzinska, Beata 1994. Women in Polish academe, in Stiver Lie, S., Malik, L. and Harris, D. (eds) *The Gender Gap in Higher Education: World Yearbook of Education 1994*. London: Kogan Page.

Giles, Judy 1995. *Women, Identity and Private Life in Britain 1900–50*. Basingstoke: Macmillan.

Gontarczyk-Wesola, Ewa 1997. Women's situation in the process of change in Poland, in Renne, Tanya (ed.) *Ana's Land, Sisterhood in Eastern Europe*. Boulder, Colorado: Westview Press.

Guymer, Laurel (this volume). Spilling the caviar: telling privileged class tales.

Havelková, Hana (this volume). Women in and after a "classless" society.

Herne, Karen, Travaglia, Joanne and Weiss, Elizabeth (eds) 1994. *Who Do You Think You Are? Second Generation Immigrant Women in Australia*. Broadway NSW: The Women's Redress Press Inc.

Hey, Valerie 1997. Northern accent and southern comfort, in Mahony, Pat and Zmroczek, Christine (eds) (1997a), pp. 140–51.

Hoffman, Eva 1991. *Lost in Translation: Life in a New Language*. London: Minerva.

Hoffman, Eva 1993. *Exit into History: A Journey through the New Eastern Europe*. London: Heinemann.

hooks, bell 1984. *Feminist Theory: From the Margin to the Center*. Boston, Mass.: Southend Books.

hooks, bell 1989. *Talking Back: Thinking Feminist – Thinking Black*. London: Sheba.

hooks, bell 1994. *Outlaw Culture: Resisting Representations*. London: Routledge.

Hill Collins, Pat 1990. *Black Feminist Thought*. London: Unwin Hyman.

Lobodzinska, Barbara (ed.) 1995. *Family, Women and Employment in Central-Eastern Europe*. Westport, CT: Greenwood Press.

Long, Kristi S. 1996. *We All Fought for Freedom: Women in Poland's Solidarity Movement*. Oxford: Westview Press.

Madhavarau, Leela (this volume). Officially known as "Other": multiethnic identities and class status.

Mahony, Pat and Zmroczek, Christine (eds) 1997a. *Class Matters: "Working-Class" Women's Perspectives on Social Class*. London: Taylor & Francis.

Mahony, Pat and Zmroczek, Christine 1997b. Why class matters, in Mahony, P. and Zmroczek, C. (eds) (1997a), pp. 1–7.

Marshall, Gordon 1997. *Repositioning Class: Social Inequality in Industrial Societies*. London: Sage

Maynard, Mary 1994. Race, gender and the concept of "difference" in feminist thought, in Afshar, H. and Maynard, M. (1994), pp. 9–25.

Morawski, Witold 1992. Social and economic change in Poland, in Clancy et al. (eds) (1992), pp. 91–101.

Nowicka, Wanda 1997. Ban on abortion in Poland. Why?, in Reene, Tanya (ed.) *Ana's Land, Sisterhood in Eastern Europe*. Boulder, Colorado: Westview Press.

Oakley, Ann 1974. *Sociology of Housework*. London: Pantheon Books.

Oleksy, Elzbieta 1995. Introduction in *Selected Proceedings of the Women's Studies Conference*, Lodz, Poland, 17–21 May 1993. Women's Studies International Forum, 18(1), 3–8.

Penelope, Julia (ed.) 1994. *Out of the Class Closet: Lesbians Speak*. Freedom, Ca: The Crossing Press.

Pine, Frances 1992. Uneven burdens: women in rural Poland, in Rai, Shirin, Pilkington, Hilary and Phizacklea, Annie (eds) *Women in the Face of Change: the Soviet Union, Eastern Europe and China*. London: Routledge.

Reay, Diane 1997. The double-bind of the "working class" feminist: the success of failure or the failure of success, in Mahony, Pat and Zmroczek, Christine (eds) (1997a), pp. 18–29.

Skeggs, Beverley 1997. *Formations of Class and Gender*. London: Sage.

Stanislawski, Jan 1982. *Wielki Slownik Polsko-Angielski (Polish English Dictionary)*. Warsaw: Wiedza-Powzechna.

Steedman, Carolyn 1986. *Landscape for a Good Woman*. London: Virago.

Sword, Keith with N. Davies and Ciechanowski, J. 1989. *The Formation of the Polish Community in Great Britain. 1939–50*. School of Slavonic and East European Studies, University of London.

Sword, Keith 1996. *Identity in Flux: The Polish Community in Britain*. School of Slavonic and East European Studies, University of London.

Teleky, Richard 1997. *Hungarian Rhapsodies: Essays on Ethnicity, Identity and Culture*. Seattle and London: University of Washington Press.

Temple, Bogusia 1994. *Polish Identity and Community*. University of Manchester Occasional Papers, 38.

Temple, Bogusia 1997. Contested categorizations: auto/biography, narrativity and class, in Mahony, P. and Zmroczek, C. (eds) (1997a), pp. 78–86.

Thompson, E.P. 1979. *The Making of the Working Class in Britain*. London: Penguin.

Thompson, Paul 1997. Women, men and transgenerational family influences in social mobility, in Bertaux, Daniel and Thompson, Paul (eds) (1997), pp. 32–61.

Tokarcyk, Michelle and Fay, Elizabeth 1993. *Working Class Women in the Academy*. Amherst: University of Massachusetts Press.

Walkerdine, Valerie 1990. *Schoolgirl Fictions*. London: Verso.

Watson, Peggy 1997. (Anti)feminism after communism, in Oakley, Ann and Mitchell, Juliet (eds) *Who's Afraid of Feminism: Seeing through the Backlash*. Harmondsworth: Penguin, pp. 144–61.

Weclawowicz, Grzegorz 1996. *Contemporary Poland: Space and Society*. London: UCL Press.

Westwood, Sallie 1984. *All Day, Every Day: Factory and Family in the Making of Women's Lives*. London: Pluto Press.

Wiatr, Jerzy 1992. The state and society in Poland, in Clancy et al. (1992), pp. 3–11.

Wnuk-Lipinski Edmund 1992. Transformation of the social order and legitimation of inequalities, in Clancy et al. (1992), pp. 169–77.

Wright, Erik Olin 1997. *Class Counts: Comparative Studies in Class Analysis*. Cambridge: Cambridge University Press.

Zajicek, Anna M. and Casalanti, Toni M. 1995. The impact of Socioeconomic restructuring on Polish women, in Lobodzinska (1995), pp. 179–92.

Zandy, Janet 1990. *Calling Home: Working Class Women's Writing*. New Brunswick, NJ: Rutgers University Press.

Zandy, Janet (ed.) 1995. *Liberating Memory: Our Work and Our Working Class Consciousness*. New Brunswick, NJ: Rutgers University Press.

Zawodny, J.K. 1971. *Death in the Forest: the Story of the Katyn Forest Massacre*. London: Macmillan.

Zmroczek, C. Class: women's studies students respond (provisional title). In progress.

Zmroczek, Christine and Mahony, Pat 1996a. Lives beyond the text, in Bell, D. and Klein, R. (eds) *Radically Speaking: Feminism Reclaimed*. Melbourne: Spinifex; London: Zed Press.

Zmroczek Christine and Mahony, Pat 1996b. Women's studies and working-class women, in Ang-Lygate et al. (eds) *Desperately Seeking Sisterhood: Still Challenging and Building*. London: Taylor & Francis.

CHAPTER SEVEN

Class matters: Yes it does

Janice G. Raymond

When I was growing up among the labouring people in my part of the world, class had no articulated vocabulary. I was not familiar with the language of class until I studied sociology in college where the discourse was not even about economic class (which smacked of communist class struggle and conflict), but rather about "socioeconomic status". To speak of socioeconomic status in the United States is to imply striving for a better position. So if you are striving for a better position, which nearly everyone is, you are supposedly not located in the working class. It is as if because everyone *aspires* to be middle class, everyone *is* middle class. Nor did we talk about social inequality in college; rather we talked about social stratification. I did not know my family was part of the *proletariat* until graduate school where the class discourse picked up and the status discourse left off.

When I entered the professional teaching class of the academy, everyone still presumed that "we" all come from middle class backgrounds. I teach at a large US state university that is well known as a centre of radical economic thought. It is also known for its substantial percentage of faculty who come out of, or at the very least are sympathetic to, leftist traditions of thought and activism. Women's studies, at my university, has been much more allied with a historical socialist feminist tradition than with a radical feminist analysis and activism with which I identify. Thus women's studies, like other progressive departments in the university, engages in class analysis, but that analysis is conducted from the fictional starting point that those of us who are white academics come from the middle class and are different from the proletariat.

It is no surprise that this assumption prevails. Who teaches at the state universities that most working-class students in the United States attend? Who in these public institutions is the teaching class, a class which includes the substantial group of leftist faculty who "do" class analysis? As Tokarczyk and Fay note in their introduction to *Working-Class Women in the Academy: Labourers in the*

Knowledge Factory, "A look at faculty rosters at the state university level shows that tenured and tenure-track professors are for the most part graduated from the Ivy or near-Ivy leagues . . ." (1993: 15). Only a small percentage of faculty who teach at these major public research universities have themselves graduated from state schools (not having the elite status of a University of California, Berkeley, for example). Even fewer faculty on the state university rosters have graduated from Catholic universities which historically have been identified with a class-bound education tethered to an unthinking, simplistic and "dupes of the papacy" mentality. The traditional academic prejudice toward Catholics in elite private higher education in North America follows a similar historical trajectory as that towards Jews, with the crucial difference that Jewish quotas at secular elite institutions were linked with feared intellectual superiority. In contrast, Catholic quotas were linked with assumed intellectual inferiority.

I grew up Catholic in a Rhode Island milltown called Phillipsdale in the same home where my mother had been raised. The house had been moved across the railroad tracks and plunked on what had been a former factory dump, a.k.a landfill, to put a distance of 500 yards between it and the nearest factory. But I thought it was the nicest of a row of millhouses on our street, originally built by the local plants. What made the house even nicer was that it was a duplex which my family shared with my mother's sister's family. Between the two families there were seven children – six boys and myself. Luckily, I was the oldest.

My father worked in one of several mills in the town and when the work orders grew scarce, as they often did, he laboured as a janitor at the mill, or was laid off. For many years he alternated shifts in the factory, frequently working the grave-yard stint between 11 pm to 7 am. Years later, when I was in graduate school, he too "graduated" to heading up the one man "food service" for the local mills in the area. The "food service" was a 10 foot by 17 foot shed attached to the largest mill which my family called "the cafeteria", and the workers simply referred to as "the greasy spoon". And greased it was, not with the lard of cooking – for my father kept it as clean as he could – but with the oil, soot and particulate matter on floor, walls and equipment layered by years of residence in a factory building.

My maternal grandfather had worked in another of the local factories – Glenlyon Print Works – for 40 years. Mother always proudly told us that he was the mill's chief "engineer" which meant that he was the man in charge of keeping the furnaces blasting winter, summer, fall and spring. Her stories included her daily childhood task of bringing my grandfather his noon meal – a "hot meal", she would emphasize – in his "lunch pail". Together with her sister, my Aunt Mae, she was soon employed at a nickel a day by the local wives of the factory workers to bring their husbands' hot meals in their lunch pails.

When my mother first told me this story, I thought it was a great way of making money. I too could aspire to young entrepreneurship and decided, with a neighbourhood friend, to set up a lemonade stand at the gates of the mill when my father's shift disgorged from the building. The workers thought it quite charming, but not my father who reasoned that it looked like he needed to send his kid into child labour. My mother quietly told me I was never to set up shop at the factory gates again, so I moved curbside to the front of our house where I tried to catch the workers on their rush home from work in cars that seldom stopped. I resented how my entrepreneurial growth had been stunted at the factory gates.

I am to this day the only person in my immediate family to have attended college, never mind to have graduated and completed a higher education. Although my parents had never attended college, neither lacked a native "higher education" and existential intelligence. My mother and my father tried to read what they could, although beyond a secondhand and outdated collection of the *Worldbook Encyclopedia*, there were few books in the house. My mother was a refined woman who taught me to play the piano as her own mother, who had not been formally schooled beyond grade 4, had taught her. But my mother would, in this same refined way, do many things which indicated the class from which she came. When she was in her sixties, and I took her to the doctor one day, my mother was asked to bring a urine sample. This was before the days of "clean catch" procedures and standard sample cups. So my mother used the plastic container in which she placed her dentures at night. At the end of her appointment, she asked the doctor to return the plastic container, because she needed it for her teeth!

In high school, my mother had wanted to pursue a college course but switched to a business track to prepare her for bookkeeping and secretarial work upon graduating. Throughout her childhood my mother, with my Aunt Mae, Uncle Walter and my grandmother ran a newspaper service out of their garage folding thousands of the daily *Providence Journals* and then delivering them locally to businesses and residences. My mother would describe with some pride how she and her siblings helped her mother earn money for my Uncle Frank's college and medical school education, assembling and folding by hand thousands of newspapers day after day. And after high school, when she went to work as a bookkeeper and secretary at one of the local mills, she would give each paycheque to her mother to be put aside for my uncle's ongoing education.

Years later when my Uncle Frank was a successful surgeon, my mother worked for him cleaning his family house and doctor's office. And when his wife was dying of cancer, she took care of my Aunt Doris. When we were children, my Uncle Frank would give me and my brothers $50 each Christmas. Small change, I thought, for the years of work my mother had contributed to his education. And I would be invited once a summer to their lakeshore home where I learned to swim and even to water ski all of which, I remember, contributed to my first consciousness of the difference that money makes to the material quality of life one can lead.

My mother and father married when she was 30 and he was 21, and thereafter my mother would always be self-conscious about their age difference which she would hold responsible for their differences in temperament, interests and goals. Not exactly a storybook marriage, it prompted my asking one day why she married my father. "I felt sorry for him," she said. "His mother died shortly after he was born and his stepmother treated her new husband's children very badly."

She told me that my father, being the youngest of the children, received the worst abuse – so much that his father sent him off to boarding school to remove him from the family home.

Like my mother, my father was an intelligent man. I loved his small, smart set of leather-bound classics in our one bookcase that stood next to the tattered set of encyclopedias that had been passed down to us by my Uncle Frank. But as my class-consciousness emerged, I always thought it odd that a man who went through five years of a private boarding school would end up working in a factory. There is a tale here, I thought. And the story is that my paternal grandfather had shipped his two boys off to boarding school to get them out of harm's way. But in return for their room, board and education, my father and his brother had to earn their keep by cleaning the rooms and making the beds of their more well-off classmates in addition to waiting on their tables at mealtimes. This is no cause and effect tale in which privately educated schoolboy rejects the culture of upward mobility to work in a factory. It is simply an observation on the ironies of class and class reversals. Working-class boy with upper-class education doesn't always make good by upwardly mobile class standards.

As for me, my mother was concerned that I would need to make a living after high school, but she didn't want me to work in the factories. She reasoned that her own education of bookkeeping, accounting and shorthand, all tailored to equip the young female secretaries of the male work world, would prepare me for something better. But I resisted being tracked into a business course and won the day. I told my mother I wanted to be a school teacher and after graduating from high school would go to a teachers' college. She weakly insisted that we had no money for "normal school", as she called the teachers' colleges of the day, and we didn't. But I told her I would work and earn much of the money during summers. So thus began, at age thirteen, my work life as a camp counsellor, lifeguard and swimming instructor each summer of my high school years and, during my senior year in high school, I worked almost every day as a "soda jerk" and attendant at a local pharmacy.

The high school I attended, St Mary Academy, was a Catholic girls' school with superlative teachers, several of whom I respected and admired. Coming from an all-boy family, I experienced my first sense here that sisterhood could be powerful. Girls and girls' minds were important, and we girls revelled in this culture of sisterhood.

I had ended up at St Mary Academy because my mother wanted me to have a good Catholic education. Convinced that education was moral as well as mental, my mother took on odd jobs and extracted sums from her food money to be set aside for my Catholic school education. My father, who had converted to Catholicism, mainly as a condition of marriage imposed upon him by my mother, went along with this arrangement.

Long before Robin Morgan would write that "Sisterhood is powerful", sisterhood was certainly succouring and scintillating for me. The prospects of marriage, working in the local factories as labourer or secretary, and even the dimmer possibility of attending a teachers' college were all unappealing. I craved the companionship of women and the life of the mind that I had experienced firsthand with my classmates and teachers. Unlike many Catholic schools, St Mary Academy was not a working-class, ethnic Catholic, neighbourhood school. It was a fairly large day school with a smaller boarding section, mostly attended by the children of upwardly mobile and economically advantaged Catholic professionals and entrepreneurs. Like my father, I would be outclassed during my high school years, but at least I eluded cleaning the rooms of my classmates and waiting on them at meals.

At St Mary Academy I received an excellent education that prepared me for further education and for working in the world. During these years I experienced a strange mixture of working-class inferiority and superiority that, to some extent, are still with me – inferiority that came from what I perceived to be my lack of comparable resources and the fear that I would be discovered and treated as an interloper in this classier world than mine; superiority because I knew in many ways that I had more grit and ambition than many of my classmates. And I knew that I would never, in my opinion, "settle for" marriage and motherhood. My independence, and later what would become my lesbianism, are equally the result of my class and gender background. In this context, the dissonance in class background between me and my classmates produced in me an awareness of how far I wanted to go, not only beyond my economic class but beyond accepted affectionate and gender class.

In the scarce feminist literature on class, there has been some discussion of the fact that women, especially, do not pass easily from one class to another (Tokarczyk & Fay 1993). Although one may move into a different economic class, the marks of earlier class experience may still remain. This is more of a vexed passage when working-class women who emigrate to middle-class livelihoods and professional locales remain close to many family members – in my own case, parents, brothers, nieces and nephews – who are identifiably working class, culturally and economically.

Within my own family, the pattern of the generation younger than me has been to leave high school before graduating, end up in dead-end and part-time jobs, have no health insurance or benefits, and find solace in a mindless culture of televised sports and soap operas, gambling, drinking and drugs. One of my nephews has been in jail for drugs and theft. And because they are white, have periodic steady jobs, own televisions and lease cars, and do not receive welfare payments, they view themselves as middle class. Everyone of my nephews and nieces might be said to have "regressed" educationally, economically and culturally compared with me and my brothers. More needs to be written about the "skidders", as they are called in the sociological literature, who challenge the supposed natural law of American upward mobility that presupposes more opportunities for the next generation.

In the small body of literature that exists on working-class academics, the nature of work has been a frequent theme. The scope of this discussion ranges from the alienating character of much academic work to what working-class academics understand their real work to be. For example, Monika Reinfelder writes: "Academic work is not something that I identify with, that is essential to my self, it is merely something that pays my bills at the moment" (Reinfelder 1997: 106). Other academics of working-class background have commented on how their working-class families view their academic work, i.e. as not having to work as much as, or to do the kind of "real" work that working people do. For example, when I am at home preparing classes, writing an article, or working at my computer, this is not perceived as work by many members of my family. My mother who, before she died, would live with me for parts of the year and would see me diligently engaged in writing at home, would often remark, "It's good you don't have to work today."

In contrast to my family, however, I do view my home, in which most of my writing is done, as my workplace. I like to work at home. I am more comfortable writing at home than I am at the university. In general, I find the university an uncomfortable place to be. I am told by other working-class colleagues in the academy that this is a telltale sign of working-class background – what I call the class "comfort level". I am also more comfortable shopping for groceries in the working-class town of neighbouring Greenfield than I am in the college town of neighboring Amherst. Why? Simply because I'm much more at home there. At the same time I note, with great discomfort, the class differences in physical shape, weight, clothing, and the classic giveaway of many working-class people – bad teeth.

Relative to work, it has always struck me as a class statement that the same faculty members who are union activists within the university are singularly inactive when it comes to book contract negotiations that will determine financial remuneration and conditions under which their work is published. In contrast to many of my middle-class state university colleagues, who organize unions, fight for adequate salaries and the right to determine the conditions of their work within the university, I fight additionally for adequate financial remuneration for what I write and publish, as well as the right to determine under what conditions my writing will be published, such as retention of copyright (including the copyright to this article). Many academics would not question or negotiate their publishing contracts, as they would their teaching contracts, nor join writers' unions, as they would unions of teachers. Many would never be tainted by lobbying for higher book advances (or any book advance, for that matter). There are fundamental myths that publishing is a privilege, and that academics do not publish to make money but to disseminate ideas. But these myths are contradicted by the fact that many academic authors think it more prestigious to be published by an elite university rather than a mainstream trade press. Thus, they do not aspire to be (nor are they rewarded for being) public intellectuals whose work is disseminated to a larger group of people, nor would many of them know how to write for public consumption.

In academia, I soon learned that class was not only about money but about sensibilities and values. And this lesson was taught most graphically in the way middle-class peers spoke about their parents, in particular their mothers. Bell hooks writes: "... I was profoundly shocked and disturbed when peers would talk about their parents without respect, or would say that they hated their parents. This was especially troubling to me ... [but] It was explained ... as healthy and normal (hooks 1993: 102). Likewise, in a dialogue with Kate Ellis, Lillian S. Robinson remarks on the way middle-class women speak of their mothers and the presumption, often verbalized, that mother–daughter alienation is natural and normative, which it seems to be for many middle-class women (Ellis & Robinson 1993: 38).

On reading hooks' and Robinson's words, I was struck that I had heard much the same disrespectful comments from many middle-class female academic colleagues. When I first joined the five-college faculty in Amherst, Massachusetts, I was shocked at the way many female academics talked and joked about their mothers in what seemed to me, enormous efforts to *disidentify*. I do not want to idealize working-class mother–daughter relationships, but I think it is accurate to say that for many female academics of working-class background, the difference is in "not being alienated from our mothers" (Ellis & Robinson 1993: 38).

If anything, what becomes part of the history of many female working-class academics I know is a tendency to *identify* with our mothers, perhaps especially with our mothers' struggles and hopes. We are well aware of our mothers' often frustrated and unmet aspirations – aspirations which we may have transformed into our own successful life histories of education, independence and economic mobility. I was profoundly moved each time my mother struggled to read every one of my five books. She would read each of them very slowly, then again, then once more, and finally would ask many perceptive questions which the books raised for her. For whatever I was writing about, she would become a clipping service of articles she thought would interest me. What working-class women reject is not our mothers but their "way of experiencing a woman's life" (ibid.). Although my life was and has been very different from my mother's, it was she who, in large measure, helped to make my life different and provided some of the early signposts for the roads I travelled.

Finally, it is telling that, *analytically*, "class matters" in progressive academic departments and in women's studies but, in practice, few acknowledge that some members of the faculty may have a personal working-class history that indeed matters to the class analysis. *There is the notion that theoretical class analysis supersedes actual class experience.* For those faculty who come from working-class backgrounds, sitting in on discussions/analyses of socioeconomic class in academia is like eavesdropping on a conversation about your life where the fact that "this is your life" is simply not recognized. A similar lack of acknowledgement would not happen in the same "pronounced" way if the faculty member participating in a discussion about race or sexuality were a person of colour or a lesbian. My lesbianism, for example, is referenced in women's studies much more than my working-class background.

Nor do I wish to blame this lack of acknowledgement simply on my academic colleagues. As an academic, I have found it particularly difficult to know how I make visible my own working-class background – as compared to my lesbian existence, for example. I agree with Susan Wolfe when she writes: ". . . the influence of class has been at once so pervasive, and so woven into my sensibilities and reactions, that I've never been able to isolate or analyse it before" (Wolfe 1994: 291).

Because the definition of working class in North America is so fluid, because the academic is no longer situated economically in the working class, because the academy levels class differences in a way it cannot level racial or gender differences (if only because these latter differences are usually apparent), and because there is a stereotype of "residual" working-class behaviour that we of working-class background are supposed to exhibit in appearance, accent or manner, the result is often disbelief if we are not true to type. It is as if a faculty member of working-class background is a "pretender" to working-class status. Combine this with the fact that many female academics who come from working-class backgrounds often feel like frauds within the academy (see, e.g., Miner 1993: 81), and this can make for a peculiar schizophrenia.

"Schizophrenia" and personal invisibility are worsened by a "community of scholars" that acknowledges class in theory, but in practice assumes that white folks teaching in the academy all come from the middle class. "The academy theorizes class, but unless it is subsumed by gender or race, and particularly by race, it does not figure in the practical calculus by which we assess our efforts at creating equal opportunity" (O'Dair 1993: 239–400). That assumption in itself is profoundly silencing to many white working-class academics. The collegial inability to acknowledge an academic peer's working-class experience functions as a kind of "disbelief". This disbelief goes far beyond the lack of individual acknowledgement given to a person of working-class background.

Disbelief has profound political implications for the ways in which affirmative action is practised in US universities, particularly in the hiring of the teaching class. As Sharon O'Dair has astutely observed, given the theoretical importance of class in academic criticism, and the intellectual community's general embrace of affirmative action policy and programmes, even in the face of these policies and programmes being subverted by state legislatures and the courts, one would think that academics would strive to put their own house in order (O'Dair 1993). One would think that left-liberal academics especially would push to extend the benefits of affirmative action, expanding the teaching class to those who have been subject to class disadvantage and discrimination. That class has not figured in affirmative action criteria used for academic hiring is due to a variety of middle-class, self-interested and elitist reasons (ibid.). The result is that class as a variable in academia is most often theorized but hardly ever implemented. Affirmative action is *practised* around issues of race, gender and sometimes sexuality but *theorized* around the issue of class.

Affirmative action programmes and policies have failed in structural ways to address the disadvantages and discrimination based on socio-economic class. This is most tangible in the matter of higher education. Working-class people contribute through taxation to the financing of higher education, whether public or private. But as O'Dair points out further, thinkers from both the right and left make the point that "... public expenditures on higher education transfer wealth from one socioeconomic class to another, in this case from the working classes, who make less use of these services, to the middle and upper classes, who use them much more heavily" (ibid.: 247).

As far as affirmative action goes, a numerically large group that has been historically class oppressed and class disadvantaged has been left to raise itself up "by its own bootstraps". This is not the place to develop the fuller meaning of this class reality nor what might be the merits/demerits of expanding affirmative action policies and programmes to include class in an age when affirmative action as we know it is under siege from several quarters. It is rather to affirm that class matters; yes it does.

References

Ellis, Kate and Robinson, Lillian S. 1993. Class Discussion: A Dialogue between Kate Ellis and Lillian S. Robinson, in Tokarcztk, M.M. and Fay, E.A. (1993), pp. 25–46.

hooks, bell 1993. Keeping close to home: class and education, in Tokarcztk, M.M. and Fay, E.A. (1993), pp. 99–111.

Miner, Valerie 1993. Working and teaching with class, in Tokarcztk, M.M. and Fay, E.A. (1993).

O'Dair, 1993.

Reinfelder, Monika 1997. Switching cultures, in Mahony, Pat and Zmroczek, Christine (eds) *Class Matters: "Working-Class" Women's Perspectives on Social Class*. London, Taylor & Francis.

Tokarcztk, Michelle M. and Fay, Elizabeth A. (eds) 1993. *Working-Class Women in the Academy: Laborers in the Knowledge Factory*. Amherst: University of Massachusetts Press.

Wolfe, Susan J. 1994. Getting class, in Penelope, Julia (ed.) *Out of the Class Closet: Lesbians Speak*. Freedom, CA: The Crossing Press.

CHAPTER EIGHT

Coming out

Frances A. Maher

I came out in 1960. I wore an ivory-coloured, off-the-shoulder satin gown, with lace and seed pearl decorations, a 1950s' wedding dress but without the sleeves. Along with 99 other debutantes in Boston, Massachusetts that year, I curtsied to the floor of the Grand Ballroom of the Copley Plaza Hotel on the arm of my father and my escort, paying court to the dozen or so assorted grande dames of Boston who were to accept me into polite society. Boston Brahmins, the nickname classically given to the elite of Boston, are white, Anglo-Saxon, Protestant, and culturally and financially the dominant class, less so now than 30 years ago but still identified with the leadership of Boston's major cultural and business institutions.

While the American aristocracy, particularly this New England version, gets its cultural flavour from England, it is of course not quite so hereditary, not quite so landed, and nowhere near as old. Although my mother can trace her blue-blood ancestry back to a president of Harvard in the eighteenth century (a man who sided with the Tories in the American Revolution), my father's family, originally from Providence, were small farmers until my great-grandfather made the family fortune in the years after the Civil War. It was his family, the Aldriches, who were the richer and more prominent in my childhood, and yet they had been "upper class" for less than a century.

I believe that the English version of "coming out" is about "curtsying to the Queen". While I hope British readers will make connections on their own between, for example, Harvard and Oxbridge's renditions of class and gender distinctions, this is not a comparative piece. Perhaps they will let me know what they discover. While I made my curtsies along with the other girls, I did not, however, have my own "coming out" party; my parents could not afford it. These were gala affairs in tents with hundreds of eighteen-, nineteen- and twenty-year-olds dancing to the music of Lester Lanin and his society orchestra and drinking themselves prone (mostly the boys,) under the potted palms. The reasons my parents could not afford it was that my grandfather had dissipated his chunk of the family fortune on artists' models and we were left to make our way in a somewhat more humble fashion than many of my friends. This meant giving a dinner before the ball, but no lavish party, going to private school but having a scholarship to buy the uniforms, and living in a vast old winterized summer house in an upper-class summer community that was only fashionable from Memorial to Labor Day.

These experiences, and many like them, have contributed over the years to my nervous perplexity about just what class I was from anyway. If upper class, then how come we didn't see ourselves as rich and how come I often felt I didn't belong? If I was only middle class, then how come there were lots of girls, even in my private schools, whose families, unlike mine, were not in the *Social Register* (the telephone directory of American upper-class families) and who were not invited to "come out" as I had been? It seemed as though these markers were important barriers, and that I was in a club many couldn't join. Ten years later, when I had become a socialist wife and mother and a member of a small revolutionary Marxist party, the term "coming out" had come to mean something else, and I want to use this "coming out" essay to grapple with some of the issues raised by such a background in my current, very different life. How has it mattered to this life to have been born into an upper-class family, and how has my gender operated within this frame? What has my class background bequeathed to me that I use, consciously or unconsciously; what has it taught me that I have had to unlearn? How could this ever-changing process of self-definition possibly matter to anyone else?

My purpose, then, in writing this chapter is to excavate some of the workings of my social class privilege in my own life and practice as an American academic and still-socialist feminist. In common academic parlance, I want to examine my contradictory position of dominance in relation to social class, both within and surrounding my subordinate gender position. I want to sort out particularly those aspects of my life which, in Peggy McIntosh's description of whiteness, constitute "an invisible package of unearned assets" that I "can count on cashing in on each day, but about which [I was] meant to remain oblivious" (McIntosh 1992: 64). These assets isolate me, often unconsciously, from important issues and concerns in the lives of the people I work with and on behalf of, issues such as long-term economic security. On the other hand I want to figure out which of my "advantages", if any, have been or might be of positive use to them and to me. I hope this story will help push the boundaries of our thinking about the ways in which we all occupy contradictory and ambiguous positions within networks of both domination and subordination. Often these contradictions have baffled me – for example, when I feel powerful and productive is it my class privilege working, or my gender oppression being overcome? Or both? Is this why every professional accomplishment carries both the joy of being recognized and a tinge of guilt, the desire not to put myself forward too much?

While I have written elsewhere with Mary Kay Tetreault, my co-author, about white privilege in relation to our research (see Maher & Tetreault 1994, 1997), here I will concentrate on social class, although the importance of the "white" bit for the term WASP (i.e. "White Anglo Saxon Protestant") cannot be over-estimated and deserves a full treatment on its own.

Why "coming out?" The "closet" is not that of presumed heterosexuality, but presumed middle-classness. Partly, my title reflects the deep ambivalence I have just referred to about whether or not this chapter will be worth reading, exacerbated by the feeling that once again this very writing is a display of class privilege. Much has been written, what more need be said? (If you read this, you will see that I overcame my doubts to publish it, doubts I have not overcome as I write it.) It is an irony that Americans have always famously denied the existence of our class system (even though the rich/poor divide has never been wider) and yet there is much work already on the American upper class – even on its women (see Ostrander 1984). Moreover, and this is a double irony, some of it is not only figuratively but literally about me. My brother wrote a book called *Old Money* about the declining but still powerful WASP ascendancy in America; as an ethnographer of class values and mores he mined our family traditions and stories (Aldrich 1986). And yet there were few women in the book at all, except in the acknowledgements, and no mention of women as a group. Of course when I complained he said, "Everything I said applies to women, too," and when he retreated from that notion, his final comment was simply, "You write it, then." So in the "History" section below I look a little for mess-ages from my female forebears.

Later, a feminist social psychologist and researcher on women's lives, inter-viewing members of my college class, did a book chapter on social class at the college in the 1960s based on in-depth interviews. Her upper-class case study was me, under a pseudonym (Ostrove & Stewart 1994). Her (my) theme was one of persistent feelings of marginality solved by finding a home in feminism, and I will be quoting her (me!) in the "Education" section below. Since my current theme is to explore and deconstruct precisely that sense of sisterly in-clusion I emphasized before, I think I have more to say, now, but again, the "coming out" theme reflects my uncertainty in that regard.

"Coming out", in the sense of becoming visible, standing out from the crowd, has another meaning to me as well. The three parts of this chapter are all animated by the same theme, which is that of inclusion and exclusion, belonging and not belonging, connection and isolation. Even while wanting to separate myself out as being, for example, the "smartest" one in my elite all-girls' board-ing school, I envied others, sprouting their multiple monogrammed cashmere sweaters, for their belongingness and popularity. As a professor in education who also teaches women's studies, I have embraced the comfortable mantle of "middle-classness" that feminists, writing about their working-class back-grounds, have cast on their more privileged sisters. (Indeed, I have been surprised at how seldom these writers mention the upper class.) I also teach at a middle-of-the-road institution, a small undergraduate liberal arts college, which is neither elite nor at the bottom of America's higher education pecking order. Our upper-class students are often those who could not get in to more elite schools; the ones from the working-class are often the first in their families to go to college. It is an environment, like many, in which class is extremely important and never mentioned, so that I can feel happily invisible much of the time, and occasionally very self-consciously visible indeed. (Once a good friend of mine, an economics professor, had his students guess the "three upper class people on the faculty" by our clothes and our general "look", making the point that class differences were based on more than economic differences.) "Coming out", then, as *not* a middle-class feminist but as even *more* privileged than middle-class women are, makes me feel exposed, cast out, once again not included. In a world where the whole group is "smart", it turns out that I am once again different, the only one, as it were, with the cashmere sweater.

Other memoirs of class and education have focused on the themes of power and resistance. At a recent conference of the British Sociological Association (whose actual theme was "Power and Resistance"), a British male colleague, the son of a Church of England priest, made the point in his presentation that even as he was resisting his middle-class family by becoming an intellectual, the kind of "muscular intellectuality" he embraced led to real social power of an important kind; in the words of one article:

> Peter's fascination with the muscular intellectualness he identified with (a certain teacher) can be understood in terms of the access it promised to give him to the entitlements of conventional masculinity . . . the world of ideas and knowledge [was] powerfully middle-class, a source of personal strength and a means to exercise personal control over others (Redman 1996).

These contradictions, I would argue, are particularly masculine ones, as they are articulated in the hierarchical language of unequal power relationships, relative strengths, and control. While I want to come back to the notion of the relative powers and deficits of my position, as both an academic and a "woman of privilege", the metaphor that captures my anxieties about this project is not one of hierarchies but of networks and webs. I want to explore, not what powers or resistances I have in relation to societal inequalities, but how my advantages both work to include me and isolate me (see Gilligan 1982: 62). I want to trace this theme in three parts, looking first at my own family history for the origins of my political commitments, next at my education for the origins of my own inclusions in and exclusions from feminist identities, and finally at the implications for others' and my own current feminist work of exploring hitherto unmapped positions of social privilege.

History and power

> Class experience is deeply rooted, retained and carried through life
> rather than left behind (or below). In this sense it is more like a foot
> that carries us forward than a footprint which marks a past presence
> (Mahony & Zmroczek 1997: 4).

When the events of the 1960s gradually convinced me and my peers that
the American government was not only mistaken, in the case of Civil Rights
and Vietnam, but consciously exploitative on a global scale, I became – as it
has turned out – a lifelong socialist. My first adult relationship with my family
and class of origin was thus not a leave-taking but an outright rejection
and rebellion; an early memory of the period is of a confrontation between
my father and my then-husband, also from an upper-class privileged family,
whose father's fortune was even more recent than my own family's dwindling
one. One day my father asked him, "Does your group [meaning our Marxist–
Leninist "vanguard" party] want to take over all of this?" gesturing around our
house and evoking his whole way of life, and my husband said, "Yes." I later
learned that many student radicals were from similar backgrounds to my own,
also outraged and disillusioned at their parents' key positions in such a corrupt
and venal system (and at the same time feeling the personal entitlement to
change it!).

At the time and for many years afterwards, therefore, I thought I had largely
managed to evade my background, a footprint erased or smudged over. Thus,
over the years I have repeatedly been embarrassed by and just simply silent
about my social class origins. "Rich" or not in my generation, my forebears
were capitalist exploiters of the first order, and the kind of energizing look at
class, ethnic and/or racial origins engaged in by my radical feminist peers was
quite painful. How could I look back and celebrate my ancestors? At a women's
studies conference about ten years ago, I remember seeing a wonderful film
about a Women's Labor Summer School at Bryn Mawr College, the school my
mother went to for one year during the Depression, before her tuition money ran
out. During the discussion after the film many of the women in the audience
recalled their working-class origins, and described the strong labouring women
who had bequeathed to them their feminism, their class-consciousness – and,
ironically, their upward mobility. I found myself in tears and excused myself to
friends on the basis of some crisis in my private life. I had come by then to think
it was better, often, to remain silent and confused, to call myself privileged
simply by being one of those comfortably indeterminate middle-class white
heterosexual women whom other feminists justifiably wanted to get out of the
centre of the movement. On the few occasions in feminist academic circles when
I mentioned my family of origin to try out the admission that I was not middle
class, I got the feeling that people thought I was kidding or boasting, and, in any
case, what difference did it make now?

However, that film, the publication of my brother's book and Susan Ostrander's study of upper-class women, and the interviews with the social psychologist mentioned above made me think again, and over the past ten years I have been mulling over how that foot has indeed carried me forward in my life. The searing message of the film had filled me with shame, shame that my forebears, particularly on my father's side, were the very people who were the class enemy in the film, shame that my mother's association at Bryn Mawr had been a privileged one, even shame that with all that privilege, she had not been able to finish college. Although I didn't write about it, I began about then to look for forebears I could take pride in, and to think about the messages I was given at home about my place and responsibilities in the world. Here is what I said to my interviewer:

'In boarding school we were told we were very privileged people and you absolutely have to make a difference in this world, you can't just sit back and enjoy it. I was always the smart one in the family, so I think I was expected to do something intellectual; I was supposed to do good in an intellectual way. But the message was not specific in the sense of you must become a teacher or you must do this kind of volunteer work. It was much more of a general sort of "the purpose of life is to achieve, get good grades, be respectable, and then turn over all your advantage to the less fortunate" (Ostrove & Stewart 1994: 298).

Well, then, I could look to the good works performed on this basis by the members of my family. But how does a socialist make sense of an injunction to help the "less fortunate", knowing that the real solution is the withering-away of such economic distinctions in the first place, and that the struggle for this must be led by these people, certainly not by you? The question I agonized over, then and now, was to what extent, if you don't come from an exploited group, you can help anyway? My brother had written eloquently about the way in which my father, a Boston architect, had been a "public man", contributing much time and effort to community institutions, but of course his activities were about the maintenance of class privilege disguised as, or concurrent with, community development (see Aldrich 1988: 285–6).

But what about the women in my family? How did they exercise their responsibilities towards making the world a better place? Unlike my father, they worked directly with the poor and "less fortunate". I knew that my mother had assisted in an inner-city nursery school before she settled down to putting in endless and tireless volunteer hours at Massachusetts General Hospital, albeit the famously WASP premier hospital in the city. In an interview held with my grandmother 20 years ago, before her death, I had learned that her major volunteer activity as a young bride in Cambridge, Massachusetts, had been to go around to poor Irish neighbourhoods and collect money from the women in the family. "Excuse me, collect money *from* them?" "Yes, we had a Poor Women's Savings Association,

I would bank their money for them because they couldn't get to the bank by themselves, and that way their husbands wouldn't come home and drink it all up." When I revisited this story in search of my noblesse oblige background, this mixture of paternalism (maternalism), ethnic superiority, and genuine concern for these women struck me dumb all over again.

Susan Ostrander locates her upper-class women subjects' charity work squarely within their activities to maintain their class exlusivity and superiority, which is certainly where I would have to place my eager, earnest grandmother's commitments:

> The women do community work to return some of what they have to the community, to carry on family traditions, and to oversee the organizations to whom they contribute money . . . As they share their energies and wealth with those less fortunate, they also protect and justify those class privileges that they consider to be their birthright . . . A central aim of upper-class women's community volunteer work is to keep private control over community organizations. Private control is defined as the control of their own class (Ostrander 1984: 148).

If I am heir to these values, these sentiments, in any ways, how does their persistence subconsciously colour my own work? What is the basis of my conscious solidarity with working-class women (about whom I tend to overgeneralize and essentialize, even as I envy them and feel guilty about their "impeccable" origins as compared to mine)? Does this solidarity cover a deep-seated subconscious sense of cultural superiority? On the other hand, if I divest myself of certain unearned privileges, certain abilities, which set me apart from others, am I making myself less or more useful to the movement?

My most recent encounter with these questions was perhaps the sharpest, poignantly raising but also provisionally settling the question of my ethical and ideological relationships with my ancestresses. As part of a book my co-author and I were writing on feminist teachers and our own "emancipatory" educational projects, I was making a visit to an historically black women's college in the deep South (Maher & Tetreault 1994). She and I, who are both white, wanted to explore and publicize the work of African American women, teachers and students, who were transforming the curriculum in higher education. I arrived on campus late at night and spent the night alone in the Faculty Guest House; no other campus we visited had invited us to stay, practically free, on campus. I got up bright and early. Beginning to cross the quadrangle, the first thing I saw in front of me was a dormitory sign. I was looking at *Aldrich Hall*, named after my great-aunt, whose famously and historically wealthy husband had donated the money for this building and many others besides. Shivering in the early morning light, although it was spring in Atlanta, I had never been so glad for my married name. I felt both exposed and invisible – my surname up there for all to see, and yet if they really knew they would not see *me* at all. I was afraid that they would see a name, another "missionary" presence, and they would never understand, never see that my own commitments, my own purposes there, were completely different.

During the next three weeks, however, having been joined by my co-author, we were repeatedly asked, as white visitors, "Why are you here?" As I listened to my own answers becoming fuller and more thoughtful, I began to realize that I was forging a new sense of myself as an anti-racist feminist activist. My ancestors and family thought of themselves, certainly self-servingly but no less sincerely, as the guardians and builders of a better community. My beliefs are that such a community can only be forged through the breakdown of racial, gender and class inequalities. I thus came to see my presence there as a way of making common cause with African-American feminist peers. Could I then maybe make a small, secret connection with the spirit of my great aunt – both of us wanting to foster black women's education? Writing this, though, I realize that unlike my grandmother and great-aunt, unlike Ostrander's women, I mean my activities to be geared not towards the preservation of my class but its dismantling. But I also come from a different historical time and context, and from another generation in my nuclear family, one whose men (unlike my great aunt's family) have drastically less money, but whose women have considerably more education. Instead of a lady bountiful, then, I became an academic. In the next sections of this chapter I want to explore the contradictions of class and classlessness, inclusions and exclusions within my own education and then within academic feminism.

Education and alienation

Public discourses in American society are notably silent and confused about questions of the significance of class in shaping either the social structure or people's life experiences. This denial, among other factors, has made socialism and radical political perspectives difficult to convey to most Americans. Apparently Thatcherism has had a similar effect in Britain. Whereas in Britain both the Tories and New Labour have challenged traditional class distinctions, here in the States they are thought never to have existed in the first place. Differences in income and status are freely acknowledged, but are seen only in individualized terms. In the States, moreover, class and race are confounded, in that the terms "black" and "poor" and "white" and "middle-class" are frequently used interchangeably; middle-class blacks and poor whites are seen as exceptions to general rules. In the academy, a place where expert thinking about social matters is meant to take place, class is a particularly obscure topic. University is the place where working people go precisely to *change* their class by gaining credentials, again solely as individuals; middle-class people go to maintain and enhance theirs. (It is hard to teach Marxism to people whose very presence in the classroom seems to deny its premises.) This process is central to the American dream, and indeed the widening of opportunities for higher education in Britain may be seen in the same way. One way of looking at the academic arm of the Women's Movement, namely women's studies and feminist scholarship, is as a reflection of women's use of the educational system for personal upward mobility.

Within the academy, then, there is a spurious air of class equality and class denial; as is often said and as working class feminists have often commented, there is the common statement, often said with a kind of puzzlement, anger, or guilt, that "If I were *still* working class I wouldn't even be here." . . . ("Would I?") Those of us who stay in institutions of higher education for our working lives thus go through many "out-of-class" experiences. For my part, there is probably no other life I could myself lead that would as effectively hide, smooth over, and render invisible my own (or anyone else's) class origins. But, not completely.

In this section of the chapter, I want to trace the theme of belonging and not belonging through the meanings I have given to my own education, finally grappling with the present satisfactions and mystifications that my subsequent career in education has bequeathed me. Speaking to my interviewer six or seven years ago, I related a narrative of exclusion from and rejection of my social class peers by becoming "an intellectual", followed by my embrace of a radical political stance for which my earlier outsider stance had prepared me. Central to my early experience of university was also the by now much-explored sense of gender exclusion and confusion; on what grounds were we women supposed to join Virginia Woolf's "company of educated men?" Adrienne Rich captures exactly my own experience at the same college she attended, the "woman's arm" of Harvard University:

> From my (all-girls) school, I went on to Radcliffe, congratulating myself that from now on I would have great men as my teachers . . . I never saw a single woman on a lecture platform, and never again was I to experience, from a teacher, the kind of prodding, the insistence that my best could be even better, that I had known in high school. Women students were simply not taken very seriously. Harvard's message to women was an elite mystification: we were, of course, part of Mankind; we were special, achieving women, or we would not have been there; but of course, our real goal was to marry – if possible, a Harvard graduate (Rich 1979: 238).

This confusion, never being sure on a subconscious level whether to try to *become* a successful person or to try to marry one, was maybe partly what led me to separate myself from the social world of my background:

> "At Radcliffe [I] first operated within Harvard's preppy world – social clubs and 'final clubs' [Harvard's exclusive fraternities]. At the end of my sophomore year I left that world behind, pretty consciously. I

decided those people were boring, and in my Junior and Senior years I ended up mixing it up with all sorts of Bohemian types, mostly through the men I was involved with . . . I was beginning to move out, move away" (Ostrove & Stewart 1994: 299).

This narrative of alienation from my social class peers at college had a kind of double aspect. Many of my male social class peers were at this college because it was the most prestigious one in the country, and because they were training to take over the reins of power in various professional, business and political settings. This was still a time where elite private schools could get their less brilliant graduates into Harvard. The women, however, were not there for such training. And yet we were *more* intellectually qualified because it was harder then for women to get in: only a quarter of the undergraduate student body, we were always seen as "more intellectual", and much smarter than many of our upper-class male peers. (There were lots of smart guys at Harvard, but the "preppies" – the upper-class "prep school" boys who had gone to the American equivalents of Eton, Harrow and Winchester – were famously "dumb"; the gentleman's "C" was still alive and well.) To date a social class peer was often, for me, an act of "dumbing down"; after all, I had been the "smartest girl" in my boarding school! And yet at Radcliffe, compared to other *women*, I wasn't that smart at all. My interviewer describes me as follows, beginning with a quote from me:

> "Until I got to Radcliffe, I thought I was smart for a girl. When I got to Radcliffe I didn't think even that any more, because everybody at Radcliffe was smart for a girl." Painful as (her) experiences of marginality and feelings of inferiority were, they provided her with a basis for empathic connection with others' experience of class-based and race-based oppression (Ostrove & Stewart 1994: 299).

As have so many others before and after me, I even doubted whether my admission to Radcliffe was based on my abilities at all. Was my admission only a token of class privilege? My father, after all, was a Radcliffe Trustee, so of course they had to admit me. It was partly in flight from this double sense of class and gender disorientation (neither of which were consciously categorized that way at the time), and to escape these vexing contradictions, that I joined the Civil Rights and anti-war movements along with my first husband, a similar class rebel. I forged my life-long identification with progressivism, social change, and finally the socialist project. As I now see these times, the formation of these convictions, still firmly held, were thus based not only on empathy for the "oppressed", but were also a kind of personal way out for me from the confused positionings I was facing.

It was not until fifteen years later, though, that I became a feminist. My co-author, Mary Tetreault, has just reminded me that in the early days of the Second

Wave and 1970s' feminism, I was too much of a socialist to see feminism as more than a distraction from attention to the "class enemy". Perhaps, she suggests, the image of men I was familiar with, from the powerful ones in my family to the powerful (and often class-privileged) males I knew in the movement was too strong to resist. It may take longer for upper-class women to see their own oppressions and realize their possibilities precisely because their men are so powerful. Nevertheless, after 15 years as a wife, mother, and high school teacher, I became a divorced college professor, and discovered feminism through a curriculum project in feminist theory and scholarship at the college where I teach. Thus the next phase of my educational journey was, and has been, my discovery of a satisfying community through becoming a feminist academic. By being a teacher and a college professor, I have transcended my class alienation, or so I have thought; by becoming a feminist I have joined a new community which allows me to put myself, as a woman, among the company of people whose liberation I was seeking. Rather than working for oppressed others and feeling guilty about the privileges which set me apart from them (black people and workers in particular), I can claim sisterhood with them all through sisterhood with all women, black and white, rich, middle class, and poor. Indeed it was this conviction of sisterhood which sustained me in my research visit to the African American women's college in 1990. However, more recently, this satisfying narrative of feminist inclusion has begun to show some cracks and discrepancies, and I now want to turn to its deconstruction to discover some new bases for my old searches for community.

Feminists, academia and social class

One of the confusions of this chapter that has persisted through several drafts is the question of "when I knew what". Memory work is always about constructions and reconstructions, and I have revisited and made new meanings out of all the stories here a number of times. One of the specific difficulties I can name, however, is that the ideology of middle-class individualism often keeps us from understanding ourselves as acting within, while always also resisting and recreating, structures of gender, race and class inequalities. For example, the agonizing over whether or not I, as an individual, "deserved" to get into Radcliffe obscures my class advantages as the beneficiary of a substantial amount of cultural capital. In the early 1980s I suddenly located all my experiences in terms of gender oppression, but it has probably not been until recently that I have even fully grappled with, let alone understood, what *not* being middle class has meant to me. And yet I remember the feelings and actions I describe here vividly. I must have known, and not known, for a long time. This current version emerges into view through lenses I have gained from work by Tetreault and myself, and others, on whiteness, and more broadly, through the feminist and postmodern work on multiple identities and positionalities (Alcoff 1988; Maher

& Tetreault 1994, 1997; Morrison 1992; Fine et al. 1997). This work allows and enjoins complex and shifting locations at the intersections of complex and contradictory relations of power and oppression for us all.

In her chapter on social class at Radcliffe, my interviewer described her middle-class informants by saying that, quoting the work of Benjamin De Mott, "as men or women of the middle class, these people can only with an act of will imagine themselves to be members of a class. Normally they feel themselves to be solid individual achievers in an essentially classless society composed of human beings engaged in bettering themselves". One informant's "strategy for managing her own marginal identities was to emphasize her own individual uniqueness, a strategy that may have had much to do with her class background" (Ostrove & Stewart 1994: 301–2). The academy both fosters these assumptions of individualism and provides the quintessential setting for the proving and betterment of the self. Perhaps as a result, both working-class and upper-class women may feel alienated there – for different reasons, of course, but also perhaps for some similar ones – and perhaps one aspect of writing about marginal class identities is to isolate some hitherto hidden features of the pervasive middle-classness of university life.

I was led to think about both of these points by reading Pat Mahony and Christine Zmroczek's essay, "Why class matters", which introduces a book of essays about working-class women's experiences in the academy, and being shocked to discover that they were saying a few things about my experiences as well. How could that be? I was the opposite of working class. They say, for example,

> Women who have gone through higher education often see themselves as being required to continue an ethic of service to others less "lucky" than themselves. At the same time there are feelings of insecurity about positions attained but not deserved, and these are often expressed in the fear that one day the fraud will be exposed (Mahony & Zmroczek 1997: 5).

Me, too! Is it only people who securely occupy an individualist ideology who can be comfortable deserving what they get, and therefore who do not feel that they must serve others? Or is it once again just another gender thing? Is it the act of transgressing class boundaries into the middle class that makes the rest of us feel like frauds? As an academic and teacher all my life, I too have joined the middle class. But because I was coming from another direction, class mobility has had both similar and different meanings for me than for either working-class women or for those middle-class women trying to go beyond their father's (and mother's) accomplishments. What are those similarities and differences, and how can they illuminate mine (and our) multiple identities?

I want to experiment here with a narrative of being the marginalized "other", but one who comes from a privileged position. I am not writing about the

structural factors which position classes in relations of dominance and exploitation to each other worldwide and which are organized by dimensions of race,
ethnicity and gender as well as class inequalities, although it is of course those
factors which shape the ones I am discussing here. My contexts here are specific
ones, though very broad: namely my own small college, the world of the academy and the international feminist community within it. How that world is
situated more widely is of course a much bigger topic.

In that context, is it possible to be marginalized by privilege? The idea of
privilege carries with it complex meanings; when we think of white privilege or
class privilege, it means assets, special treatment, and it implies hegemony over
those without privileges, even the enactment of power over them. To go back
to Peter Redman's (1996) metaphors of power and resistance, but to entwine
them with metaphors of inclusion and exclusion, it feels to me as though both
my experiences and practices of class privilege share aspects of both of these
dynamics. At the most superficial level, when I deny my differences from my
middle-class colleagues because most aspects of my life are exactly the same
as theirs, I feel included. When I begin to acknowledge the differences, as now,
I can find many places of unearned advantage and power, but I can also find
places where I feel excluded and, yes, even disadvantaged as well. How can I
acknowledge these advantages (and disadvantages) and either reject them or put
them to productive use, so as still to be personally included in the world of
people whose liberation from these inequalities I seek?

Some of my advantages are easy to chronicle. My nest-egg, in the form of the
divorce settlement from my first husband, is small compared to the rich people
I know and large compared to most fellow-academics. It has allowed me to:
1) never teach summer school or evening classes; 2) take a whole year for a
sabbatical, and travel during that year; 3) not worry about paying for my children's education or my mother's old age; 4) pay for lots of therapy to get my
private life straightened out; and 5) do research at times without applying for
grants. (This last has perhaps been a mixed blessing, as I have yet to acquire
those competitive skills necessary for writing successful grants and propelling
myself forward in the profession that way.)

The above have to do with financial capital; my cultural capital is a little
harder to put my finger on. I grew up in a small summer resort town where both
sets of grandparents had maintained summer houses. Both families were part
of the aristocracy of both this small town and of Boston; their social networks
guaranteed that in college and in later life I would always know people in
Boston and Cambridge (Massachusetts) and always know exactly where I came
from. This security (which is hard to locate precisely because I have never not
had it) has probably meant feeling comfortable knowing and meeting people
from all walks of society, and in fact, paradoxically, probably helped me to rebel
in the ways described above. One of the ways my parents defended the idea of
sending me to an elite boarding school was to say that I would meet people from
all over the country (from our social class) and while I kept in touch with none

of them, it is true that the Harvard/Radcliffe connection crops up everywhere, rather like Oxbridge, I suspect. "You all act like you know each other," my husband jokes. My cultural capital also includes specific social skills, and a certain ability to feel comfortable in most situations. I know how to express myself, make people feel at ease, run a meeting or a class discussion – like a dinner party in which everyone will be made to feel at home and urged to contribute. I write easily and colloquially most of the time, because I had to write weekly essays from the age of about ten. Writing these things down makes me squirm because I hope I use them in the pursuit of feminist goals and practices but realize that often I must use them thoughtlessly, thinking of them as part of who I am as an individual only. Moreover, writing them down fixes a source of isolation and difference, sets me apart a bit.

There is another layer of feeling, however, below this one, whose presence embarrasses and astonishes me, and that is my sense of actually being discriminated against, not only by my gender position within my class, but also by my class position within my gender. Unlike many middle-class women, especially those from intellectual backgrounds, my family culture, while full of books, was not in any sense academic. The oldest of three girls, I was actually the first female in my family to graduate from college! This was only partly because of my mother's family's decline during the Depression; it had more to do with the tradition of upper-class women to come out, get married and do good works in the community after finishing school was completed. The men, of course, went to college. My maternal grandparents, with three daughters and a son, had enough money for two college tuitions; my uncle got his four years and my mother and her sisters each got a year apiece. My mother has always been bitter about not being able to finish college, and she herself might have benefited from it in ways that her own mother, the grandmother of the "good works" described above, would not. Indeed, women's higher education in the States, and I suspect in Britain too, was not pioneered by upper-class privileged women but by middle-class women, often encouraged by their middle-class professional fathers. (At the turn of the century, one historian has commented, "several educators feared that the respectability of a college education for women would remain suspect until upper-class families sent their daughters to college, for amongst the leisure class college remained unfashionable" (Antler 1982: 18).

Of course, by my generation my sisters and female peers all went to college, but very few of my social class peers, even at Radcliffe, went on to become academics. Unlike many of my academic friends and colleagues, I knew nothing about graduate schools, nothing about the professoriate, nothing about the culture of the professional intellectual life. While I thought I wanted to continue to study history after college, I was easily deterred from graduate school by a faculty advisor who casually told me I could not get in, and it was not until years later I realized that she meant I could not get into Harvard, the only school on her map! I did not know enough about other graduate schools to apply, which sounds crazy on its face, but I think it was a prime example of both the ways in which Radcliffe women were ill-advised about careers at the time, and my own confusions about identity, gender expectations and politics referred to above. Initially out of college, then, I used my interest in history to become a secondary school teacher. It seemed a perfect combination of a classically women's job and a chance to practise my radical politics. It was not until years later that I realized that I wanted to be a professor and an intellectual, and that I *could* get into graduate school. (At that point, though, it was in education and not history.) But graduate school wasn't part of my family culture. It wasn't hostile to my family culture, as has been true for so many working-class (and probably middle-class) feminists, but it was kind of alien nevertheless. In saying this, I am of course aware that any middle-class feminists whose mothers neither worked nor went to college, and whose family cultures were not academic, could say the same thing – what strikes me is that my occupation of the so-called "position of dominance" by class did not include the legacy of a particular kind of intellectual cultural capital, and I have at times felt its lack.

Like middle-class and working-class academics everywhere, I was socialized by the academy – but unlike them, this move for me has been a kind of zig-zag: across, or down, socially while being "up" intellectually. And yet, another layer here: as a potential wife of a rich and dominant-culture WASP, I would have occupied a more privileged social position. As a woman, however, I was upwardly mobile, climbing out of the private sphere into the professional classes. In so doing, I actively sought and claimed the feminist academic community I have inhabited ever since. My status is mine, not my husband's, not ascribed but achieved, and my "good works" are, I hope, professional and political rather than moral and charitable. I have in crucial ways always been an undeserved beneficiary of much of the capital, both cultural and financial, that my working-class (and middle-class) sisters have worked for. Nevertheless I still feel part of an intellectual and political movement which is larger than myself, a part of a wider community, and I feel that the more I am aware of my position, the more I can consciously use the powers it has given me to enhance that community. As for feelings of inclusion? I think I can speak and write, now, about social class and race in the feminist community, but probably use the personal stuff, now that I have excavated it, pretty sparingly. Most of the time, I think I am not going to "come out" about "coming out".

Conclusion

How can this admittedly brief excursion into my odd position of marginalized privilege help with thinking about social class and feminism more generally? The recent work on whiteness, particularly, has made me and many others examine "the position of dominance", to see the ways in which, in Mary Kay Tetreault and my words, the dominant frameworks continue to call the tune, to maintain the conceptual and ideological frameworks through which suppressed voices were distorted or not fully heard (Maher & Tetreault 1997).

If the dominant voice in the academy is actually the discourse of competitive meritocratic individualism, then looking at experiences of upper-class privileging perhaps helps to expose the class (as well as race and gender) basis of different structural arrangements whose workings are drowned out by this voice. For example, what are the combinations of personal/psychological, familial, cultural and structural factors that account for all peoples' life trajectories into and within the academy? Structural arrangements create frames for all of us, upper class, working class *and* middle class. They are always unequal, and they position us all in complex relations to the prevailing assumptions of class mobility, and gender and race identities. But their operations are not always predictable.

I want to continue to take account of my areas of "difference", not to separate myself from others, but to locate more precisely my connections to them in the shared goals of, as Diane Reay puts it, "the erosion of status hierarchies based on educational qualifications and wealth. Only through work which centres class injustice, as well as the injustices of race and gender, can we keep at bay 'the alienation of advantage'" (Reay 1997: 23). Moreover, class is in my view the only "difference" which, as socialists, we want to destroy as such. I want to be able to celebrate and honour race and gender diversities; it is their unequal experiences in terms of wealth, power, status and social agency that I want to eradicate. I hope that further work in excavating the "hidden injuries" and advantages of class will help that project along.

References

Alcoff, Linda 1988. Cultural feminism versus post-structuralism: the identity crisis in feminist theory, *Signs*, 13(3), 405–36.

Aldrich, Nelson W., Jr. 1988. *Old Money, the Mythology of America's Upper Class*. New York: Alfred A. Knopf.

Antler, Joyce 1982. Culture, service, and work: changing ideals of higher education for women, in Perun, Pamela (ed.) *The Undergraduate Woman: Issues in Educational Equity*. Lexington, MA: Lexington Books, pp. 15–42.

Fine, Michelle, Weis, L., Powell, L. and Wong, Mun (eds) 1997. *Off-White, Readings on Society, Race and Culture*. New York: Routledge.

Gilligan, Carol 1982. *In A Different Voice, Psychological Theory and Women's Development*. Cambridge, MA: Harvard University Press.

McIntosh, Peggy 1992. White privilege and male privilege: a personal account of coming to see correspondences through work in women's studies, in Andersen, Margaret and Hill Collins, Patricia (eds) *Race, Class and Gender, an Anthology*. Belmont, CA: Wadsworth Publishing, pp. 70–81.

Maher, Frances A. and Tetreault, Mary Kay 1994. *The Feminist Classroom, An Inside Look at How Professors and Students are Transforming Higher Education for a Diverse Society.* New York: Basic Books.

Maher, Frances A. and Tetreault, Mary Kay 1997. 'Learning in the dark, how assumptions of whiteness shape classroom knowledge, *Harvard Educational Review,* 67(1) Summer, forthcoming.

Mahony, Pat and Zmroczek, Christine (eds) 1997a. *Class Matters, Working-Class Women's Perspectives on Social Class.* London and Bristol, PA: Taylor & Francis.

Mahony, Pat and Zmroczek, Christine 1997b. Why class matters, in Mahony, Pat and Christine Zmroczek (eds) 1997a, pp. 1–7.

Morrison, Toni 1992. *Playing in the Dark, Whiteness and the Literary Imagination.* New York: Vintage.

Ostrander, Susan 1984. *Women of the Upper Class.* Philadelphia, PA: Temple University Press.

Ostrove, Joan M. and Stewart, Abigail A. 1994. Meanings and uses of marginal identities: social class at Radcliffe in the 1960s, in Franz, Carol and Stewart, Abigail J. (eds) *Women Creating Lives: Identities, Resilience and Resistance.* Boulder, CO: Westview Press, pp. 289–307.

Reay, Diane 1997. The double bind of the working class feminist academic: the success of failure or the failure of success?, in Mahoney, Pat and Zmroczek Christine (eds) 1997a, pp. 18–29.

Redman, Peter 1996. Schooling sexualities: heterosexual masculinities, schooling and the unconscious, *Discourse: Studies in the Cultural Politics of Education,* 17(2), pp. 243–56.

Rich, Adrienne 1979. *On Lies, Secrets and Silence, Selected Prose, 1966–1978.* New York: W.W. Norton.

CHAPTER NINE

Class and transnational identities: a Korean-American woman in England

Miri Song

Introduction: placing myself

When I was asked to meditate upon my sense and understanding of social class, I realized how little most literature about class has seemed to speak to my own experience. Like many other women, my own sense of class position and identity is much more complicated than most theorizing around class has suggested. In particular, mainstream understandings of the class system and of class consciousness have tended to treat women's experiences of class in terms of their fathers' or husbands' class positions, which are most typically associated with their occupations (e.g. Goldthorpe 1983; Wright 1985; Marshall et al. 1988). While women, in my view, do not constitute a class *per se*, their class positions cannot simply be derived from those of their male counterparts (see Acker 1973; Britten & Heath 1983; Delphy 1984; Walby 1986; Zipp & Plutzer 1996).

Exploration of the various relationships between women and class, as exemplified in this volume, is an especially important endeavour, given that we live in "new times" in which the significance of and meanings around social class are now said to have changed irretrievably (Hall & Jacques 1989). In the midst of globalization, some analysts such as Beck (1992) have suggested that the significance of class is declining, as Western capitalist nations have moved from industrial societies to a "risk" society. "Risk" is said to affect every member of society regardless of location and class position: "The multiplication of risks causes the world society to contract into a community of danger" (Beck 1992: 44). Unfortunately, most theorizing on globalization has had very little to say about the implications of these processes for women. As long as much social theory relies upon often vague and sweeping pronouncements about trends in the world, it is crucial that empirically based studies which situate the diverse experiences of women critically investigate propositions about the declining significance of class.

There has generally been a growing recognition of the inadequacies of main-stream theorizing on class, not only in discussing women, but also in capturing the complex interweaving of class position with other aspects of peoples' iden-tities, such as ethnicity and sexuality (see Bradley 1996). However, most litera-ture addressing women's class positions has tended to focus upon the experiences of working-class women, and the ways in which the intersections of their sex and class have often resulted in their relatively oppressed status. For example, Gamarnikow et al.'s volume, *Gender, Class and Work* (1983), addressed issues of work and the interrelationships between gender and class at the workplace and at home. This volume was important in documenting the work and family experiences of working-class women, and pointed to the need to differentiate these women's positions from those of working-class men and middle-class women.

However, in the case of ethnic minority women, class has often been talked about as part of the "triple" oppression of gender, class and "race" suffered by them. For instance, in her study of West Indian migrant women in Britain, Phizacklea (1982) argues that given their subordinate status in economic and politico-legal relations, such women constitute a particular "class fraction" which differentiates them from the positions occupied by white working-class women. Although there is much that does apply in studies of working-class women to middle-class ethnic minority women, situating my experiences as an ethnic minority middle-class woman, *vis-à-vis* most existing feminist literature, was no easy task.

Mapping out my experiences of class, and of how class has shaped my understandings of being a woman, entails some messy back-tracking. How would I describe myself? I am a middle-class Korean-American woman living and working in England (I believe for the foreseeable future). I was born in South Korea, and I left for the USA with my parents and my three siblings in 1969, when I was five years old. Our emigration to the USA was enabled by the selective immigration practices in place at that time; medical doctors, such as my father, were in short supply in the USA, so we had little difficulty in gaining entry to America. My mother was a full-time housewife and mother, and our numerous moves around the USA, taking us from New York to Wisconsin, were centred around my father's practice as a gynaecologist/obstetrician.

I was naturalized as a USA citizen when I was fifteen years old. At the time, I had not thought much about it. My parents had arranged for their four children to gain US citizenship (thus forgoing Korean citizenship), because it was very likely that we would remain in the USA, rather than return to Korea. I raise these details about my nationality because I believe that an analysis of the intermingling of my ethnicity, nationality, and class background is necessary for an understanding of my experiences as a middle-class woman.

Middle class background

For as long as I can remember, I have always had an awareness of being a privileged middle-class person. Although this awareness took on new significance when I moved to the USA as a young child, it was an important part of the way in which I viewed not only my immediate family, but also my large extended family in Korea. In particular, this awareness of coming from "a good family" (according to my parents and relatives) was emphasized in relation to my paternal grandfather, who was said to be an eminent physician, who was active in medical associations and affairs in Korea. Virtually every story I was told about my family and my ancestors centred, somehow, on the insistence that my class background mattered a great deal. In this sense, I was inculcated with the idea that because my family and relatives had been privileged and implicitly superior relative to other "ordinary" people, I had a responsibility to uphold this track record.

In addition to my awareness of my family tree, I was also told, from a very early age, that of course I would go to a top university, and of course, become a professional – "to make my grandfather proud". In this sense, I was very much aware that my personal and career trajectory had ramifications extending beyond my own life decisions. Therefore, this ever-present awareness of my parents' and my relatives' expectations of me laid the foundations for my own ambitions and sense of social self. I found such mythologizing about my relatives simultaneously irritating, oppressive and interesting. Although I dislike feeling "boxed in" by other people's expectations of me, those high expectations also instilled in me a strong sense of competence and social confidence.

Furthermore, I believe that the narrative about familial expectations of my success took on new meaning and urgency as my family and I arrived as immigrants to the USA. Like my father, who had to prove himself as a doctor in a new and foreign place, I knew that we were all expected to learn and to be "successful" as immigrants to the USA.

Class privilege and insulation from racism

Given that my sense of being a privileged person was formed in Korea, my arrival in New York and starting primary school brought into sharp focus the significance of my class background. Throughout my childhood and adolescence in the USA, I encountered various forms of racism. Racist experiences were especially acute in school. On occasion, I still encounter racist remarks or taunting here in Britain. As painful and difficult as such experiences were, particularly in my childhood, I realize, looking back, that my parents' support and my middle-class background were absolutely fundamental in insulating me, to a certain extent, from the worst effects of racism.

This was due to a number of factors related to my class background: firstly, I remember my parents warning me about various forms of racism and racialized stereotyping. Certainly my parents had experienced racism first hand. Although I did not confide in them about my own experiences of racism, I was always comforted by the fact that my parents reinforced my sense of self-worth and competence – I was smart and strong, and would not crumple at such attacks. This reinforcement usually related to reference to my class background and the high educational background of my family and extended relatives. As a result, I was implicitly taught to rely upon my sense of being educated and middle class as a resource and bulwark against racist encounters, which were presumably perpetrated by ignorant and "lesser" beings (see Kuo (1995) for a discussion of Asian-Americans "coping" with racism).

Secondly, my parents told me that, as an Asian immigrant, I would have to do better than my white peers in order for me to succeed, both educationally and professionally in the USA. I was a good student throughout my school days, and indeed, my self-esteem and sense of self were fundamentally linked with the knowledge that I could perform well in school, and carve out a niche in which I could excel. When I turned 15 years old, my parents decided to send me and my siblings to a private day school located in a much more affluent town; the public schools in Watertown, Wisconsin, they believed, would not provide the appropriate support and preparation for university entrance that "prep" schools would. Looking back, I believe that I did benefit a great deal from my four years at this private school; I received a great deal of attention in the small classes, and I'm certain that such a school prepared me well for my entrance into an Ivy League university. Therefore, my attendance at a privileged school not only provided better tuition, but it also provided a more socially protected environment for me, in terms of racist encounters with my peers.

This is not to say that students in private schools are not racist. My private school was lily-white (like my public school had been), but a different kind of culture was in place at this school, in which overtly racist behaviour (such as racial epithets) was clearly frowned upon. There was no question that my ethnicity mattered in this school. Initially, my siblings and I were subtly socially excluded, and I felt very self-conscious about the fact that we did not have the "preppy" clothes, parents and life-styles that the majority of other students had. In spite of the fact that I was aware of such subtle forms of exclusion or stereotyping of me (e.g. as a brainy and serious Asian), such behaviour was much less threatening to me than taunting by a group at my former school.[1]

Thirdly, everywhere I lived in the USA, it eventually became known to those around me (particularly in smaller towns, such as the one in which we settled in Wisconsin) that my father was a doctor. This meant that I was immediately accorded a certain amount of respect and privilege, just by virtue of being his daughter. So in addition to my material comforts and my access to private education, which derived from my father's status as a professional, I was known as a doctor's child by my school teachers and also by many other people I came into contact with. I realized just how valuable my class background was to me when I was 13 years old. I was in my art class, and my art teacher asked me if my father was the cook at the one Chinese restaurant in town (a very white town). I remember being taken aback and surprised by this stereotypical assumption, but I don't think I betrayed this feeling, for I replied that my father was a doctor in town. My art teacher did, however, betray *his* complete surprise at this information. He had evidently not come into contact with Asian people who were professionals. Although I had experienced this kind of stereotyping before, this incident always stuck in my mind, and reminded me of the ways in which many people viewed me.

To a lesser extent, I believe that my class background has helped to insulate me against forms of sexism as well, for instance, in higher education and in professional employment. For instance, I was aware of the formally prescribed adherence to non-sexist practices not only in my private secondary school, but also at my university, which was quite active in its commitments to both recruiting women and to aiding women students' educational needs and interests.

I do not wish to overstate the degree to which my class background insulated me from forms of racism and sexism. In most cases, I felt I had little or no control over people forming assumptions about me, or viewing me in particular ways, and acting on these formulations in ways which were offensive and often hostile. Nevertheless, by virtue of my middle-class background, I felt able to counter racist stereotypes and to assert myself in many situations. And in situations in which I didn't assert myself, I drew upon my sense of self-esteem and competence, which my family had instilled in me.

Funnily enough, being stereotyped as a Chinese person, in relation to the Chinese catering industry, would accompany my move across the Atlantic. However, both the material and psychological privileges of being middle class also accompanied me from the USA to Britain.

A Korean-American woman in England

My sense of self and the ways in which I was perceived and frequently stereotyped took a slightly different turn when I came to England to do a PhD in 1991. It became clear to me that few Britons had had much exposure to Asian-Americans such as myself, because I was (and still am) almost always assumed to be a Japanese tourist or student learning English, or a Chinese person connected to the Chinese catering industry. Until I actually opened my mouth, revealing the typically rounded vowels of American speech, I was assumed to be one of these two racialized types by the majority of Britons, including ethnic minority Britons.

When I spoke, many people seemed to experience a kind of cognitive dissonance, because they were unable to place me, and to reconcile my Asian features with my American accent (see Song & Parker (1995) for more on this). Nor did most people seem enlightened by my answer to the question, "Where are you from?" In most cases, people were inquiring about my ethnic origins, but I couldn't resist replying that I was from the US. There are very few Koreans in Britain, except for a small number of Korean businessmen and their families.

It was ironic that I was often assumed to be a British person of Chinese heritage because my doctoral research focused upon the work and family experiences of young people in Chinese families running take-away food businesses in Britain (Song 1999). In fact, my experiences of researching Chinese people in Britain were fundamental in highlighting the ways in which I felt able – by virtue of my privileged class position – to assert and counter racialized stereotypes. Not that there is, of course, anything wrong with being a Japanese tourist or a Chinese person working in a take-away. However, I soon learned, in the course of my research that being Chinese in Britain did entail racialized associations with Chinese take-away food businesses which were demeaning. A commonly reported feeling by Chinese young people was that they were treated by their customers (virtually all non-Chinese) in a way which suggested that these young people were naturally there to "serve" them (Chung 1990; Parker 1994). As one respondent, Lisa, explained, about her experience at university in Britain: "Like, you know, people will always see you as Chinese. It was because they hadn't seen an Oriental person from behind the counter [take-away] walking out, freely, as it were."

Through listening to and talking with numerous Chinese young people, most of whom were British-born and raised, I became highly aware of the fact that many of these individuals were constantly subject to degrading stereotyping of themselves as Chinese people. Unlike my own experience, in which I was able to tell my art teacher that, no, my father did not cook Chinese food, these young people could not refute this long-standing stereotype. Although many of the Chinese young people I interviewed resisted such stereotyping and fought back in various ways, their ability to insulate themselves from such racist depictions was limited by the fact that many of them had to "serve" and endure harassment from their customers; Chinese families running take-aways relied upon their customers, including those who were overtly racist, for their livelihoods. Most of these young people's parents had come from lower-middle and working-class families in the New Territories of Hong Kong (see Watson 1975, 1977), and had struggled to attain shop ownership – often after long years of waged employment as waiters and kitchen staff in Chinese restaurants across Britain.

There is growing research in the USA about the importance of class in delineating the "ethnic options" (Waters 1990) that various groups exercise. That is, not all ethnic minority groups or individuals within them are able to define or to assert their ethnic identities in the ways that they wish. For instance, Portes and Macleod (1996) conducted a study of the implications of adopting an Hispanic identity for young people in the USA. As a pan-ethnic term for people of Latin American origin, the category "Hispanic" lumps together Spanish-speaking groups of diverse backgrounds and ethnicities. The authors found that young people from more socially advantaged groups, such as Cuban-Americans, were more likely to have positive self-esteem and to consider themselves "Americans" or "Cuban-Americans", and less likely to consider themselves to be "Hispanic" – unlike most individuals of Puerto-Rican and Mexican origin, who are much poorer than Cuban-Americans. More middle-class groups such as Cuban-Americans resisted the imposition of the term "Hispanic", which was reportedly regarded as an imposed (by the white majority and government bureaucrats), rather than a chosen ethnic label.

Thus my work with these Chinese families highlighted the gulf of experience between me and the respondents in the study. There were some awkward moments in interviews, in which a few respondents alluded indirectly to our different class backgrounds and positions within British society. For instance, Kam, who was 26 years old, abruptly stopped her description of what it was like to work in her family's take-away, and asked, "Have you ever worked in a Chinese take-away?" I replied that I had not. I was initially puzzled by this question. Was this a sincere question? Did she have any reason to believe that I worked in a Chinese take-away, although she knew I was Korean? I concluded that the posing of this question (which was not hostile) was a way for Kam to underline the differences of our experiences – not only in terms of the two different countries within which we had been raised, but also in terms of our respective experiences of class and family life (Song & Parker 1995). Therefore, my interactions with Chinese young people in Britain enhanced my sense of agency and ability to define myself in my own terms – despite the fact that I was even more mistakenly identified here than I had been in the USA!

Class as a constant across nationalities

Although I had to undergo some adjustments in the ways in which most Britons superficially perceived me, particularly in terms of recognizing me as an American (and then in dispelling some irritating stereotypes about Americans!), my sense of self as a middle-class person, who was able to transplant herself from one society to another, remained stable and was in fact reinforced. I knew many others, including friends from my university days, who had not only travelled a great deal, but who relished their experiences of living abroad, with the confidence that they could take advantage of whatever other societies had to offer. Although we live in times where not only middle-class people engage in tourism and the sampling of foreign places and cultures (Hannerz 1990), it seems to me that privileged people can more easily traverse disparate lands, with their armour of social credentials and cultural capital (Bourdieu 1984).

My career as an academic has perpetuated my ensconcement in predominantly middle-class environments, surrounded by (still) predominantly middle-class people. Although there are lecturers and students of working-class backgrounds at many universities, the dominant tone and cultures of most academic institutions are, in my view, middle class; it is this middle-classness which I am familiar with, despite my transplantation from the USA to Britain. It is possible that my entrance into the new and unfamiliar arena of British academia has been less jarring and alienating – despite my being a Korean-American woman – than such a transition might be for lecturers from a working-class background.

Therefore, a stable sense of class background and privilege can serve as an important resource (both in material and psychological terms) and bulwark against racism, and to a lesser extent, sexism, for people (such as myself) who have experienced a lot of displacement across national boundaries. Furthermore, my middle-class identity has served as a constant, as a kind of ballast, accompanying me from Korea to the USA (and across it) and from the USA to England. Although my sense of my class position takes on slightly different nuances across countries, for instance, in the USA and Britain, it is precisely because of my indeterminant sense of nationality and "belonging" that I have experienced my class position and identity as such stable constants in my life.

This is not to suggest that one's class position necessarily stays static. The dynamics of both continuity and change in class terms must be related to macro-level processes and transitions affecting women and employment. Not only has economic restructuring resulted in changing patterns of work for women (which were not unitary in their effects upon diverse groups of women), but there is evidence of new patterns of migration by women seeking work (Morokvasic 1983; Zulauf 1996). Such labour flows clearly have implications not only for women's sense of class, but also for their sense of nationality and ethnicity (Ang-Lygate, 1996).

Conclusion

Given my experiences of being a middle-class Korean-American woman, who has experienced a signficant number of moves from country to country, and who has been a relatively privileged ethnic minority woman, I have tended to be wary of feminist frameworks which automatically assume common experiences of class and "race" oppression across all "women of colour". Such well-meaning frameworks are usually premised (implicitly) upon the experiences of working-class women, and do not adequately address the contingencies and complexities of many women's experiences, by examining factors such as nationality and diasporaic displacement.

Although such rubrics are often important and valuable in political movements and other solidaristic efforts, a reliance upon assumed (and often uninvestigated) notions of commonality across "women of colour" does not advance our theoretical thinking about the complexity of many women's lived experiences (see Song 1995) – unless such theorizing is qualified by and concretized by the specific circumstances and experiences of a variety of women, including ethnic minority middle-class women.

A key work experience in my life helped to shape my views about the need to be careful in making assumptions of either commonality or difference between ethnic minority women. Before I entered graduate school, I worked as a social worker in a shelter for homeless women in New York City. Most of my clients were black and Hispanic women from working-class backgrounds. Never before had I felt such a gulf between me and other women: I had (with hindsight, naively) entered this job with the expectation that being an ethnic minority woman was an important and sufficient basis for trust and mutual understanding. However, most of these women resented a middle-class woman advising them and telling them what to do. I had to respect their suspicions of me and their implicit and sometimes explicit insistence that they had little in common with me (see also Edwards 1990).

I believe that these suspicions arose not only because I was a social worker (and because they were my clients), but also because Asian-Americans in the USA are often perceived to be a privileged "model" minority in relation to Hispanic and black people. This is, however, a gross simplification about Asian-Americans, who constitute a very diverse group. Some groups of Asians, such as the Japanese and Chinese, are much more affluent and privileged than others, such as some Americans of Filipino and Vietnamese heritage (see Espiritu 1992; Ong et al. 1994). In my work as a social worker, class disparities, power differences between me and my clients, and the historical differences in the reception and experiences across different minority groups in the USA, structured the relationship between me and the women in the shelter for the homeless.

In my view, such structured differences need not be unbridgeable; there are many ways in which we as women can share a great deal in common. However, we must not rest upon easy notions of common experience either in our personal interactions with people or in feminist theorizing. Thankfully, there is more and more awareness and insistence upon the multiplicity and potentially shifting nature of women's identities – particularly since there is now more scepticism in much feminist theory about essentialist notions of what it means to be a woman. The challenges ahead for feminist theory are great, but exciting: rather than viewing an emphasis upon the multiplicity and nuances of women's experiences as a divisive project, not only are analyses of women's class positions absolutely necessary, but they need increasingly to be crafted in tandem with understandings of historical specificities and (trans)national moves and identities.

Note

1. See Reay (1995) for an interesting discussion of the operation of a peer group "habitus" in the classroom, in which white privileged pupils excluded and rendered invisible ethnic minority pupils.

References

Acker, J. 1973. Women and social stratification: a case of intellectual sexism, *American Journal of Sociology*, 78, 936–45.

Ang, I. 1994. On not speaking Chinese, *New Formations*.

Ang-Lygate, M. 1996. Women who move: experiences of diaspora, in Maynard, M. and Purvis, J. (eds) *New Frontiers in Women's Studies: Knowledge, Identity and Nationalism*. London: Taylor & Francis.

Beck, U. 1992. *Risk Society*. London: Sage.

Bourdieu, P. 1984. *Distinction*. London: Routledge & Kegan Paul.

Bradley, H. 1996. *Fractured Identities: Changing Patterns of Inequality*. Cambridge: Polity Press.

Britten, N. and Heath, A. 1983. Women, men and social class, in Gamarnikow, E. et al. (eds) *Gender, Class and Work*, London: Heinemann.

Chung, Y.K. 1990. At the palace: researching gender and ethnicity in a Chinese restaurant, in Stanley, L. (ed.) *Feminist Praxis: Research, Theory and Epistemology in Feminist Sociology*. London: Routledge.

Delphy, C. 1984. *Close to Home*. London: Hutchinson.

Espiritu, Y.L. 1992. *Asian-American Panethnicity*. Philadelphia, PA: Temple University Press.

Edwards, R. 1990. Connecting method and epistemology: a white woman interviewing black women, *Women's Studies International Forum*, 13, 477–90.

Goldthorpe, J. 1983. Women and class analysis: in defence of the conventional view, *Sociology*, 17, 465–88.

Hall, S. and Jacques, M. (eds) 1989. *New times*, Marxism Today/Open University Press.

Hannerz, U. 1990. Cosmopolitans and locals in world culture, in Featherstone, M. (ed.) *Global Culture*. London: Sage.

Kuo, W. 1995. Coping with racial discrimination: the case of Asian-Americans, *Ethnic and Racial Studies*, 18, 109–27.

Marshall, G., et al. 1988. *Social Class in Modern Britain*. London: Hutchinson.

Morokvasic, M. 1983. Women in migration: beyond the reductionist outlook, in Phizacklea, A. (ed.) *One Way Ticket*. London: Routledge & Kegan Paul.

Ong, P., Bonacich, E., and Cheng, L. (eds) 1994. *The New Asian Immigration in Los Angeles and Global Restructuring*. Philadelphia, PA: Temple University Press.

Parker, D. 1994. Encounters across the counter: young Chinese people in Britain, *New Community*, 20, 621–34.

Phizacklea, A. 1982. Migrant women and wage labour: the case of West Indian women in Britain, in West, J. (ed.) *Women, Work and the Labour Market*. London: Routledge & Kegan Paul.

Portes, Alejandro and Macleod, Douglas 1996. "What should I call myself?" Hispanic identity formation in the second generation, *Ethnic and Racial Studies*, 19(3), 523–47.

Reay, D. 1995. "They employ cleaners to do that": habitus in the primary classroom, *British Journal of Sociology of Education*, 16, 353–71.

Song, M. 1995. Between "the front" and "the back": Chinese women's work in family businesses, *Women's Studies International Forum*, 18, 285–98.

Song, M. 1999. *Helping Out: Children's Labour in Ethnic Businesses*. Philadelphia: Temple University Press.

Song, M. and Parker, D. 1995. Commonality, difference, and the dynamics of disclosure in in-depth interviewing, *Sociology*, 29, 241–56.

Walby, S. 1986. Gender, class and stratification: towards a new approach, in Crompton, R. and Mann, M. (eds) *Gender and Stratification*. Cambridge: Polity Press.

Waters, M. 1990. *Ethnic Options*. Berkeley: University of California Press.

Watson, J. 1975. *Emigration and the Chinese Lineage: The Mans of Hong Kong and London*. Berkeley: University of California Press.

Watson, James 1977. The Chinese: Hong Kong villagers in the British catering trade, in idem, *Between Two Cultures: Migrants and Minorities in Britain*. Oxford: Basil Blackwell.

Wright, E. 1985. *Classes*. London: Verso.

Zipp, J. and Plutzer, E. 1996. Social class, gender and class identification in the U.S., *Sociology*, 30, 235–52.

Zulauf, M. 1996. The occupational integration of female European Union migrants in Britain, Germany, and Spain: a case study of the nursing and banking professions. Unpublished PhD thesis. Department of Social Policy, London School of Economics.

CHAPTER TEN

Personal reflections from the margins: an interface with race, class, nation and gender

Anita Franklin

In this chapter I attempt to flesh out the role of social class in my life and how it intersects with other social concepts. This has not been easy as class remains a slippery category to define and analyze even in one national context. As an African-American who has lived and worked in the UK for 14 years I have found that attempting cross-national analyses increased the difficulty. And trying to tease out class from other concepts and categories such as race and gender is not straightforward either. Nonetheless intellectually and politically, Marxist definitions of class appeal to me even though I remain unconvinced of the primacy of social class over and above other kinds of social stratification.

However, in my experience, Marxist conceptions of class do not fit with popular conceptions and my personal account here is more about how I have added to and/or amended my class identity over time. For example, it is "obvious" to me that I am working class. I work for a living. I do not have wealth or other sources of unearned income. I am dependent on my salary. Yet according to popular conception university lecturing is a middle-class occupation because as intellectuals we work with, maybe even create, knowledge. But we work for salaries in conditions that we do not choose and more and more of us are working on contracts that make fast-food burger slinging look secure.

Perhaps that is why I have never understood why lecturers in the UK seem ambivalent over organizing in their interests. It has always seemed evident to me that professionalism and indeed academic freedom demand that we organize to protect conditions of work. Because I grew up poor, black and female, life has taught me that I (and others on the social margins) cannot afford *not* to organize.

I became an academic because from the time I was small I was interested in trying to figure out why poor people were poor and why when I looked around, the poorest people were all black. I thought that to understand why black folks

145

were poorer in the US than whites would be an important step towards rectifying that poverty. By the time I was able to get to university some of those questions about the relationship between race and poverty had been "answered" for me. That is to say I learned, in and out of classrooms, about the role of slavery, segregation, and institutional racism in the creation and maintenance of anti-black racism in the US. And so I went on to try to discover why poor countries, especially those of Sub-Saharan Africa, were poor. In the pursuit of that knowledge I became a postgraduate scholar and finally secured an academic post in one of the "new" universities (formerly polytechnics) in the UK.

The interface of class, race, nation and gender remains intriguing and difficult territory especially in the British context (Mirza 1997, 1992; Mama 1992; Yuval-Davis & Anthias 1992; Bryan et al. 1985). I hope that these personal reflections may be illuminating in sparking further discussion about women and social class.

Family and class

I was born into an aspiring black "middle-class" household in the US. All this meant is that education was important on both sides of my family. My parents enjoyed fairly high status within the black community in Philadelphia in the 1950s. I was born at the end of that decade, a time of great hopes within black communities in the US. My mother injured her foot trying to witness a Democratic Party presidential candidate campaigning just outside her door while simultaneously trying to attend to a crying baby – me. My own first memories of craning to have a look outside our door were a few years later and tinged with frost. I remember feeling abandoned and registering in my mind the grey of the trees and the street pavement and the houses. The very air itself was silvery white and crystalline. My mother believes this is my memory of my father leaving when I was about three years old.

My parents' divorce brought with it downward social mobility as they both lost the home they owned. For my mother there was loss of married status too, poverty and later on poor health which worsened our social position.

And yet for my parents and grandparents, success was never just about money. "Making it" was more related to one's status within the black community and what you were doing to help that community, than how you were seen by whites. In other words the first definition of class that I encountered was one shaped by a sense that black and white worlds were separate and that black society had it its own social hierarchies and class structures which were related to but not the same as the social hierarchies and class structures of the white world (hooks 1991; George 1992).

I grew up in black neighbourhoods in New York which at that time in the late 1960s and 1970s, were teetering on the brink of ghettohood. The whites I saw were "outside" of this world and the southern black world that my mother came from. Whites were usually downtown, in suits, working in offices, on television. Later on with the influx of white teachers to black schools I began to experience whites as less distant figures because of the roles they played in my education. I had never seen or known poor white people until I came to the UK in the mid 1980s. There was the odd individual like Miss Margaret, an Irish-American woman who lodged with my cousins in Brooklyn. But unlike my parents who knew better, I grew up thinking that virtually all white people were well off. By the time I was ten years old I had already formed two ideas about class. One idea was that black communities had their own society made up of several classes (with poor people making up the majority) and the other that white society's class structure was different from black society's. White society had from my point of view few poor people with well-off people making up the majority.

Historical context

The migration of millions of black people from the south of the US to the north and west during the first half of the century is becoming more widely known (Marable 1983). As has been shown by Marable the migration was a search for better economic and social opportunities. Black people who left the South found themselves in very different political economies from that of the southern states. The story of our adaptation to and influence within the different regions of the US is still only partially appreciated and understood. The US is not a single political economy but consists of several regional economies (Braverman 1974). Certainly one could argue that this regionalism is in the late 1990s by and large irrelevant, or that it is fading in relevance, or perhaps that it has been trans-formed. Nevertheless these differences in social and economic opportunities had a bearing on black life when I was growing up and on black Americans' relationship to social class.

It is, however, clearly not the case that black people moved up the class ladder as they left the South. Indeed, many black people lost status as a conse-quence of moving to a different state or region. There are no doubt many factors which contributed to dramatic fluctuations in status but a major factor was the extent to which occupational qualifications and experience which blacks had acquired in the South were or were not recognized elsewhere. Sometimes this was due to direct racism on the part of an employer. Other times the increased professionalization of a job might render qualifications and experience from other states redundant. For instance, many black women who were recognized as teachers in the segregated South found that when they moved North, their qualifications and experience were not adequate for employment within another state system. Although many women did gain the professional qualifications that the states of Pennsylvania and New York required to teach within their systems, many women did not and became domestic workers, thus losing their class position in the move from South to North (Hill-Collins 1990).

Generally black people in the South and North lived in their own neighbourhoods because of *de jure* segregation in the South and later because of the *de facto* segregation in the North. As a result black neighbourhoods had a tendency to have a mix of classes. In Bedford Stuyvesant or Harlem, for example, it would not be unusual in the 1960s and 1970s (when I was growing up) to find teachers, pharmacists, nurses, artists, lawyers, dentists and doctors in fairly close proximity to domestic workers, restaurant workers, factory workers and the unemployed. That kind of mixture seems to have changed.

Certainly one of the pressing issues in black community is the difficulty of keeping a mix of social classes in black neighbourhoods. In general there has been what Cornel West has described as "a shattering of black civil society – black families, neighborhoods, schools, churches, mosques, [which leaves] more and more black people vulnerable to daily lives endured with little sense of self and fragile existential moorings" (West 1993: 16). Ironically, integration policies which formed part of the legacy of the Civil Rights Movement have allowed a greater degree of black mobility of middle-class families out of places such as West Philadelphia and Bedford Stuyvesant in Brooklyn, New York into slightly more racially mixed, but more importantly, distinctly middle-class settings. According to O'Hare et al. (1991) the United States in the 1990s is just as racially segregated in housing, education and employment as it was in the 1960s. It appears that although attempts at integration have by and large failed, an unexpected side effect, the collapse of mixed-class black neighbourhoods, has taken place.

I remember when I first started school in the mid 1960s this same integration policy seemed to be moving white teachers into our schools while moving black teachers out of our lives. I recall having black teachers in Philadelphia as a very young pupil then having most of them replaced by white teachers. When I moved to Brooklyn it was similar. Black teachers were present this time in predominantly black schools but I lost them as I was propelled into "intellectually gifted" educational settings in junior high school and a specialist math science high school. I had no African-Americans lecturers while I was at university, although while living in Hawaii I was taught by one Hawaiian and one Chinese lecturer.

From my experience class position seems to be shaped by race and gender. As I have discussed above, it is also adversely affected by dramatic shifts in income and status caused by micro-level social events such as divorce and illness. Other factors adversely affecting African-Americans have included shifts in policies on employment opportunities and professional qualifications during the 1920s and 1930s migration which deskilled untold numbers of men and women. Current observations of what has happened in the 1980s and 1990s suggest that drugs (especially crack cocaine), the continued failure of the criminal justice system and the "gentrification" of inner-city neighbourhoods at the expense of the communities, all within the context of a market-driven morality, are contemporary factors which have grave effects on social mobility within black communities in the US (West 1993).

African Americans and class

The standard occupational income groupings (such as those used in the US census) show us a country where the majority of families live in middle-income groups, with racialized minorities represented throughout the entire range but still disproportionately overrepresented at the low-paid and lower skilled end of the spectrum. However, occupational income groupings can be misleading indicators of social class as such groupings do not take wealth into consideration. When we do take wealth into consideration the picture changes dramatically. At the beginning of the 1990s, 1 per cent of the population in the US owned 37 per cent of the wealth and 10 per cent owned 86 per cent of the wealth (West 1993: 6).

Among blacks there have been extraordinary changes in social stratification since the 1950s related to the political and legislative legacies of the Civil Rights Movement (Landry 1987). Some writers have even claimed that there is a very real schism between middle-class blacks and working-class and unemployed blacks. This is a controversial claim when it is used to bolster the idea that race is a declining factor in analyzing black prospects. The classic texts in this area of black neo-conservatism include Sowell (1975) and Wilson (1978).

The Rodney King case[1] and later the O.J. Simpson[2] "circus" should have reminded anyone who might have forgotten that race was and is still a major factor in the shaping of black people's lives in the US. This is not to say that the income and wealth divide does not matter but that the armour afforded some black people by virtue of money is not strong enough to protect us from every and all aspects of racism.

According to the US Bureau of Labor Statistics, 25 per cent of all black families in 1972 were middle class. However, Alphonso Pinkney points out that "part of the difficulty with such discussions stems from the varying definitions of middle class" (1984: 10). If, as in the 1972 work, researchers include as middle class for blacks being "plasterers, painters, bus drivers, lathe operators, secretaries, bank tellers, automobile assembly line workers" then Pinkney is correct is querying the credibility of writers alleging dramatic black economic progress in the 1970s. The debate over black progress in the 1970s is related to 1990s political debates. One debate is over whether or not the continued use of Affirmative Action policies with regard to African-Americans is still justifiable if there has been some kind of measurable erosion of the income gap between black and white. Another question is to what extent has Affirmative Action actually been responsible for any increase in social stratification within black communities.

Black communities may have become increasingly stratified by social class. There are indeed middle-income groups, perhaps even an occupational "middle class" that would be recognizable in white terms, like the Huxtables in the Cosby show on American television. The Huxtables are, with one parent a physician with his own practice and the other an attorney in a prestigious law firm, recognizably middle class from the perspective of any television audience around the globe.[3]

It may be that lumping bank tellers with bankers under the heading "middle class" obscures more than it reveals about the very vulnerable position many middle-income blacks are in. Moreover, black professionals and managers do not enjoy the same kind of political, economic or ideological security as their white counterparts, mainly because of persistent racial discrimination. This middle class is not necessarily able to reproduce itself. It is a class with its origins in slavery and in the black working class and it still maintains some ambivalence about its position and relative power *vis-à-vis* other black workers. And in terms of structural change to the racial bias of the economy, the black middle class has made little difference to African-Americans' net worth. If, for instance, we compare African-American median household incomes with those of whites in 1979, black households made 62 cents for every white household's dollar. In 1989 black households made 63 cents for every white household's dollar (Edwards 1993).

There is also the problem that black businesses find it difficult to start up and maintain viability in the face of subsidized competition from other groups. Therefore I share the idea voiced by writers such as West (1993), hooks (1991) and Marable (1983) that integration has had the unintended consequence of making black community more difficult to sustain and the class factor is one element of the problem.

The divisions between middle-class blacks (however defined) and others have not yet been manifested in party political differences in black voting behaviour. By and large we are still Democrats and that has remained unchanged since F.D. Roosevelt was president from 1933 to 1945. But it may be that the traditional black leadership of church leaders and the professional black leadership of politicians are now more "out of touch" with working-class and especially unemployed black people and young people than they were in the 1960s. Church leaders have in the past played an important part in our intellectual and activist tradition (for example Reverend Martin Luther King, Reverend Jesse Jackson and Reverend Al Sharpton) and are organic to our "communities", but professional politicians (as a group), notwithstanding their electoral accountability to geographic constituencies, have not in general had the same kind of organic accountability to black communities (Marable 1983; Robinson 1983).

Socialist expression in the US is muted and has been since the 1930s. There have been small but important pockets of socialist thought since then, for instance as expressed by the Communist Party and the Black Panther Movement, but the shift to the right in the US and Europe has made socialist alternatives very difficult to put on the political agenda. With such a big political vacuum on the left, black nationalist/separatist politics have enjoyed a renewed vigour, with the Nation of Islam led by Louis Farrakhan and in more conventional Islamist terms by Warith Deem Muhammed, offering a political programme which promises in some ways to reconcile middle-class and working-class and men and women into a black nation through black entrepreneurship and self-determination.

The appeal of Islam in the US has more of a relationship with class than may at first be evident. Although the Nation of Islam, which became popular under the leadership of Elijah Muhammed, successfully captured the imagination of many professional and entrepreneurial black women and men, Islam's appeal to working-class blacks, men in particular and especially those incarcerated, is unparalleled. With the charisma and analysis of Malcolm X on the side of the Nation in the early 1960s, this organization provided a new vision of black community. This is a vision of a community with its own schools, businesses and other institutions; a programme for meaningful and complete self-determination as the primary goal for black liberation rather than integration (Cone 1993). Islam has transformed many people's lives from angry embittered underclass to aspiring middle- and working-class individuals. It has been estimated that 40 per cent of the approximately eight million Muslims in the US are African-Americans. Of these, some twenty thousand are led by Louis Farrakhan in the Nation of Islam sect and well over a million are claimed by Warith Deem Muhammed's group (Barboza 1995). The practice of the religion also calls for direct contact with communities, sharing resources and in that way tends to promote community consciousness and class mixing. This social welfare aspect is of course evocative of the best of the black Christian traditions as well (Henry 1990).

The chasm

When I think about being poor in the US, working for low pay or having no job at all, "making it" is a euphemism for having reached somewhere above where you are now and is where you want to be. It is related to having a college degree, a secure job doing something that you like and that offers prospects for promotion. To get there from the projects of Fort Greene or the tenements in Bedford Stuyvesant is a bit like taking a running leap across a wide and seemingly bottomless pit and landing "safe" (or so we think) on the other side. Many of us do not make it first time and we land in the pit (which does have a bottom after all) or sometimes we are lucky enough to get a "toe hold" on the edge of the other side of the pit. This pit symbolizes for me the chasm between, on one side, the poor and powerless and on the other side not so much the rich, as those who "count", those who are seen as "real", as having some kind of prospects. In terms of relationships, class rears its head as "having something to offer" to a potential marriage partner. Many educated and professional black women are thought to have too high standards, expecting black men to have "more to offer" in terms of education, occupation and income than is possible for most black men in the US. In other words there is sometimes a tendency to mimic white sex-role relationships where men typically earn more and provide for families. Some black women have accused educated professional black men who have "made it" in terms of the American Dream, of choosing white women in preference to black as "trophies" of success in a white world (Wallace 1978). In other words, the historical legacies of slavery and racism have included from time to time black men and women denouncing each other for failing to fit white America's patriarchal patterns.

Britain and class

The British relationship to social class is of course very different. Race and ethnicity are popularly understood as defining features of American society but for Britain it is still thought to be primarily social class. In the broadest sense it seems to me that black (in this instance I am referring to people of African and/ or Caribbean origin) people in Britain are either seen as a part of the working class or as transient and hence outside of national class relations. The lack of segregation policies in the UK has meant that black and white workers share (albeit not without problems) many of the same inner-city neighbourhoods and many of the same schools.

The Conservative "revolution" of the 1980s has undermined the British welfare state (Gough 1982), allowed for parental choice in schooling (which has been employed in racist ways by allowing white parents to exercise their choice for predominantly white schools) (Palmer 1986), imposed new restrictions on Commonwealth immigration (which has affected black abilities to benefit from the European Union) (Back & Nayak 1993) and lessened local authorities' capacity to implement anti-racist policies in employment and the provision of services (Gibbon 1992; Ben-Tovim et al. 1992). All of this had had tremendous impact on social class in the UK among African, Asian and Caribbean communities.

When I first came to Britain a trade union leader could talk about a need for political loyalty to the working classes. Throughout the latter half of the 1980s and 1990s trades unions and other "left" organizations have been discredited and crippled with legislation that wreaks havoc on collective action. New Labour is in power having pretty much abandoned its socialist platform and all but abandoned its ties to the trade union movement. Predominantly black uprisings in the UK protesting abusive policing and joblessness won a few concessions in terms of community centres and local authority jobs, but the bulk of such gains have been all too easily eroded by subsequent recessions and public sector cuts.

On the other hand, another important factor in shaping class identity for black people in the UK is related to their class identity "back home". The majority of blacks currently living and working in the UK have roots and relations outside the UK and this community coupled with the black community in the UK may gauge class differently from whites (or South Asians, or Arabs, or Chinese) in the UK. Research has shown that although blacks and other people of colour enjoy high levels of education they remain unemployed, underemployed and/or underpaid as a result of racism. There does not seem to be the same sort of correlation between occupation and education in the UK for black and white. Therefore many black people entitled through educational qualifications and experience to move up to more prestigious positions find that they are unable to do so (Brown 1992).

Moreover, the nature of class in the UK is not (as yet) related to some sort of congruence (however real or imagined) of occupation, income and education. In spite of the use of occupational income categories in the census and other kinds of survey, there remains the plain truth that social class in Britain is shaped by the presence, wealth and power of the aristocracy. Class can in a very real sense be measured by the relative distance families are positioned from the Queen. This makes meritocracy difficult to establish and sustain in Britain in spite of neo-Conservative claims to the contrary.

Day-to-day interactions

In my personal life I am aware of race, gender, "national culture" and class shaping my interactions with groups and individuals. But it is rare that any of these concepts can be separated from the others which are operating. For example, it is obvious to me and other black people I know that being black and living in Britain means that most whites will assume that you are working class and many whites (especially working class) are not happy to find that you are not. And yet while members of the black community may be relieved to find that there are black lecturers in higher education, community activists will wait patiently (or not) for professionals and intellectuals to demonstrate the use of their skills and knowledge and position in ways that are helpful rather than hurtful to (quite often unspecified) visions of black community. And there are times, too, when judgements of me and other non-British black intellectuals are influenced by a suspicion and wonder that British born black (especially African Caribbean) people still remain largely *invisible* in the professions in northern cities in the UK. As a woman I also know that clothes, makeup, accent and patterns of speech, deportment, body shape and weight, marriage prospects, child rearing and the way you manage a household all scream class heritage and aspirations (feminism notwithstanding).

However, as an Afro-diasporaic woman I also know that in addition to these factors, a woman's social mobility is frequently related to and affected by facial features, hair texture and skin colour. It is not that long ago that the average brown-skinned black women would look at the wives of black leaders and entertainers and recognize very little of themselves in them. Such wives were for the most part very light skinned with straight hair. As a child I could not help but feel a judgement was being made on the relative value of my own nappy hair and dark skin and my prospects in the marriage stakes. As an adult I see little evidence that African looks – skin colour, hair texture, body shape and facial features – are highly regarded in black communities or white. Novelists seemed to have focused on these issues more than social scientists. Toni Morrison's novel *The Bluest Eye* (1970) is among the best at delving into the psychic scars around "race" and beauty, as is Dorothy West's *The Wedding* (1995).

Political allegiances

Having the background I have of growing up poor but with parents who had experienced some middle-class privileges and who both had a mixture of middle- and working-class family backgrounds in the African-American context, I have strong views about education and saw education as the key to a good life. Education was something that neither illness, nor joblessness, nor divorce, nor racism, nor sexism could take away from me. The credentials earned through education could, I felt, take me anywhere and bring me home again. Education was also something that was easily shared and could/should be used to inspire, organize, agitate and transform individuals and groups. Having gained my credentials and been admitted into the academy, "the Promised Land", I saw the world had changed. Or perhaps I simply got my face out of a book long enough to take a proper look around. And what I saw chilled me. I saw that much of what was now "education" simply served to preserve the status quo, or even worse to move social barriers back a century.

What I have come to realize is that higher education (especially in the UK) has been a privilege of the elite and that moves in the 1960s and 1970s to erode that elitism have been partial and short-lived. While it is true that there are plans to continue to pursue mass higher education in the UK I have grave concerns over what that education will look like. What I have come to realize is that I was lucky to do my initial higher education learning during a time when critical awareness of social issues was affirmed. It does not feel that way today.

In order to survive an institutional climate that on the one hand degrades women's studies as a field of inquiry but milks popular women's studies modules for the money they bring in, I have had to get in touch with intellectual traditions that have sustained my people (however I define them). I have learned to measure my achievements in non-linear ways. I remember who I am and where I am from and what I am working for. I organize. I try to teach so that students are engaged and challenged to think critically and globally. In my teaching I try to include what interests me and sustains me. I make sure I act outside of higher education institutions to stay reminded, lest I forget, of what kind of intellectual I am, committed to exposing and challenging social inequalities. Class is one of them.

Notes

1. In April 1992 riots broke out in Los Angeles in social outrage at the Rodney King verdict whereby two police officers were acquitted for assaulting King in spite of video evidence showing extreme police brutality. Of those arrested 36 per cent were black (West 1993).
2. In October 1995 O.J. Simpson was acquitted of the 1994 slayings of Nicole Brown Simpson and Ron Goldman after a lengthy and televised trial. I agree with these

comments by Toni Morrison who voices her concerns over what I term the "circus" of the Simpson trial. Morrison continues, adding another layer of analysis:

> I'm also concerned about the number of national issues that are being played out with Black men: sexual harassment, rape, wife battering, murder. All of these issues are being worked out in television epics, and so a legal case becomes a case of national anxiety. People used to make up epics to describe a war or a romance or a tragedy. Today in the absence of Homer, we have these long sustained media spectacles, and we frequently cast Black men in the lead roles because the theatricality and the emotional baggage are more intense (Morrison 1995).

3. An interesting study on the black middle class perspectives of the Cosby show has been undertaken by Leslie Inniss and Joe R. Feagin (1995). Their study defined middle class as holding a white-collar job, whether professional, managerial or clerical and university students preparing for entry into white collar jobs.

References

Back, L. and Nayak, A. (eds) 1993. *Invisible Europeans: Black People in the 'New' Europe.* Birmingham Race Relations Unit, AFFOR.

Barboza, S. 1995. Facing Mecca, *Essence.* November, pp. 106–8, 156 and 161.

Ben-Tovim, G., Gabriel, J. and Stredder, K. 1992. A political analysis of local struggles for equality, in Braham, P. et al. (1992), pp. 203–17.

Braham, P., Rattansi, A. and Skellington, R. (eds) *Racism and Anti-racism: Inequalities, Opportunities and Policies.* London: Sage.

Braverman, H. 1974. *Labour and Monopoly Capital.* New York: Monthly Review Press.

Brown, C. 1992. "Same difference": the persistence of racial disadvantage in the British employment market, in Braham, P. et al. (1992), pp. 46–63.

Bryan, B., Dadzie, S. and Scafe, S. 1985. *The Heart of the Race: Black Women's Lives in Britain.* London: Virago.

Cone, J.H. 1993. *Martin and Malcolm and America: A Dream or a Nightmare.* London, HarperCollins.

Edwards, A. 1993. The black-white money gap, in *Essence,* April, pp. 85–6.

George, N. 1992. *Buppies, B-Boys, Baps and Bohos: Notes on Post-Soul Black Culture.* New York: HarperCollins.

Gibbon, P. 1992. Equal Opportunity policy and race equality, in Braham, P. et al. (1992), pp. 235–51.

Gough, I. 1982. *The Political Economy of the Welfare State.* London: Macmillan.

Henry, C.P. 1990. *Culture and African American Politics.* Bloomington: Indiana University Press.

Hill-Collins, P. 1990. *Black Feminist Thought: Knowledge, Consciousness and the Politics of Empowerment.* New York: Routledge.

hooks, bell 1991. *Yearning: Race, Gender and Cultural Politics.* New York, Turnaround Press.

Inniss, I. and Feagin. J.R. 1995. The Cosby Show: the view from the middle class, *Journal of Black Studies,* 25(6), 692–711.

Landry, B. 1987. *The New Black Middle Class*. Berkeley: University of California Press.

Marable, M. 1983. *How Capitalism Underdeveloped Black America*. Boston, MA: Southend Press.

Mama, A. 1992. Black women and the British state, in Braham et al. (1992), pp. 79–101.

Mirza, H.S. 1992. *Young, Female and Black*. London: Routledge.

Mirza, H.S. (ed.) 1997. *Black British Feminism: A Reader*. London: Routledge.

Morrison, T. 1970. *The Bluest Eye*. New York: Chatto & Windus.

Morrison, T. 1995. The world according to Toni Morrison, *Essence*, May, p. 274.

O'Hare, W., Pollard, K., Monn, T., Kent, M. 1991. African Americans in the 1990s, *Population Bulletin*, 46(1), July, pp. 1–39.

Palmer, F. (ed.) 1986. *Anti-Racism: an Assault on Education and Value*. London: Sherwood Press.

Pinkney, A. 1984. *The Myth of Black Progress*. New York: Cambridge University Press.

Robinson, C. 1983. *Black Marxism: The Making of the Black Radical Tradition*. London: Zed Press.

Sowell, T. 1975. *Race and Economics*. Washington, DC: American Enterprise Institute.

West, C. 1993. *Race Matters*. Boston, MA: Beacon Press.

West, D. 1995. *The Wedding*. New York: Doubleday.

Wallace, M. 1978. *Black Macho and the Myth of the Superman*. New York: Dial Press.

Wilson, W.J. 1978. *The Declining Significance of Race*. Chicago: University of Chicago Press.

Yuval-Davis, N. and Anthias, F. 1992. *Racialised Boundaries: Race, Nation, Gender, Colour and Class*. London: Routledge.

CHAPTER ELEVEN

Owning up to being middle class: race, gender and class in the context of migration

Maher Anjum

The aim of this chapter is to look at the debate on "class" from a personal point of view. By this I mean to look at the issue of class and how it has affected my life living as a black woman in Britain.

It is through my own experiences that I have come to understand the debate on class, especially in the context of migration of the first generation and the full effects of failure to recognize fully the position of black people and black women in Britain. Class has had an enormous effect on my life and it has taken me some time to understand and accept this. Understanding the issue from a theoretical perspective has enabled me to deal with situations and issues of everyday life far better. Hence this chapter will point to some of the contradictions and difficulties that I have come across in the debates on class, race and gender. To do this, it is necessary for me to look at who I am, and then look at some of the events and issues which have influenced how I think and what I believe today. I hope this process will throw some light on the gaps in the debate on class, race and gender and why it is essential to study the three issues together as one.

The beginning

I like to think there is nothing significant or special about my life or my family. I was born into a professional middle-class Bangladeshi family in Bangladesh. I had the privileges and lifestyle that accompanied my family's social position and these would be the same for anyone else from a similar background. My maternal grandfather, following his migration after the partition of India in 1947, was a High Court judge in East Pakistan. My paternal grandfather worked in various Civil Service roles which culminated in his appointment as the Assistant Secretary in the Bengal Legislative Assembly Department in British India.

157

Both my parents are doctors. My uncles and aunts on my maternal and paternal sides are academics, performing artists, business people, engineers, architects and politicians. Furthermore, members of my family, like many others, have made tremendous contributions to the history, economy and social structure of India for generations and following partition in 1947 in East and West Pakistan and since 1971 in Bangladesh. Even today in Bangladesh I am a "somebody". This means I am able to do things there which I will never be able to do here in Britain. For instance, getting a job in Bangladesh would depend on my ability but my family connections makes me part of the existing status quo and thus more acceptable. Similarly, when introducing myself to someone I would do so by saying whose daughter, granddaughter or niece I am or they would immediately start questioning who my parents and other members of my family were in case they knew them.

My family's migration to Britain in the 1980s was definitely the turning point of my life. It brought me into direct contact with issues and facts of life that I knew nothing about. The shock of migration was followed by two definite phases. In the first phase I went into total denial and shame about my background and upbringing. This saw me declaring my solidarity with all that I saw to be black and working class or rather anti-establishment. This has been followed by a more analytical approach and understanding of the process of migration and its effects on race, class and gender. Through my studies, I came across the works of Marx, Engels, Lenin, Rosa Luxembourg and some of the early debates by Michelle Barrett (1980). I read everything I could get my hands on, went to war against my family for being bourgeois and oppressing the proletariat and declared myself to be working class by what I called the "sympathy" clause.

However, now I have begun to see how these triple factors of race, class and gender have to be viewed together to understand the experiences that I have had in Britain. But I see also how my social position and all the trimmings that came with it from Bangladesh, affected my life and experiences in Britain. In fact I have come to accept that I need to see the experiences of before and after migration to Britain together and as a continuum.

The process of acceptance of who I am was also due to some additional factors. As mentioned earlier my family, like countless other black people around the world, has given blood, sweat, tears and their lives for European colonizers and it is impossible not to acknowledge it. So while I was busy denying my social position and that of my family, I was also inadvertently denying the contributions made by my own family and countless black people over hundreds of years.

It was impossible not to acknowledge my social position, particularly as a result of my involvement with the Bangladeshi community living in Britain. The majority of Bangladeshis in Britain are from a particular region of Bangladesh, that is Sylhet. Sylhet is mostly a rural area with some very large towns. For example, due to its connection with the West, Sylhet has its own international airport terminal, the only place in Bangladesh to have one outside the capital city Dhaka. Historically, men from this region have sought work around the world and a large number of them settled in Britain following the end of the Second World War, when Britain needed labour to rebuild itself (Visram 1986; Adams 1987; Ballard 1994). This region not only has its distinct norms and culture but also the majority of the first generation migrants came from rural, deprived areas which were dependent on agricultural outputs or the British-established "tea gardens". Hence not being a Sylheti in the UK means there is more than a likely chance that the individual will be seen as an outsider and as being of a different socio-economic background. When these differences are not acknowledged, which was my own response initially in order to show solidarity with fellow Bengalis, it made matters almost farcical, as people who know the Bangladeshi community nodded their heads in a knowing manner to my claims of, "No, I am not from Sylhet but from Dhaka" (Dhaka is the state capital). Many people felt and still feel that my family's social position means that I have no understanding or affinity to what their Sylheti Bangladeshi situation was.

I have now come to accept that I have not personally gone through or ever will go through the same set of circumstances as people of other social classes whether they are from Bangladesh or not. However, I also feel very strongly that my own social position in Britain, where I am just another black/Bangladeshi woman means I do go through and understand some of the issue and problems faced by them.

Acknowledging oneself to be from a middle-class family and to have appreciated the lifestyle and the trimmings that go with it, is a way of understanding the differences of opportunity open to individuals, particularly to women. The resources and opportunities that I grew up with and took for granted were and are fundamental to what I have been able to achieve and to my lifestyle at present, though I did not understand or accept how hard my parents had to work or the sacrifices that they made, especially when they took the decision to migrate to Britain. However, this does not mean I accept the limitations or even some of the outright exploitation presented by the social class system. I have tried to use it to my benefit by understanding and applying it to the work that I do within the Bangladeshi community and to the ways I lead my life as a black woman in Britain.

The migration

Acceptance of who I was was a long and slow process. The actual process of migration was fairly simple and painless and a direct indication, I believe, of the effects and influence of social class and its privileges.

The normal pattern of migration is often assumed to involve the man who has lived in the country for some time trying to bring his family over to join him. For families from Bangladesh, waiting to join their father or husband can take anything from two to ten years or even more (Bhabha & Shutter 1994). In my case, I came to the UK with my two sisters, to join our mother who was already here working as a medical research fellow in a specialist research unit in a London teaching hospital, rather than to join my father. We joined our mother within three months of her arrival to Britain. In our case, just my younger sister and I had to go to the British High Commission in Bangladesh for an interview as my elder sister held a British passport. Our interview lasted for about twenty minutes and we received the entry visa at the end of it. We came to Britain within five to six weeks of that. The whole process was so simple and fast that we were all caught up within it. It was only on our arrival to the UK on a cold, bleak September day that we suddenly realized that everything that we were familiar with was gone. Reality hit us within minutes of entering the UK, as only I and my younger sister were taken aside at immigration control for a chest x-ray to see if we had TB. My older sister was spared this humiliation on the grounds that she held a British passport, which indicates the racist nature of this procedure.

My father joined us some six or seven months later, having taken a leave of absence from his position as a professor of general medicine and cardiology in a teaching hospital in Bangladesh to complete a series of courses in the UK. My father's decision to remain in England with his family has meant that he has given up his career and taken jobs as they have arisen. This is because his initial medical degree was not recognized in the UK and because of his age. No consideration was given to his 30 years of experience and knowledge. However, for me and my sisters, all these changes created a totally new world.

When my two sisters and I joined our mother in Britain, the reality of our living conditions were two rooms, a kitchen and a small bathroom on the ground floor of a house in south London. This alone was a shock to the system when compared to our standard of living in Bangladesh. We did not have a television for the first two or three years. We had to go to the launderette at the end of the road to do our weekly washing. There was and is nothing wrong with having to do any of these every-day chores. However, when compared to our previous lifestyle, when everything had been done for us and it had never occurred to us to question who did them or how they happened, there was an enormous difference. Those first four years of living in Britain were one of the most educational periods of my life and crystallized for me the essence of who I am and how lucky I had been.

My younger sister and I and went to a girls' comprehensive school. My older sister went to a college to do her "A" levels. We remained living in the small flat for a further three years after my father's arrival. We then moved to another flat which my parents bought. Again this highlights the fact that however drastic we felt our own position to be, the fundamental reality was that due to their professional backgrounds and hard work, my parents were able to get us out of the situation that we were in. This is the same for other people of professional background, whether they are from Bangladesh or not whereas for the average Bangladeshi family reunited in Britain this would not be a very typical picture.

In fact for most of the families, living and social conditions deteriorate quite rapidly as they are forced to rely on the state or local authority for accommodation and related benefits.

The transition

As said earlier, it was the first three or four years after my arrival in Britain that had the most significant influence on me and my understanding of who I was. I realized I was a black person living in a country which is cold, damp, grey and most of all did not care who I was or what I wanted or needed. I was, I realized, a nobody here. In Bangladesh I am part of a social class which does what it wants and takes what it needs rather than worrying too much about the rest of the 60 per cent of the population of one of the poorest countries of the world. This is, I think, the same for others in similar privileged class positions the world over. I believe what I have achieved professionally and academically overall is still linked to the benefits of my social class position. However, I do not regret the experience at all. It made me realize that the existing definitions of social class were inadequate and did not address or acknowledge the position of black people and definitely did not recognize the position of black women. For instance, it is assumed that for most women the migratory process is when they join their husbands or fathers. This view fails to recognize the thousands of Afro-Caribbean women from the West Indies in the 1950s, Asian, African and other women over the past 20 years who have migrated in their own right. The difficulties and many of the issues that they have faced in the process of migration, including class, race and gender discrimination, continue to be hidden.

The gaps

The early 1980s saw the opening of the debate between black and white feminists around the issues of race (Carby 1982; Parma 1982; Amos & Parma 1984; Bhavnani & Coulson 1986). By universalizing the category of women, the feminist debate had actually accepted that the issues for black, disabled, lesbian and other minority women were the same as those for white women. While the academic debates raced on, the effects of such broad assumptions or stereotypes meant resources in terms of service delivery of health, social services, housing, employment and education were not reaching large sections of "multi-cultural" Britain.

As a youth worker working with Bangladeshi young women and then a community development worker and a legal advisor, I repeatedly came across service providers from the statutory and voluntary sector who justified not having services for a specific group such as Bangladeshi women. The reasons given were that "their", that is the women's, culture forbade them to mix with "outsiders" or do anything outside the home and that they had to have separate and segregated services if any at all. The contradiction between my own position and those with whom I worked became very stark and made me realize the benefits of my own social class position. Once I came to terms with this, it became easier to understand and work with the groups as I felt more confident in myself.

My social class had given me access to resources and opportunities not only in Bangladesh but also here in the UK. When I came here initially and started school I went straight into the top stream of my class. It was not till half way through the school year that, purely by accident, my mother and I realized that for one of my courses I was doing CSE level rather than, what we thought, the standard "O" level. No sooner had we found this out than, to my teacher's and school's amazement, my mother met with the headteacher, head of the 5th year and the subject co-ordinator and insisted that I be put into the "O" level group and that I be provided with additional tutoring by the subject tutor to catch up and complete the syllabus. I did not, needless to say, attend this meeting to give my point of view but the end result was that I did sit the subject with the rest of the group taking it as an "O" level and passed.

I point this incident out because it exemplifies one of the privileges of my class position. Although at that point none of my family was very aware of the education system in the UK, we were aware that "O" and "A" levels were the accepted forms of qualifications to gain entry to higher education. The influence and continued presence of the British system through the British Council in most New Commonwealth countries, means that a large proportion of middle-class families from such countries put their children into education systems which enable them to achieve the necessary qualifications to gain access or entry to universities of the West. It is possible to gain entry to higher education institutions without these qualifications but individuals still have to prove that they are financially able to support themselves and that they have the required level of English. All of this costs money and is thus very much linked to class position. My mother, an educated professional person, was not daunted or intimidated by the education system in England even though she did not know her way around it. What my parents and others of the same social class know, regardless of their race, is the system and what they want out of it and they have the language and confidence, even as black people, to go and get it.

By contrast, I continually come across young Bangladeshi boys and girls, recently arrived from Sylhet and even those born and brought up in the UK, who have very low expectations of themselves and what they will achieve. The transition that they have to go through is not just that of getting familiar with their new "home" but also learning that they are a nobody in Britain. As Bangladeshi men have settled in Britain over the last 30 years or so, while waiting to join them here their families "back home" have been living on money sent from "abroad". This created a better lifestyle for many including giving access to education, housing and even employment (Gardner & Shukur 1994). However, like me, on their arrival here they suddenly find themselves at the bottom of the heap. It is at this point that your original social position makes a difference to what you get access to and how others view you.

Young Bangladeshi girls and boys get discouraged as they and their parents repeatedly receive negative messages, for example, that their chances of achieving anything within the education system are very small, that they need to learn to speak English to be able to get anywhere, that their aspirations and hopes are ill-founded and unachievable and that their parents have no interest in their future. What the parents have been able to do to have their voices heard has been very little and very slow. This slowness is not because the parents do not care about their children's education but because they bow in "reverence" to what is the "English education" system, an unfortunate throwback to the colonial days. It has been unthinkable for parents to believe that the education system has failed them and their children. Also the system treats the majority of working-class parents, regardless of race, as uninterested in their child's future. Now there are organizations set up primarily to work with parents of school-age children. They inform parents of the school-system, expectations of the children by the school, etc. What a lot of these working-class parents from Bangladesh face is no different to what happens to white working-class parents and their children. All of this is a far cry from my own school experience in Britain in which I benefited from the confidence generated by my family's social class position.

Having come full circle, I believe that my position as a black person and as a black woman has not been fully addressed or explored within the existing debates on class. It is not in question that I suffer from double forms of oppression as a woman and as a black woman. Class becomes an integral part of oppression and access to resources and opportunities. Racial discrimination does not stop because one happens to be of a higher social class. It just occurs in sometimes a more subtle manner as well as directly. For example, it is assumed that as a Bangladeshi woman, my professional or academic achievements are all due to my social class privileges as the statistics are there to prove it, that Bangladeshi women do not reach this level, at least not many (Bhavnani 1994). This not only disregards my own personal efforts but also fails to acknowledge and encourage those who have achieved despite their social class position or any other barriers!

Stereotypes and assumptions based on them place barriers to all our achievements. For example, it was assumed when I went for a university interview that the institution needed to acknowledge that I was Muslim and encourage me more to stay on and complete my degree as otherwise my parents might have decided to marry me off! Being a Muslim woman has become equated to being oppressed and exploited. It has become the new category of all oppression. Just as when people said to me, "Oh, you are from Dhaka," I have had people say to me, "Oh, you are Muslim" as if I deserved all their heart-felt sympathies for all my sufferings – past and future. I have no more suffered as a Muslim woman than I have as a middle-class woman. Again, I believe it has been my social class position which has overridden any form of religious orthodoxy. After all, it is not the religion which is orthodox or fundamental but rather the way it is interpreted and practised. Women of a working-class background could possibly, but not necessarily, be subjected to more rigorous routines of the religion and as they are less economically mobile they have to live with it.

The question here is how and where did these assumptions come from? How can institutions in the name of equal opportunity and multiculturalism limit my achievements based on their narrow definitions and expectations? This is an example of how racist assumptions can and do cut across class lines. Yesterday black women suffered and did not get access to services due to these racist assumptions. Today Muslim women, refugee women, lesbian women suffer due to similar attitudes and beliefs. Which group will be targeted tomorrow?

It is not just in employment, housing, education and health that we find that in the case of black women the private is public. What is public for some women, for example, in immigration rules and regulations, just does not exist for others. What this means is that black women are more likely to have to prove to the state and its agents publicly that their status or their relationship is what they say it is. The immigration rules have always allowed men, even black men, to bring their wives and children over to join them and settle with them once they were in Britain. This was very much based on assumptions of wife and children following and settling with the head of the family, i.e. the husband. The Labour Home Secretary James Callaghan in 1969 said:

> to prevent a man's wife and children from joining him here leads to social problems in the community. The only way to prevent those problems is to allow families to be reunited (quoted in Bhabba & Shutter 1994: 56).

However, at the same time the establishment feigned concern that

> abuse of the arranged marriage system is in itself sexually discriminatory . . . it uses girls in such a way as to enable men to enter illegally . . . (quoted in ibid.: 68).

thus justifying the introduction of the "primary purpose rule" in March 1977. This immigration rule meant the couple had to prove that their marriage or engagement was genuine and lasting. If the immigration officers had "reason to believe" it was not genuine they could refuse entry to the spouse. This rule led to the introduction of very intrusive and biased questioning of the couples applying for entry. But also it led to the introduction of the "virginity test" in the mid 1970s which only came to light in 1979. The virginity test is an embodiment of racist and sexist assumptions. It was believed that Asian women entering the UK as wives or fiancées must be virgins otherwise their engagement or marriage was not genuine.

Conclusion

There are those who would argue that class oppression is far greater than gender or race oppression. What I have tried to highlight in this chapter is that class can not be seen separately in a vacuum and by itself. The effects of class and how class positions alter and affect individual's lives, especially women's, is too complex to just distinguish it as either bourgeois or proletarian. With the process of migration, class takes on a new face. At one level, all black people are viewed as working class regardless of their social class position prior to migration. However, those who came from a middle-class position have more flexibility and opportunity to achieve more and even to integrate. They might still face racial discrimination but materially they are possibly better off. For me class, gender and race are interlinked and the effects are directly a result of this link and hence have to be understood in that context.

References

Adams, C. 1987. *Across Seven Seas and Thirteen Rivers – Life Stories of Pioneer Sylhetti Settlers in Britain.* London: THARP Books.

Amos, V. and Parma, P. 1984. Challenging imperial feminism, *Feminist Review*, Special Issue, *Many Voices One Chant*, 17, 3–19.

Ballard, R. (ed.) 1994. *Desh-Pardesh: The South Asian Presence in Britain.* London: Hurst.

Barrett, M. 1980. *Women's Oppression Today.* London: Verso.

Bhabha, J. and Shutter, S. 1994. *Women's Movement – Women Under Immigration, Nationality and Refugee Law.* London: Trentham Books.

Bhavnani, K. and Coulson, M. 1986. Transforming socialist feminism: the challenge of racism, *Feminist Review*, 23, 81–92.

Bhavnani, R. 1994. *Black Women in the Labour Market – A Research Review.* Manchester: Equal Opportunities Commission.

Carby, H. 1982. White women listen! Black feminism and the boundaries of sisterhood, in Centre for Contemporary Cultural Studies (1982), *The Empire Strikes Back – Race and Racism in 70's Britain.* London: Hutchinson.

Centre for Contemporary Cultural Studies 1982. *The Empire Strikes Back – Race and Racism in 70's Britain.* London: Hutchinson.

Gardner, K. and Shukur, A. 1994. I'm Bengali, I'm Asian and I'm living here: The changing identity of British Bengalis, in Ballard, R. (ed.) (1994), pp. 142–64.

Parma, P. 1982. Gender, race and class, Asian women in resistance' in Centre for Contemporary Cultural Studies (1982), pp. 236–75.

Visram, R. 1986. *Ayahs, Lascars and Princes.* London: Pluto Press.

CHAPTER TWELVE

Officially known as "other": multiethnic identities and class status

Leela MadhavaRau

In the classrooms of radical discourse, the darkness of my skin is like a badge of honor. I am marked as an empath. Guilty and solicitous white male scholars tiptoe around my privileged understanding of texts. And I think: I was not raised in the barrios, in the ghettos, under the British colonial empire, so how is my color a window? (Bhat in Visweswaran 1994: 122).

This is a tale of "race", "colour", privilege, class and confusion. When young, I would have said that I was middle class because we would travel 80 miles to Toronto to go to bookshops. Later, it meant that there was never a doubt that I would attend university and aspire to some type of "professional" standing. Yet my family did not seem to fit in, we were "betwixt and between". Being middle class always seemed problematic, and the uncertainty appeared to centre around colour and "race": I was told quite openly that I didn't fit into the standard categories of my small Canadian city. At the age of nine, I heard that I was a "Paki" and at the age of 13, my classmates surrounded me and said, "We've been talking about you and we've decided that you must be Chinese 'cos you don't look Canadian." To one extent or another, ethnicity ("race") has mediated my social position in three different countries: Britain, Canada and the United States as well as my place in my family in India.

The process of locating oneself is a political, as well as a geographical, act. As Hall says, "the 'I' who writes here must also be thought of as, itself, 'enunciated'. We all write and speak from a particular place and time, from a history and a culture which is specific. What we say is always 'in context', *positioned*" (1994: 392). I assume "race" to be a social construct, albeit one so deeply entrenched in theoretical and experiential literature that it becomes difficult to avoid granting further legitimacy simply by employing the term. I have begun to use the term "ethnicity" in preference to "race" although this term has also taken a battering from theorists in the recent past.

While I find it far easier to comment on dislocation, some characteristics are immutable: I am a woman, "multiethnic" (South Asian/white), middle class, privileged, born in Britain, an immigrant as a child in Canada and again as an adult in the United States. Of the above categories, I would point to ethnicity, gender and "colour" as the characteristics which I have viewed as the most important determinants of my personal and political position in various societies. Yet it is class which enables me to write about these experiences and to live the life that I do now. My need to grant importance to "colour" while treating class with almost casual contempt is, I suspect, not unusual but does not appear to be an admission that women make too often. If it is possible further to compartmentalize oneself, I have made the very specific characteristic of my own multiethnicity the focus of this piece. Imperfect as it is, I choose to employ the term "multiethnic" or "of mixed ethnicity". The more commonly used term is "mixed race" (in Britain and Canada) and "biracial" (in the United States) and for comfort in casual conversation that tends to be the phraseology I use. For me, all such terms imply that one's parentage is a combination of two ethnicities which are considered (by the majority) to be "different", usually by virtue of chromatic distinctions. Johnson and Warren note:

> ... [the] social equality implicit in the mixed marriage violates socially sanctioned patterns of privilege and superiority. In fact, it is this characteristic which causes a society to label it "mixed" – mixed between two groups which are in different positions in the pecking order. The further apart the groups are in their access to social rewards, the greater the sense of "mixture" (1994: 4).

These authors go on to make the point that social context will influence what is considered each society's ultimate barrier setting groups apart. While frequently that factor is race, in some places it may well be religion and elsewhere longstanding ethnic/tribal conflicts. Thus, while children of some of these other "mixed" relationships may not share my experiences, the fact that they are named as "mixed" (i.e. "other") will likely lead to some negative encounters. In 1996, the American Statistical Association was forced to distribute an apology after issuing a press release which described multiethnic people as "Americans of mixed or *murky* racial and ethnic origins" (my emphasis). Such usage serves as a commentary on the negative interpretation of "mixed" which is prevalent. Those of us who combine Indian and British ancestry are privileged to have a specific terminology to call upon should we choose. Yule and Burnell's *Hobson-Jobson* includes one comment from 1789, "Mulattoes, or as they are called in the East Indies, half-casts" (1903: 410) with another entry defining "Eurasian" as

> A modern name for persons of mixt European and Indian blood, devised as being more euphemistic than Half-caste and more precise than

East-Indian. ["No name has yet been found or coined which correctly represents this section. Eurasian certainly does not. When the European and Anglo-Indian Defence Association was established seventeen years ago, the term Anglo-Indian, after much consideration, was adopted as best designating this community" – April 13, 1900] (ibid.: 344).

While the genesis of this piece is an exploration of feminist views of class, I am greedily using the opportunity to examine this topic in conjunction with other aspects of my life. In the past few years, I have been struggling with writing autobiography alongside theoretical considerations. I am slowly persuading myself that such writing is not self-indulgent navel-gazing, but rather will shed light on the operation of my own social and political identity. When writing in my anthropological guise, I sometimes find this issue dominating all others. Visweswaran (1994: 131) discusses the angst that accompanies an increasing number of "halfie-ethnographers" ("those whose national or cultural identity is mixed by virtue of migration, overseas education, or parentage" (Abu-Lughod 1991: 137)) attempting to do anthropology while negotiating "multiplex identities". Yet the question remains, where does one draw the line between ethnography and resolution of one's own identity issues? In my readings of anthropologists such as Ruth Behar, I am slowly discovering that in contemporary discussions, this line must be flexible:

> In anthropology, which historically exists to "give voice" to others, there is no greater taboo than self-revelation . . . Lately, anthropologists have been pushing at that irony, seeking another voice in anthropology that can accommodate complex I's and we's both here and there (Behar 1996: 26).

In this account, my voice remains persistent throughout, thinking aloud about the relationship between colour (race), gender and class. However, the power I exert is seen in one very important facet of this chapter. Writing autobiography is perhaps more selfish in its inclusion of individuals who have not asked to be a part of theoretical meanderings. I therefore include, within the text, an acknowledgement to my family, particularly my parents, who are an integral part of this work. While I am making the choice to write about my personal theories on this subject, such writing, of necessity, includes the emotional aspects of my family's life, subjects which they are not entirely comfortable in opening up for public consumption.

"Ethnicity" versus class

Although I grew up hearing about the "class struggle", I would argue that for me, ethnicity (race and to some extent colour) is of greatest significance and plays the most important role in identity formation. Where class is given primacy, it is often a powerful determinant of one's future. An individual's ability may be subsumed beneath the class position into which they were born. However, when arguing that class is not primordial, but rather that gender or even race are of paramount importance, one seems to develop, in some circles, the cloak of a heretic. Race and gender are still frequently viewed only as manifestations of class, not a sole determinant of life position. My as yet incomplete thinking on the separation of race and class has much in common with Gilroy and Hall's view as articulated through Anthias and Yuval-Davis (1992) as "separate but connected sets of relations, but with an agnosticism concerning which is primary" (1992: 171). Hall states that

> This gives the matter or dimension of race, and racism, a practical as well as theoretical centrality to all the relations which affect black labour. The constitution of this fraction as a class, and the class relations which ascribe it, function as race relations. Race is, thus, also, the modality in which class is "lived", the medium in which class relations are experienced, the form in which it is appropriated and "fought through" (1996: 55).

This "assumes that class consciousness, presumably unlike race consciousness, is never at the point of being, but always in the process of becoming, and therefore requires something else (that is, race) as its representational or phenomenal form" (Anthias & Yuval-Davis 1992).

Despite my ambivalence on the question of "ethnicity versus class", I cannot ignore the findings of researchers such as Tizard and Phoenix in their survey of young people, each of whom had one white and one Afro-Caribbean or African parent:

> Being of mixed parentage was a different experience for young people from working-class and middle-class families. We have already reported that those from working-class families were more likely to say that they experienced racist abuse than those from middle-class families, and more likely to say there was racism in their schools. They were also more likely to be adherents of black youth cultures. They were more likely than those from middle-class families to say that they felt more comfortable with other people of mixed parentage, perhaps because they knew more of them, or because they were more likely than middle-class young people to have experienced discrimination from both black and white young people. They also tended to refer to themselves as 'half-caste', whilst middle-class young people more often described themselves as being of 'mixed race' (1993: 168–9).

Is class an equal opportunity category?

In my writing on Asians in Britain, I am toying with the notion that, on the simplest level, class appears to be for the white population in Britain a category for their own self-definition that is not needed by a population defined by others on the basis of race or, less controversially, ethnicity. Modood adds credence to this idea with his explanation that British thinking has been heavily influenced by American models which assume that descendants of immigrants

> would lose all their 'difference' except colour and would therefore be thought of as a relatively undifferentiated 'black' mass both by them- selves and by the white British, and that the only area of conflict would be socio-economic – or more broadly of inclusion–exclusion into white British society (1994: 5–6).

This is not to say that Asians and Blacks cannot have a class identity but frequently status in an intra-community sense does not translate into the same status in broader British society. The very titles of two recent books, Daye's *Middle Class Blacks in Britain* (1994) and Srinivasan's *The South Asian Petty Bourgeoisie in Britain* (1995), speak to the presence of class change in British society. However, as both authors make clear, "race as a modality of class" is perhaps the most accurate summary of the situation:

> By the racialist nature of the society it is difficult for people like myself to participate fully in Britain. It is difficult to actually categorise your- self. If you felt that you could participate politically in the country, as well as have an economic stake in the country, as well as feeling com- fortable in the country then you would have justification for saying this is the class I belong to . . . But if you are denied a large part of your aspirations and they are not fulfilled then it is difficult for you to have an intellectual conception of what class you belong to (Daye 1994: 179).

In response to the question, "Do you think it is possible for black [African- Caribbean] people to be middle class in Britain?" over three-quarters of Daye's respondents said "yes". Daye groups her respondents' comments to this question into three broad categories of explanation: first, it is possible and problems such as racism will be overcome over time; secondly, individuals have constructed an "ideal type" of what they see as the existing middle class in Britain today. They will then strive to fit into this pattern. Her third explanation is most pertinent to this chapter:

> having acknowledged that class position on the basis of acceptance by the class of arrival can never be a reality for black people in the British context, they resolve to argue that used purely as a descriptive concept

(as opposed to one which necessitates common acceptance by members of the receiving class as a pre-condition for 'gaining entry') Black people can be described as a middle class in objective terms (Daye 1994: 197).

Srinivasan's work on the Asian "petty bourgeoisie", while not as developed, documents similar trends. Approximately half of her sample see themselves as being middle class but most agree that their position in Britain is lower than that they would have held in the country of origin (Srinivasan 1995: 76). What is addressed less in her work is the perceptions held by Asians born or largely educated in Britain. I conducted fieldwork in Leicester, where I focused my research on Gujarati Hindu women, most of whom had come to Britain from East Africa. We often talked about issues of identity as well as the difficulty these women have in finding their "place" within British society. One Gujarati woman in Leicester, now in her mid thirties, voiced what many others told me: "People think our culture will die out in my generation but it won't. It'll always get stronger because whatever we do, the English will never accept us. Our colour will always make us different." There are a growing number of Asian millionaires in Britain, and an even greater number whose hard work has led to their move into Daye's "objective middle class". Yet in the 1980s, Norman Tebbit could still introduce his "cricket test", which suggested that a Pakistan-born migrant watching a cricket match between Pakistan and England could not be regarded as assimilated if he [sic] cheered for the land of his birth (Paul 1997: 188). This incident, when taken with the furore which surrounded it, seems to confirm that

> black Britons . . . still must endure a question mark over their status as "true Britons" . . . This potential for flexibility and shifting boundaries exists because there is a perception, based on decades of reconstructive language and a succession of immigration and nationality laws, that black-skinned people are generally immigrants and that immigrants are less than fully British (ibid.: 188–9).

Class mobility is often *talked* about as a relatively simple process in countries such as the US and Canada – the we-are-countries-of-immigrants-and-anyone-can-make-it school of politically expedient discussion. However, I am convinced that the real process of class change is as complex in North America as it is in overtly class-ridden Britain. I would argue that a deliberate effort is made to ensure that people of colour, and in particular African-Americans in the United States and blacks in Canada, cannot exercise the type of class mobility which is alleged to be available to all. Class privilege accrues differentially to people of colour, based primarily on chromatism and stereotypes. This appears to be the same in the US which has, until recently, claimed to follow the "melting pot" pattern of ethnicity or in Canada which has always claimed itself to be a "mosaic". Bonacich deconstructs the myth of the US being a country in which all are equally free to attain upward class mobility:

The notion that the American system can be "color blind," a common conservative position, is, of course, predicated on the idea that one is color blind within a system of rules, and those rules are the White man's. Even though he claims they are without cultural content, this is nonsense. They are his rules, deriving from his cultural heritage, and he can claim that they are universal and culturally neutral only because he has the power to make such a claim stick (Bonacich 1992: 105).

People of colour cannot be treated as a monolithic block. In the three countries in which I have lived, there is immense privilege to be gained from being a part of what is considered a "model minority". This terminology is commonly used in the United States to refer to the Asian (particularly South Asian, Korean, Japanese) populations. The racism inherent in its usage accentuates the greater privileges that can be gained by, at the very base, not being black. Does this become a post-colonial form of "class"? The advantages of being other than black are rooted in colonial history and in the diverse ways in which "colour" is determined to be a marker of difference. Young's *Colonial Desire* contains a pertinent examination of the equation "civilization = white culture = upper class Briton":

> Civilization and culture were thus the names for the standard of measurement in the hierarchy of values through which European culture defined itself by placing itself at the top of a scale against which all other societies, or groups within society, were judged ... Fear of miscegenation can be related to the notion that without such hierarchy, civilization would, in a literal as well as a technical sense, collapse ... As the defining feature of whiteness, civilization merged with its quasi-synonym 'cultivation', and thus the scale of difference which separated the white from the other races was quickly extended so that culture became the defining feature of the upper and middle classes (1995: 94–5).

While the "fear of miscegenation" has survived into this so-called post-colonial era, Henriques notes that "contemporary manifestations of racial mixing have been very largely determined by the historical matrix of colonization" (1974: x). Thus, chromatism became a part of our lives, whether we are (descendants of) colonizers or colonized. However, it quickly becomes apparent to "minority" individuals living in Britain, Canada or the United States that these tiny demarcations of colour are largely irrelevant and invisible to the white citizens of these countries. In the United States, "Some Asian Indians were counted as members of a Hindu race in the censuses from 1920 to 1940; then they became white for three decades" (Wright 1994). In 1973, South Asians remained in the white category along with others who "have origins in any of the original persons of Europe, North Africa, the Middle East, or the Indian subcontinent" (ibid). In 1977, "Asian Indians" were subsumed beneath the far too broad Asian/Pacific Islanders category. In the contemporary United States, individuals from the Middle East are still considered "white". A 1997 US case confirms the arbitrary nature of racial classification by government decree:

> A dark-skinned Egyptian immigrant is suing the federal government to change his racial classification from white to black. Mostafa Hefny said the classification, based solely on his country of origin, has kept him from seeking jobs, grants, scholarships and loans as a member of a minority group. He said that even though he's from Egypt, his ancestry is from the ancient black kingdom of Nubia, now part of modern Egypt and Sudan.
>
> Hefny said his hair is kinkier, his complexion darker and his features more African than blacks such as Detroit Mayor Dennis Archer and retired Gen. Colin Powell. "I was born and raised in Africa and they were not," said Hefny, a 46-year-old naturalized U.S. citizen. "And yet they are classified as black and I am classified as white" (Associated Press 1997).

Personal history

The inclination to argue in favour of ethnic identity as more significant than class to people of colour and those considered "multiethnic" has much to do with personal experience. My own personal history spans some of the complex interactions between race, class and gender, that now commonly quoted triad of the post-colonial age. For much of my life, I would say that class has been the least important of the three; it took me some time to understand that my privilege was the result of my middle-class background. I was brought up in a household which believed in a philosophy epitomized in the 1970s' American song/book, "Free To Be You And Me" that is, a belief in social justice and working for an egalitarian world. I was given feminist books from an early age. But my family talked less about issues of race. The first time I told my mother I had been called a "Paki", she broke down in tears and blamed herself and my father for even thinking about bringing children into such a world. I was more concerned with the fact that my father was from India, not Pakistan. Her reaction speaks to the difficult decisions that "mixed race" couples made in the 1960s about having children and their expectations of the treatment that those children would receive from others. There was also a rarity value in participating in a mixed-race marriage in the 1960s. In the British context, Alibhai-Brown and Montague note, "Unsurprisingly, in 1963, from 1,000 parishes questioned, only 84 had recorded marriage across the races" (1992: 12).

I was born in Britain shortly after the above parish survey was conducted and I have little doubt that becoming parents of a multiethnic child forced my parents to examine again this unusual situation which their love for one another had created. It was a tumultuous time for both of them and in 1970 (when I was six), they made the decision to leave Britain and emigrate to Canada. We arrived in Halifax, Nova Scotia where my father completed a year-long medical residency which entitled him to practise paediatrics in Canada. My immediate family still resides in Canada, while I went back to England in 1985 to undertake graduate work at the University of Cambridge. I returned to Canada in 1990, working at the University of Western Ontario in London, Ontario. I held the position of Race Relations Officer, a role which forced me to think about issues of racism on a daily basis. Unfortunately, in the context of this university, racism (and sexual harassment) were not considered issues requiring advocacy or even, according to some of the professoriate, examination, let alone resolution. In 1995, exhausted by this struggle, I moved to the United States, beginning life as an adult immigrant in Lansing, Michigan. My personal travels have coincided with my deepening levels of understanding of who I am and the components (race, gender, sexuality) that coincide to create me. As the years have passed, discussions of racism are now very open ones in my natal household. At one point, my father became an unofficial spokesman for the non-white doctors in the local medical community and referred to me for professional advice on handling racism.

Although I have read few exhaustive studies of mixed-race marriages that took place in the 1950s, 1960s and 1970s in Britain, those that do exist confirm my personal perception that such marriages often crossed class as well as colour lines. In many situations, as with my own parents, it was the male from Africa, the Caribbean or the Indian subcontinent who was from what would be considered a higher class. This is logical; for the most part it was males whom the wealthy, more educated families sent abroad for educational purposes. It is possible that men and women from the Caribbean present a slightly different scenario. There are stories of men who were part of the RAF or other British services who met English women and decided to stay in Britain. Although their class backgrounds were various, many were from working-class or lower middle-class backgrounds as were the white women whom they married. Henriques confirms this: "Of this minority most of such unions have taken place at the working-class level to which the majority of immigrants belong" (1974: 145). Researchers such as Benson have noted that working class women were more likely to enter into relationships with early immigrants of colour in the period following the Second World War: "A more general complaint [from West Indian students in the 1950s and early 1960s] was that those women prepared to enter into some kind of relationship with them were generally of a lower social class and educational level than themselves" (Benson 1981: 7).

There was also emigration from the Indian subcontinent for purposes of employment with the expectation of returning "home". For the most part, these emigrants formed a part of a "chain migration" process. This was a phenomenon found among early emigrants, whereby men came to work while the women stayed behind. Men would hand over their positions in England from one to another – father to brother, brother to brother. Gradually the men began to settle in Britain and wives and daughters were sent for. For further discussion of this topic, various chapters in Roger Ballard's *Desh Pardesh* (1994) are of some value. As far as can be ascertained from the records, few of these migrants married British women. Some were already married and left their wives behind, others were working in Britain in order to get married, the remainder planned to marry upon their return. The majority of those who were considered "sojourners" in Britain were from families which would be considered lower-class (in Britain), although their caste designations varied.

When my father came to England in 1957 to complete his paediatric and dermatological training, he classified himself as both upper caste and upper class. His family settled in what is now Karnataka (previously Mysore) in India, are Brahmins, members of the establishment elite. His grandfather was Mysore's Trade Commissioner to London and New York between 1929 and 1932 and then became *diwan* of Mysore State, the last "governor" under the Raj. Several years ago, when I expressed amazement at my father's typing skills, he told me that while his grandfather was the *diwan* he would bring home draft copies of the Indian constitution and as he made changes, my father would type up new versions. My father's family's position as "elite" or *olle mane* (translated literally from the Kannada "from a good house/family") was based on education and position in society, although the family also possessed some wealth.

My father's ability to ascribe both a caste and class status to himself and his family is hardly unique in the Indian context. As frameworks for the organization of society, in the subcontinent and diaspora, both caste and class have value. Both allow for upward (and downward) mobility, although that fact is less recognized with caste. In many ways, the caste system is the most transparent; not that theorists can agree on even a basic conceptualization of caste, but the workings of the caste system are known to most who are a part of it. As Sharma reminded me, Karl Marx had predicted, "Modern industry will dissolve the hereditary division of labour upon which rest the Indian castes, those decisive impediments to Indian progress and Indian power" (Sharma 1993: 5). More recently, one of the senior researchers on caste in India told an interviewer that "In the future, too, caste will remain a predominant feature of Indian life. But it will be conceived more in terms of ethnicity" (Béteille 1996: 171). As India becomes one of Asia's technological powerhouses, caste will be intertwined with class in ever more complex and subtle ways:

> ... how far caste is used metaphorically for class can itself vary with caste rank for, as Béteille comments, 'the burden of caste may weigh more heavily on the lower- than on the upper-caste person'. Thus members of the urban intelligentsia belonging to high castes can more safely dismiss the importance of their birth and more readily employ caste as an idiom for class than those belonging to low castes, because the latter are more aware of and sensitive to their lowly status within an elite in which they are still a minority (Fuller 1996: 17).

In contrast to my father's family, my mother's background is defiantly English working class. Yet contradictions exist here as well. They were a large family of intellectuals, for whom education was very important as well as music, art and theatre (they went to the Old Vic on a weekly basis). Her parents were both founding members of the British Communist Party in 1920 and most of her family were involved in CP activities. She can recall being taken along to marches and rallies in her pushchair and even remembers police horses rearing up over her head in an attempt at intimidation. She was with her parents as they marched to try to prevent Oswald Moseley's Blackshirts from entering the East End of London to persecute the Jewish population. My grandparents entertained Paul Robeson in their tiny council flat when he was allowed to visit Britain for a few hours to sing. My mother left school at 16, completed her National Nursery Education Board training, started her paediatric nursing at the Children's Hospital, Carshalton in 1952, finishing in 1956. She became a staff nurse and then went to King's College Hospital (a London teaching hospital) to do her general (adult medical) training. She finished that in 1959 and moved to Hereford, England as a staff nurse. It was there that she met my father who was a senior house officer in paediatrics. She later became the ward sister in charge of the paediatric unit at South London Hospital, leaving that position a few weeks before my birth.

Marriages that take place between partners of different ethnicities are not without controversy. I believe that in most instances (particularly in the British context), it is colour and heritage rather than class that precipitates many of the difficulties. This is a point of great interest to me, the very fact that class-ridden British society chooses to make race of paramount importance. Within my own family, as in some others, my mother's family had no objections to my father at all; it was my father's family that, to put it delicately, disapproved strongly. For them, caste considerations were the overriding concern; that my mother was white was comparatively irrelevant, any non-Brahmin would have met with the same angry response, a non-Hindu and non-Indian was only marginally worse.

Authenticity

I have a friend whose father is a *hakujin* [white] American and whose mother is Japanese. She says when you grow up in two cultures, you aren't split in half. Instead there are two distinct beings inside of you. If you're separated from one of the cultures, that being dies, at least for a time. It has no light to bathe in, no air, no soil. It can, like certain miraculous plants and seeds, come back to life, but the longer it dwells in that state of nonbeing, the harder it is to revive (Mura 1996: 121).

I have long suspected that the phraseology "caught between two cultures" is an inadequate description of the situation of the so-called "second generation immigrant" population (that is, those born or raised for the most part in Britain,

Canada or the US). The term appears to have moved into common parlance through its use in two academic works: Muhammad Anwar's 1976 piece, *Between Two Cultures: A Study of Relationships between Generations in the Asian Community in Britain*, written for the Commission for Racial Equality and Watson's 1977 book, *Between Two Cultures*. The contributions to Watson's book chronicle the "catching between cultures" of Jamaican, Chinese, and Cypriot youth, among others. Watson explains as the reasoning behind the title that it represents those who are born in Britain and are caught between the cultural expectations of their parents (first generation migrants) and the social demands of the wider society (1977: 2). However, I increasingly see it as a very apt statement of the position of children of "mixed-race" relationships, especially those of us born prior to 1975. This is an arbitrary date, dividing those of us born at a time when "mixed-race" relationships were comparatively rare from those born in increasing numbers more recently. In 1985 an Office of Population Censuses and Surveys Labour Force (Great Britain) survey showed that 27 per cent of black British husbands were in mixed marriages while the figure for black women was 14 per cent. For South Asians, 10 per cent of men and 5 per cent of women were in mixed marriages (Alibhai-Brown & Montague 1992: 13–14). A 1997 Policy Studies Institute report indicates that the numbers continue to increase: "Half of British-born Caribbean men, a third of Caribbean women and a fifth of Indian and African Asian men have a white partner. Around 80 per cent of 'Caribbean' children now have one white parent" (Younge 1997: 23). The increase in numbers does not, of course, necessarily correlate with greater acceptance, although it is interesting to note the subtitle of the above-quoted article: "Multi-racial Britain is slowly turning beige".

Moving across class may be difficult and, on occasion, alienating but, I suspect, it does not propel people towards the abyss that comes with being a child of a "mixed-race" relationship. One of the difficult issues that confronts us when we begin to consider our situation is "What is my authentic ethnicity?" Am I authentically South Asian if only my father is from India? Strangely enough, people who say "no" to this question, do not appear to think that the white population may be equally quick to dismiss our claim to that ethnicity. There is a level of discomfort in both positions: in calling myself a "woman of colour" or "South Asian", I ignore my mother's contribution to my ethnicity and yet I am prevented from calling myself anything apart from "other" by mainstream individuals: that ubiquitous question: "Where are you from?" "I was born in England but grew up in Canada." "But where are you really from?" One of the men interviewed in *The Colour of Love* describes this contradiction well:

> What I'd say is strangest about being mixed race is to have been brought up so white and feel so Black. I pin that entirely on the way white society treats non-white people. I don't believe you have a choice. I am half Black and half white, my upbringing was all white. Now if I go into a room full of white people and say, 'Hi everyone, I'm white',

they'll piss themselves laughing. If I go into a room full of Black people and say, 'Hi everybody, I'm Black', they'll say 'Come on in' and 'Yes, of course you are.' I find that absolutely peculiar . . . I feel enriched by my knowledge of the Black half of my culture, but it's still half. What do I feel about the white side? I feel it's very sad that the predominant view in white society is that someone like me doesn't belong, but I think it's too bad – they're stuck with me and people like me, I'm not going anywhere and there's more of me every day (Alibhai-Brown & Montague 1992: 243–4).

One of the most painful aspects of finding that one is inauthentic is described by a mixed-race woman in Camper's collection, *Miscegenation Blues*: "What was your family name?", he asked . . . I repeated it a third time, my voice shaking. He looked confused. "How do you spell it?" he asked. With a shock, I realized the painful, humiliating truth: Peter could not understand my pronunciation. I did not know how to say my own name" (1994: 367). While such tales are also told in the US by individuals who have been deemed, somewhat controversially, "hyphenated" Americans (second-third-fourth-generation Indian-Americans, Japanese-Americans, etc.), for those of us of "mixed race", who already fear our credibility in our ethnic communities, such realizations are a further indication of our lack of acknowledged identity.

The shame that some families feel when their sons/daughters/siblings enter into "mixed relationships" was brought home to me when learning something of my husband's family history. He was brought up (in Leicester, England) to believe that he was a lower middle-class white male from a similar lineage. Nobody explained or even discussed the brown skin which led to him being called a "Paki" and even being beaten up in a racially motivated attack. At the age of 19 he discovered that a great-grandfather had been an upper-class South Asian doctor who had emigrated to Britain and married an Irish woman there. "Colour" removed him from the collective family memory for several decades. His sons were eminent surgeons, one even married into a minor branch of the British royal family. Suddenly, they were resurrected as a "dark Portuguese" upper middle-class family. Almost every new person he meets asks David to define his ethnicity and most will not believe he is "British". For him to claim a South Asian identity is far too remote but a quirk of chromatic genetics has placed him in the visual category "other".

Bureaucracy frequently requires us to complete forms which identify our ethnic/racial (although rarely class) affiliations. For "mixed race" individuals, this frequently means becoming an official "other", sometimes with the ability to be an "elaborated other". However, a growing number of forms in the United States do include a box marked "multi-racial" or "mixed-race". A recent local (Ingham County, Michigan) jury selection form requested that if I marked "multi-racial", I should continue on to check the one box that best described how *others* viewed me. There was a controversial campaign to include the category "mixed race" on the 2000 US Census which ultimately failed. This raises any number of interesting issues for future writings but Wright (1994) provides a good overview. A similar debate is being played out in Britain over whether there should be a "mixed-race" category on the 2001 Census. Chromatism, race and class can cause great conflict when we middle-class "mixed race" individuals apply for jobs in locations which operate affirmative action and equity programmes. We are frequently *seen* as "racial minorities" (i.e. "underprivileged"), yet we can only fill in categories of "race" in ambiguous ways and we often have had the luxury of tertiary education. We are well qualified for the position for which we have been hired but there is always the niggling doubt that it was our status as not being white which tipped the balance in our favour. There is the attendant guilt that we are hired because we are more acceptable to white society; that we have fitted ourselves to white America through education and what could almost be a Protestant work ethic. However, the same cannot be said of African-Americans. They are not readily accepted even when they have "proven them-selves". As was said before, the privileges that accrue to non-black people of colour cannot be underestimated. Andrew Hacker provides a thorough analysis of this state of affairs in *Two Nations*:

> The recollections of the past that remain in people's minds continue to shape ideas about the character and capacities of black citizens. Is it possible to erase the stigmas associated with slavery? After all, a very considerable number of black Americans have achieved impressive careers, winning many of the rewards bestowed by white America. Still, there is no way that even the most talented of these men and women will be considered eligible for the honorific of "white". They are, and will remain, accomplished blacks, regarded as role models for their race. But white Americans, who both grant and impose racial memberships, show little inclination toward giving full nationality to the descendants of African slaves (Hacker 1992: 14–15).

It is surprising that those of us of "mixed race" do not use class interests as a basis for coming together. After all, in many instances we cannot claim a culture of our own. As South Asian videomaker and activist Gitanjali Saxena describes:

> I checked off South Asian, and behind that box I wrote "Indo-German", because for me mixed race is not a community. It's not a cultural community and it's not a racial community, because we all come from completely diverse racial groups. How can we construct a real com-munity that's based on history and on culture. For me, I draw my cultural identity from my ancestors, my Indian ancestors and my German ances-tors. In terms of mixed race people that I meet, I can understand the issues what they might be facing when facing their own communities, I

can empathize but I can't identify with that . . . It's more of a situational community . . . (Camper 1994: 40).

I have only once come together with a group of women all of whom are multiethnic. Most of us were middle class and well educated, we were all feminists but while there were experiences we shared, we had no immediate common ground. My experiences in attempting to connect with the multiethnic "community" elsewhere have left me equally ambivalent. Two examples are the American magazine *Interrace* and the American Web Site *Interracial Voice. Interrace* describes itself as "the first magazine for and about 'interracial' couples, families and 'multiracial' people distributed nationwide". *Interracial Voice* is a multifaceted Web site, with an initial focus on getting a "multiracial" category included on the US 2000 Census. To that end, the founders took part-responsibility for organizing the first Multiracial Solidarity March on Washington, DC in July 1996. *Interracial Voice*'s somewhat controversial philosophy is partially explained in their opening statement:

> Contemporary advocacy of a mixed-race identifier is the largest and most meaningful assault on the mythical concept of white racial purity/ supremacy – an idea lustfully embraced, unfortunately, by political leaders "of color" generally and by black "leaders" specifically – to come down the pike in many moons. Consequently, the group most able to help this society bridge the gap between the race-obsessed present and an ideal future of racelessness is the mixed-race contingent (*Interracial Voice* Home Page).

Much of my ambivalence undoubtedly results from what has unintentionally become the American definition of multiethnicity: biracial children have one African-American and one white parent. Those of us who do not fit this category are often left on the margins, watching a debate drawn along black/white lines.

In many ways, it is exhilarating and even empowering to read and "talk" (even in cyberspace) with people who share with me this legacy of "ambiguous identity", yet I cannot say I feel less alone in my questioning and pondering of the "Who Am I?" question. Perhaps for me such groups serve only to provide reassurance that others share my quest, for those moments becoming my "situational community".

Conclusion

In short, it's difficult to underestimate how much as a teenager I wanted to fit in, how deeply I assumed a basically white middle-class identity. When a white friend proclaimed, "I think of you just like a white person," I'd take it as a compliment, a sign I'd made it (Mura 1996: 83).

From the time I realized that I was of "ambiguous ethnicity", I took a different view to Mura's teenaged self: I heard it as a compliment when people asked if I was Indian or just assumed I was non-white without questioning. Perhaps in that vein, the question "Where are you from?" should be seen as a compliment, confirming my non-white status. Yet I remember wanting to display the overt trappings of a middle-class existence as well. Intuitively, however, I knew that fitting in was not a matter of the right clothes or shoes, it was more fundamental.

Many of the questions posited in this chapter might have their resolution in the next generation. What will happen as "multiethnic" children become adults, enter relationships and, for some, have children? Who do we choose as our partners? What do we teach our children about identity and about their "multi-ethnic" inheritance? Will those of us who have moved into a middle-class exist-ence find that our children have fewer difficulties? My partner and I are finding that in contemporary America, as in Canada and Britain, class is no protection against racism even among children. Shortly after moving to Michigan, our then two year old came up to us at the playground and recited, "Hello, Paki boy". Some of the other children had introduced him to being different.

People never seem to inquire about my class status. Maybe it is obvious from my style of speaking, my clothes; or perhaps some puritanical ethic keeps people from asking what some see as a very personal question. Are people reluctant to ask a question which could involve financial standing? Perhaps each of us in "the West" believes we can make a judgement for ourselves on another's class standing. What a pity that the same doesn't apply to that aspect of my life I see as more personal – my ethnicity: "Where are you from?" "Where is your family from?" "You're not white, are you?" and my personal favourite "But you look more ethnic than that." What irony that the very visible marker of "colour", by its nature the marker that makes one "other", should be considered a public domain characteristic open to question.

Funderburg makes the observation that

> In a certain respect, biracial people can never re-create their family of origin, that intersection of two separate groups. They are a one-time-only generation, and so necessarily have to break new ground in their own relationships . . . A biracial person's choice of lover and spouse serves for many observers as yet another racial litmus test. The choice is seen as an affirmation of the biracial person's own racial affiliation (1994: 197).

I know that despite fearing the lifelong effects of appearing "different", I want to know that my multiethnic heritage is continued in my children. To be blunt, I do not want them to be "white". The next two decades will see an increasing number of multiethnic individuals being born and coming of age in Britain, Canada and the United States. It remains to be seen how these societies, which rely on entrenched systemic racism to function, will come to terms with the concept of multiethnicity. Given the struggles we have as individuals to find our place, the course will no doubt be difficult. I fear that I am doomed to remain a part of a "middle population", no matter how I define my own ethnic identity. South Asians in Britain, the United States and Canada are indisputably a part of an ethnic and racist hierarchy which determines position in society with more certainty than class. However, South Asians are frequently considered "model minorities", a role which could be played out in any number of ways. Until the time when ethnicity and multiethnicity no longer spell "other", class will remain for me a separate, but articulated component of my own identity.

References

Abu-Lughod, Lila 1991. Writing against culture, in Fox, Richard G. *Recapturing Anthropology*. Santa Fe, New Mexico: School of American Research Press, pp. 137–62.

Alibhai-Brown, Yasmin and Montague, Anne 1992. *The Colour of Love*. London: Virago.

Anthias, Floya and Yuval-Davis, Nira 1992. *Racialized Boundaries*. London: Routledge.

Anwar, Muhammad 1976. *Between Two Cultures: A Study of Relationships between Generations in the Asian Community in Britain*. London: Commission for Racial Equality.

Associated Press 1997. Report, 4 June.

Ballard, Roger (ed.) 1994. *Desh Pardesh*. London: C. Hurst.

Behar, Ruth 1996. *The Vulnerable Observer*. Boston: Beacon Press.

Benson, Susan 1981. *Ambiguous Ethnicity*. Cambridge: Cambridge University Press.

Béteille, André 1996. *Caste in Contemporary India*, in Fuller, C.J. (ed.) (1996), p. 17.

Bonacich, Edna 1992. *Inequality in America: The Failure of the American System for People of Colour* in Andersen, Margaret L. and Hill Collins Patricia (eds) *Race, Class and Gender*. Belmont, CA: Wadsworth Publishing, pp. 96–110.

Camper, Carol (ed.) 1994. *Miscegenation Blues: Voices of Mixed Race Women*. Toronto: Sister Vision Press.

Daye, Sharon J. 1994. *Middle-Class Blacks in Britain*. New York: St. Martin's Press.

Fuller, C.J. (ed.) 1996. *Caste Today*. Delhi: Oxford University Press.

Funderburg, Lise. 1994. *Black, White, Other*. New York: William Morrow.

Hacker, Andrew 1992. *Two Nations*. New York: Charles Scribner's.

Hall, Stuart 1994. Cultural identity and diaspora, in Williams, Patrick and Chrisman, Laura (eds) *Colonial Discourse and Post-Colonial Theory*. New York: Columbia University Press, p. 392.

Hall, Stuart 1996. Race, articulation, and societies structured in dominance, in Baker, Howard A. Jr, Diawara, Manthia and Lindeborg, Ruth H. (eds) *Black British Cultural Studies – A Reader*. Chicago: University of Chicago Press.

Henriques, Fernando 1974. *Children of Caliban*. London: Secker & Warburg.

Interracial Voice http://www.webcom.com/intvoice/

Johnson, Walton, R. and Warren, D. Michael (eds) 1994. *Inside the Mixed Marriage: Accounts of Changing Altitudes, Palterns and Perceptions of Cross-cultural and Interracial Marriages*. Lanham, MD: University Press of America.

Modood, Tariq, Beishon, Sharon and Virdee, Satnam 1994. *Changing Ethnic Identities*. London: Policy Studies Institute.

Mura, David 1996. *Where the Body Meets Memory, An Odyssey of Race, Sexuality and Identity*. New York: Anchor Books.

Paul, Kathleen 1997. *Whitewashing Britain*. Ithaca, NY: Cornell University Press.

Sharma, Arjun 1993. *Caste, Class and Politics in Rural India*. New Delhi: Khama Publisher.

Srinivasan, Shaila 1995. *The South Asian Petty Bourgeoisie in Britain*. Aldershot: Avebury.

Tizard, Barbara and Phoenix, Ann 1993. *Black, White or Mixed Race?* London: Routledge.

Visweswaran, Kamala 1994. *Fictions of Feminist Ethnography*. Minneapolis: University of Minnesota Press.

Watson, James 1977. *Between Two Cultures*. Oxford: Basil Blackwell.

Wright, Lawrence 1994. One drop of blood, *The New Yorker*, 25 July, pp. 46–55.

Young, Robert J.C. 1995. *Colonial Desire*. London: Routledge.

Younge, Gary 1997. Black, white and every shade between, *Guardian Weekly*, 1 June, p. 23.

Yule, Henry and Burnell, A.C. 1903 (repr. 1994). *Hobson-Jobson (A Glossary of Anglo-Indian Colloquial Words and Phrases and of Kindred Terms)*. New Delhi: Munshiram Manoharlal Publishers Pvt. Ltd.

CHAPTER THIRTEEN

You nurtured me to be a carefree bird, O Mother[1]

Bandana Pattanaik

A woman is not simply a woman. She is also working-class or bourgeois, dalit or upper-caste, Hindu or Muslim and so on. As a person she
is a complex and polyphonous composition (Susie Tharu, interview
published in *The Hindu*, 3 November 1996).

The woman sitting next to me in a Melbourne tram wants to know whether I am
an Indian or a Sri Lankan. "Indian," I answer. She tells me she has been to India
and we get talking about the places she has visited. She is eager to let me know
that she loves Indian food and Indian textiles.

"Indian woman" is a new marker of my identity. Like many post-colonials I
am sentimentally and passionately attached to my country. But what does the
category Indian woman signify apart from naming my nationality and gender?
While I consider both the words integral to my identity, I feel that they are too
broad to have any specific meaning. For within those two categories are identities of region, religion, language, caste, class, marital status, sexuality and so
on. Mere mention of my name and profession would be enough for most people
in India to make intelligent guesses about my multiple identities. Depending on
the context, some of them have been more important than others both for me and
for people around me. They have, however, always remained intrinsically linked
with each other. It is impossible for me, therefore, to write about my experiences
of class in India without taking into account the other factors (Liddle & Joshi
1986; Bonner et al. 1994; Kishwar 1996).

If I were writing this ten years ago, I would not have thought it important to
analyze my class position in conjunction with my other positions. Sociopolitical
tensions around caste and religion had always existed in India. But from the
privileged position of an upper-caste Hindu I had conveniently overlooked them.
The major communal riots, mass killings and destructions in the 1990s have
forced me to rethink some of my earlier held assumptions. Nor would I have

been able to see, a decade ago, the ambiguous relationship women have with their many identities. The spaces I had inhabited until then were safe and protected spaces. From my father's home in rural Orissa I had moved to residences for women students at various urban universities in India. While those campuses had made it possible for me to share the lives of women from different social backgrounds and created theoretical space for my feminist politics they had also kept me shielded from interaction with the real world.

By choosing to take up a job away from my home state and by deciding to live on my own, however, I was out in the world. My identity could no longer be defined in relation to a grandfather, a father, an uncle or a brother. Nor could I hold on to an interim position of a student; in some ways a person in the making. My job as a tertiary level teacher did place me among the educated professional class. But in the 1990s, in an urban centre where there were many highly educated women working outside their homes, my job did not give me any special status. In the locality where I lived and worked I came to be seen primarily as a woman who lived on her own. My single status, which seemed to subsume all my other identities, gave my position a peculiar advantage and vulnerability. While still enjoying many benefits I also came to live on the fringe of society. Was it a vantage point or was I a social outcaste?

I have never chosen my friends on the basis of their caste, class or religion. Many of my close friends are not Hindus. My house does not have a shrine nor do I celebrate any religious festival. My kitchen, unlike my mother's, does not get polluted if people of other religions use it. Does it mean that class, caste and religion have no meaning in my world? How many *dalit* friends do I have?[2] Why have I not met any *dalit* women in a university classroom or on social occasions?

My economic status is definitely lower than that of my colleagues who have access to their husband's pay packet, often a heavier one than mine. Most of us had similar upbringings. The manners and morals we grew up with were strikingly similar despite minor differences. Our tastes in many things are quite similar. Do we still belong to the same class? Theoretically I have access to a share of my father's property. But I have not acquired any property of my own. My sole source of income is my teaching job. Can I therefore claim to be a working-class person?

I do not have answers to these questions. All I can do is go back a little in time, retrieve words and images from my past and put them together. There is surely a process of selection in this narrative. There will also emerge a critique of the experiences as I narrate them. It is perhaps necessary to add that I could not have commented on my experiences in the same way at the time of living them. Nor am I sure whether my critique will remain the same in the years to come. Moreover, growing up in a diverse country such as India the only generalization one learns to make is that there is no pan-Indian reality. Another person living in the same places around the same time may tell a completely different story.

The images that come back to me when I think of class, caste and religion are of women's bodies. Because it is on them that I have seen the most visible markers of those multiple identities. The raised, tattooed arms of women who could balance three bamboo baskets on their heads and walk for the major part of the day selling fish from door to door; the marks of sindoor, the vermilion red powder which married Hindu women use on their foreheads and hair partings; the faces of Muslim women on the streets of Hyderabad, popping out of their burkhas (the long black outer garment which Muslim women wear while out-doors); the bodies of my grandmother, mother and my own. In telling my story I must turn to my mother's because her tensions and anxieties find echoes in mine, if only in counterpoint.

Homespun cloth and fine crockery

In an old wooden box among bits of lace, pieces of embroidery, beaded purses and other little treasures lies a yellowing notebook. My mother's attempt to chronicle her life. Translated into English the words on the first page would read:

> No one is talking to me. No one. They don't even help me with the baby. I don't know what I have done. I don't know how to please these people. I don't know why my father gave me in marriage to this family.

The date on the page is October 1956, around a year and a half after her marriage. The remaining pages of the notebook are blank. The baby in question, a toddler at that time, is my elder brother. At this time my mother was staying with her parents-in-law and my father's six younger siblings. My father was away at his place of work. It was not appropriate at that time for a man to set up an independent home separate from his extended family. I was 30 years old when I read this, on holiday in my childhood home. Back in the city I lived on my own in a picturesque little flat. My days, to a great extent, were planned and shaped by me. At my age my mother was running a large household of nearly 20 people. Looking back I see her moving from one task to the other, from one person to another trying to meet everyone's demands. What was her life like? In those crowded days of cyclical chores, what did she have that was her own?

My mother was 20 years old, the eldest daughter of an upper-caste Hindu family, when she was given in marriage to a man of the same caste and religion. The caste, called Karana can perhaps be placed, within the context of the state, immediately below the Brahmins. My father, a year older than her, was also the eldest child of his parents. While in school he had been influenced by Gandhi's ideas. He had undergone a training in basic education which sought to inculcate the Gandhian philosophy of self-reliance, simple living and social justice in the Indian system of education. He adhered to those principles all his life even though the education department's experiments with those ideas were shortlived. The families of both my parents had migrated from coastal Orissa to the western part of the state. They have continued to maintain strong cultural ties with the coastal region by celebrating its festivals and speaking its dialect. Migration meant an upward move in their economic status because they could acquire large areas of land, land being much cheaper in the west at that time. They had also been able get their land cultivated by using cheap local labour.

In many ways my parents were well matched. The only discordant note was their class difference. They were certainly not from two different classes. Only from two different ends of the same class, she being from the upper end. As a child I was struck by the hugeness of my mother's ancestral house. There was no poverty in my father's house but nor was there any abundance or luxury; things had to be carefully planned. The arrangement of marriage between two people from slightly different economic backgrounds, though not desirable, was not very uncommon. Caste and religious barriers were seen as insurmountable but minor class differences were ignored. In a newly independent country there was a strong sense of optimism in the air. All the doors were open to an educated upper-caste Hindu man, and with six male children my father's family was seen as already on its road to success. Most importantly, as a woman, my mother was expected to be malleable enough to make any adjustments that might be needed.

My earliest memory of my mother comes back with the smell of sandalwood soap, a herbal hair oil she still uses and the soft folds of her saris. She was the one who could not drink water from a metal tumbler, being used to the crockery and glassware found only in well-to-do households. The little time she had in the afternoons when we were away in school and the men were at work she spent in reading poetry, embroidering and writing letters. Her standards of cleanliness were much higher than most of our neighbours. She did not talk much but she always spoke her mind. In my childhood I have heard her being labelled proud, outspoken and a spend-thrift by the same people for whom she was slogging for hours in the kitchen. As a woman who brought upper-class ways with her she was blamed when things did not go well. So subtle were those taunts and so well disguised were they in jokes that they could never become confrontational.

In every imaginable way my mother was a model woman. She never demanded anything for herself, never showed disrespect to anyone. She accepted my father's siblings as her own and looked after them. She made it possible for my father to practise his Gandhian ideal by looking after the many people whom he brought home. What was it, then, in her behaviour which challenged my father's family and made them appear less refined in comparison to her? With hindsight it appears as if they were using two different codes and had no way of finding a common language. For example, she expected her mother-in-law or her sister-in-law to relieve her from the kitchen duties for a while so she could feed her baby. After serving everyone their meals she hoped that someone would serve her. They thought she should ask for help if she needed it. She felt having to ask for things was crude and concluded that they were insensitive and ungracious. She wanted each of her children to have their own bath towels, they thought she was being fussy and extravagant. There were numerous such misunderstandings and I grew up witnessing this daily cold war. It took me many years to understand that there was a connection between graciousness, subtlety, the finer things in life and money. I also realized that one could not just acquire those things with money. Wealth would have to be there for a considerable period of time before it became evident in that touch of class. My father's family could not talk to my mother because they did not understand her language.

Thinking back on her life I find it difficult to separate my mother's class pride from her self-esteem. Had the need arisen she would have gone out to work. That might have given her economic freedom and taken away the slum of extravagance. Had ours been a nuclear family rather than a large extended one she could have kept a better home. Had my father moved to the corporate sector or concentrated on his career development rather than choosing to work in remote tribal areas, they might have gone up the economic ladder. He in his austere Gandhian ways was a constant reminder of how extravagant her tastes were even as her extreme politeness was a constant critique of his family's crudity.

In the absence of bigger things she held on to the little treasures in her boxes. She was deeply upset if a piece of old china broke. She spent hours embroidering flowers on our clothes and she was often ridiculed for it. What I find painfully frustrating in my mother's story is her inability to effect any change. She could not take up paid work and change the economic status of her new family because both her father's and her husband's families would have seen it as unnecessary defiance. She could not give up the manners she learnt in her father's home because she was convinced they were better. Nothing in her experience helped her to be critical of her own manners. Caught in this double bind and yet too proud to admit defeat she pinned all her hopes on her children.

My parents were fanatical believers in the power of education. In fact all my relatives were fiercely proud of their children's achievements in school. We were constantly told to emulate brilliant cousins and successful uncles. Gender was not a constraint as far as educational opportunities went. My sisters and I were given the same opportunities as my brothers. My choice of humanities instead of science and technology was tolerated only because there was a possibility of becoming an administrator. Having proved myself as a reasonably clever student, my decision not to sit for the Indian Administrative Services examination was seen by the family as foolishness and pathetic lack of ambition.[3]

My awareness of myself came with a sense of my difference – that we were better than others around us, more privileged. In the little village where I grew up we were certainly economically better off than most people. The only people who were visibly wealthier were the few merchant families. But wealth was not an important marker of our superiority, in fact many people whom my family considered uncivilized were probably wealthier than we were. In many ways the migrant families from the coastal region, like mine, were the colonizers in the western part of the state. They saw the local culture as uncivilized and inferior and did not want their children to pick it up. I remember that we were strictly forbidden to use the local dialect at home. People from the coastal districts have always considered themselves to be culturally superior and have always been politically powerful in Orissa.

What set us apart, we were told, was education. Business was seen as a caste-specific trait and since there was no precedent of business people in our caste we were quite doubtful of our business acumen. We were also not farmers though we owned some land which other people cultivated on our behalf. Agriculture and business have never been very strong in the state either. Much of the local business is still dominated by migrants from Gujarat and the surplus need for agricultural produce is still met by the neighbouring state of Andhra Pradesh. The road to better social status was therefore education.

Combined with this excessive reliance on education was an ambiguous attitude towards wealth. Desire to make too much money was strongly discouraged. Stand on your feet so that you can do something for others, my parents always told us. The rigid hierarchical framework of caste, religion and class did not exclude personal kindness and concern for the needy. We were chastised if we showed reluctance to give away our toys or used clothes to poor children. My parents paid for the education of many poor students and my mother ran informal literacy classes for our neighbours and insisted that my sister and I helped her in the project.

The other side of this belief in education was that if one did not do well in studies, or worse still, became a school dropout like my elder brother, it was seen as a major disaster. If you do not study you would end up like them was the constant refrain of watchful parents. And indeed, "they" were everywhere; working in our backyards; doing menial jobs for meagre wages, often just for food; standing by tea shops because they had nothing to do. The difference between them and us, therefore, was a tenuous one. One could fall down the scales much too easily.

As a young girl it was even easier to lose my special status. Once I started menstruating many restrictions were placed on my movements. I could not go out alone. I could not smile at a stranger. My sexuality was seen as a dangerous source of power. A slight slip on my part could result not only in loss of my caste and religion, it could also bring bad name to the entire family. "What will people say?" and "Girls from our family do not behave in this way" were my mother's euphemistic injunctions to my sisters and me. The outside world held danger, yet the times demanded that we went out for education and later for jobs. We were therefore trained to be our own moral guardians by internalizing the values of our caste, religion and class.

My parents were united in their project to give us formal education but my mother was the sole custodian of our caste and religion. It was assumed that we would study and take up jobs, participate in the public sphere and make our own decisions regarding many things in life. It was also hoped that we would not upset the boundaries and hierarchies of caste and religion. For example, most parents could not rule out the possibility that their educated daughters might choose their own partners but they always hoped that the man would be from the same caste and religion.

By the time I was in my twenties the social arrangement of relationships had undergone a few changes. A considerable number of middle-class women had joined the paid workforce. It was assumed that a qualified woman would continue to work and contribute to the income of her new family. Nuclear families had also become quite common. On the surface it did look as if barriers of caste, religion and class had ceased to be important. Many educated and economically independent women did make their choices but the social costs of those choices were often very high. Friends who dared to cross the barriers of caste and religion sometimes had to face ostracism from both families. Some Hindu friends who married Muslim or Christian men were barred from entry to their parental homes because they had lost their religion. Their husbands' families insisted on their conversion into the new religion. The degree of tolerance for inter-caste marriages depended on the status of the man's caste. Some intermingling among castes quite close to each other in the hierarchy has been accepted but it is still very unusual for a high-caste woman to marry an Untouchable man. The intermingling of classes has also resulted in the most vulgar form of commodification of human beings. A man's class, in most instances, has come to be judged primarily by his pay packet and rich parents do not hesitate to pay heavy dowries for eligible professional bridegrooms from lower-class families. It is assumed that the educated, upper-class woman will help her husband's class mobility both culturally and materially. Many educated and employed women have been tortured or even burnt to death because they had not brought enough dowry (Kumari 1989; Diwan 1990).

My father's Gandhian ways had influenced me so that I became a staunch opponent of Untouchability. But in reality there was no possibility of social mingling with anyone who was from an Untouchable caste or from a different religion. In a predominantly Hindu village which was even spatially designed to keep different castes apart and the Untouchable castes outside the main village, our theoretical rejection of caste and religious hierarchies was seldom put to the test. I grew up believing that caste and religious hierarchies would soon disappear on their own. After all the Constitution did claim that there would be no discrimination on the basis of caste, creed and religion. It took me many years to realize that a Muslim might never have seen India as a secular country, nor would a lower-caste person have had any faith in the non-discrimination policies of the state (Lateef 1990; Engineer 1989).

My mother's interaction with people who were not part of our family or not related to us in some ways was limited. They were mostly women who came to help her in household tasks or to sell vegetables, fish and other consumable items. The relationship with them was largely transactional. They could not enter our living room. The hierarchy of class and caste was very strictly maintained by both the parties concerned. For example, it would not have occurred to my mother to offer them a seat and if she had they would have thought she was going crazy. It sounds strange but this rigid hierarchy did not exclude a personalized touch. Many of these women came even when she did not need to buy anything from them. On hot, quiet afternoons they used to come and rest in our courtyard. My mother would go on with her knitting or some other housework and their conversation would go on. She would insist that they ate or took some food with them before they left. They understood each others' physical experiences such as child birth, menstruation, menopause and the complications arising out of those experiences. They shared their worries over a sick child, an aging relative or a marriageable daughter. It was not unusual to see my mother or aunt cooking something special for our pregnant maid servant. It was also not out of place for a woman below our class, caste and religion to chide and scold us for not looking after our mother. An experienced woman, regardless of her social position, had some rights and authority over younger women. She also had some knowledge which was valued among women.

The other women who also visited my mother were our neighbours. They were closer to us in class and caste. They were received in the special women's living room which was different from the one used by men. They could enter our kitchen or even our shrine on a special day. But the differences between us were too many to be overlooked. We spoke the same language but different dialects. Our mothers wore their saris differently. Our festivals were different. The differences among various social groups, I grew up learning, were not always based on economic status. Region, religion, caste and marital status play a large role in the way people live their lives. Those special markers of region, religion, marital status and caste can still be seen on women's ways of dressing though they are not so clear in urban or cosmopolitan women. Therefore, a person from a particular region, caste and religion may find it much easier to socialize with someone with the same affiliations. Class differences, unless too stark, are not discernible or are easily overlooked, in the face of other similarities.

However, if there is one significant similarity among the middle class which cuts across regional and religious barriers it is the way they look upon women's sexuality. Most middle-class families were and still are obsessively concerned with the sexual chastity of their women. And the burden to bring up girls in the right way so that they achieve the exact blend of tradition and modernity is almost always exclusively placed on women (Roy 1997). My mother was already blamed for my brother's failure. It was her upper-class indulgences which caused it, she was told by my father's family. When my younger sister fell in love with a man who was below us in class, my mother was at the end of her tether. Falling in love with an unsuitable boy was my sister's crime in which mother was complicit by being a bad trustee. What was it that upset her most? Her failure or her fear that her daughter's life might mirror her own?

What was my mother's class? All her work was unpaid. If class is defined by ownership of property she did not own anything, even her jewels were part of the family's wealth. Without any agency to change her class status she was even denied the right to show any affiliations to her earlier class. What defines her social position? The softness of silk or the coarse texture of cotton cloth, of khadi? Or the frisson between the two?

Locking and unlocking my own house

My story is characterized by flights – flights of fancy to imaginary places where I could just be myself; where I could walk the streets without thinking of the dangers that lurk behind. So oppressive were the instructions to be a good girl and a high achiever that all I wanted to do was run away. The fact that I could indulge in such romantic fantasies says a lot about the privileges I grew up with.

I moved to a city for higher education at the age of 15. The college I went to was one of the oldest in the country and had a very high profile within the state. From being the daughter of a well-known family and the top-ranking student in my village school, I became one of the many brilliant students of my college. No one knew my family there. I was from a remote village living in a student residence where immersion in academia seemed temporarily to suspend the hierarchies of real life. The ranks of caste, class and religion did not seem to matter. And grades were not awarded on the basis of gender, caste, class or religion. The only hierarchies in student life, it seemed, were built around merit. Students who opted for the science stream were considered more brilliant than those who chose humanities. A degree in humanities, however, was not completely useless. One could not become a doctor or an engineer but one was eligible to enter the numerous competitive examinations for administrative jobs in the public sector or one could become an academic.

In retrospect, I realize how naive those beliefs were. University campuses were not real in the sense that a village, small town or city was and the student community came, by and large, from the privileged classes. Education, even though it was heavily subsidized by the state, was out of the reach of working-class people. Unfortunately, the situation is not very different today. Worse still, we now have many more private schools than before. Many of us went to state schools in the 1960s and 1970s. Our parents could have afforded private education but there were hardly any private schools in non-metropolitan centres. Most of my contemporaries now send their children to private schools where the fees are very high but education is better. Thirty years ago, it was beyond the means of a poor carpenter or weaver to educate his children. In the rare cases where they did go to school the situation became worse. They either got a very low paid job or none at all and they lost the knowledge of their family trade. In my childhood, a man in a low paid job could not send his son to a free school because he could not pay for his books. Or he had to choose between the education of his son and daughter because he could not afford to educate both of them. Usually the son's education received higher priority. More than three decades later, free education is still not accessible to everyone and a good education is the privilege of a limited few.

After spending seven years away from my parents' home, but in my home state, I moved out of the state to join a research programme. I had a master's degree in English literature by then and much against the will of my parents I had decided to take up teaching. The Central Institute of English and Foreign Languages in Hyderabad which offered a research programme seemed like a logical destination. The small and select body of researchers at the Institute came from all over the country. It was there that I realized how misleading the term middle class could be, at least in the Indian context. So disparate are the economic conditions among the various Indian states that someone who is middle class in Orissa would be considered quite poor in Andhra Pradesh. This became even more obvious a few years later when I moved to Gujarat, a state rich in business and industry. A university considered to be the best in one state may not even be known in another. For example, unlike some of my new friends, I had not learnt to speak English from Irish nuns. The English I spoke was recognizably influenced by my mother tongue. I was extremely upset by people's comments that long and short vowels were thoroughly mixed up in the English I spoke. However, though painful at that moment, these differences soon became subsumed under the common economic privileges. We could afford to become cosmopolitan, to make some choices. In the end it did not really matter what kind of English we spoke. Our differences came from our locations; rural, semi-urban or urban. They also came from our religions and regions. What united us was our ability to afford many things and the luxury to make some choices in our lives. I am not sure if I can call all my classmates "middle class" – the term is so vague, but we certainly had the economic privilege which many in India did not have. Some of us who have lived in many states must have shed many of our regional peculiarities. The way we dress and speak today must have changed over the years. In fact, sometimes different regional festivals, foods and costumes have conferred special identities on us. Some of us have wardrobes which boast clothes from all over the country. Over the years we have learnt to respect other regional cultures and customs and have also learnt to laugh at each others' peculiarities. Christian friends from Kerala have told me about home-brewed wine and delicious beef curries – sacrilegious things in my Hindu upbringing. Muslim friends have invited me home for Idd and introduced me to rich Mughlai cuisine.[4] If one could call this a breaking down of social barriers, it has happened at a personal level only and among those who can afford it.

In 1990, I took up a teaching job in a college in Hyderabad. The college where I worked was run by Catholic nuns and located in a predominantly Muslim area. Our students came from all religious backgrounds and the faculty was largely Hindu. In August 1990, V.P Singh, the then prime minister of India, announced that he would implement the first phase of the recommendations of the Mandal Commission. The commission's reports which had been gathering dust in the parliamentary archives for some years, had found that 52 per cent of the country's population fall within the category of socially and educationally deprived. It had recommended that the existing reservations for Scheduled Castes, Scheduled Tribes and Other Backward Castes in public sector recruitment and admissions to educational institutions should be enhanced. Within days of the prime minister's announcement tertiary level students all over the country went on protest marches and demonstrations. They felt that if more jobs were kept reserved for the disadvantaged people regardless of their merit, the meritorious ones would lose out. While the insecurity and anger of youth in a developing country were understandable, the vehement protests also made many of us re-think the notion of merit. How would one judge who is more or less meritorious, if some have not been given any opportunity at all? The media, largely owned by the middle class, gave the agitation wide coverage and in many ways fuelled it. Around the same time another political development took place. Fearing that the ruling party would win all the lower-caste votes, the opposition party de-cided to play on the religious sentiments of the masses. L.K. Advani, an opposi-tion leader, announced a *Rath Yatra* to a disputed site in Ayodhya which was allegedly the birthplace of Ram, the Hindu God. This was enormously signifi-cant for Hindus since *Rath Yatra* has religious connotations – it literally means undertaking a journey in a chariot. Apparently a Hindu temple had been de-stroyed at that spot centuries ago and a mosque had been built in its place. A countrywide carnage followed the *Rath Yatra*. Destruction and killings con-tinued for years. In December 1992, the mosque was destroyed by a group of self-styled Hindu militants. Along with it the myth of India as a secular country was also destroyed.[5]

In many ways the early 1990s was a time of rude awakenings. It was not that there were no conflicts before but somehow they had always happened else-where. If brides were getting burnt they had not got burnt in our families and if there was a communal riot it had not happened in our locality. At a personal level I was learning that economic independence and social acceptance are two different things. I was able to earn the money to pay my rent but I found it extremely difficult to find a house to rent. Many people were just too unwilling to rent a house to a woman who lived alone. And when I did find a place to stay, I felt I was always under the watchful eyes of my neighbours. This was a kind of surveillance I had not experienced. My caste, my religion and my economic status could not give me respectability. For many people I was just a woman without a man.

With my friends, I started going over our experiences of caste, religion, class and gender and realized how oblivious we had been to many social issues. We realized that our student days were largely conflict-free because most of us were from upper-caste, Hindu and what could be called loosely middle-class homes. We realized that all the well paid jobs in the entire country had gone to people like us. Caste and religious rules had kept the courtyards of our childhood "pure". The policies of the state had kept the corridors of power untainted by keeping the less privileged people out. Our higher degrees, we realized, had equipped us to analyze the class structure in E.M. Forster's *Howard's End* but had alienated us from our immediate present.

Many years ago, on hearing of feminism for the first time, I had said, "Feminism is for privileged people." Over the years, feminism has helped me to see how privileged I have always been. It has also helped me to understand how easily I can lose all those privileges because of my gender. When two people from different castes and/or religions get married it is the woman whose caste and religion changes. If an upper-caste woman has a sexual relationship with a man below her caste sometimes she is also murdered along with the man (see Bonner et al. 1994: 193–216). When a communal riot breaks out between Hindus and Muslims it is women who are raped. Even educated, employed, upper-caste, middle-class women have been tortured or burnt to death for not having brought enough dowry to their husbands' homes. It is still much easier for a divorced man to find a new partner than a divorced woman. Single women are always sexually suspect regardless of their caste, class and religion. Where would I place myself on the ladders of class, caste and religion? Where would I place women on those ladders? Every woman I know seems always to be in danger of falling off the scales wherever she is.

When I was working with the Untouchable women in a small village in Orissa one summer, I was struck by their self-esteem and their anger at mainstream society. One woman told me, "If an upper-caste man comes anywhere near us we will kill him. We do not need our men to protect us. We are not ashamed to use abusive language like high-caste women." In a flashback, I thought of the evening when a neighbour of mine, a man from my own background, had blatantly misbehaved with me. I had been embarrassed, even ashamed to tell other people of his bad manners. I wished I had had the courage of the so-called Untouchable, uneducated woman. Yet I knew I was romanticizing her situation; she has her own battles to fight; basic battles for food and shelter.

Some years ago when my mother visited me in my flat for the first time she could not get over the fact that I had to lock and unlock my own house. That simple mindless act had assumed a symbolic proportion for her. It stood for my lonely and unprotected life. She never had to lock our house. The house was never empty so it did not need a lock. During that visit, perhaps for the first time, we talked to each other as two women. She told me my life seemed a bit unreal to her. Meeting my many friends she started reminiscing about friends whom she had lost. She did not speak English so she could not talk to my friends. But she wanted to know what we talked about, what we laughed over and what upset us. I told her we were thoroughly confused because we did not know where we belonged. She asked, "Does it matter?" and added, "As long as you are together."

I have often thought about it later. Together with whom? Where? Who are my friends and who are my enemies? What has been and would be the basis of my alliances with people? Caste? Class? Religion? Race? Gender? Political ideology? The people whom she saw me with were in some way or other deviants from mainstream society; single women, refugees from Somalia and dislocated students from Palestine. Can such people constitute a class of their own? Each one of them has contributed to what I am today. Their lives and daily struggles have informed my politics. My marginal position in one category has helped me understand the privileges I enjoy in others. Sharing other women's stories has helped me formulate a feminist critique of society even as the workings of mainstream society remind me that women can perpetuate the worst kind of violence and atrocity (Sarkar & Butalia 1995).

One of the many things I have learnt from my wanderings is that hierarchical positions are unreliable. If I can indulge in utopia for a moment, I would rather exist in a circle. An ever expanding, ever-changing circle.

Postscript

I am writing this in Australia. I have been away from India for nearly two years now. On my first morning here, while driving to the city from the airport, I had looked out and watched the long fleet of cars. It was early autumn. The trees were a vibrant red, orange and yellow. I commented on the beautiful houses. The person who was driving me shrugged and said, "These are just working-class houses. You will see some of the real great houses soon." "Working-class" must mean something else here, I told myself and I realized exactly where my country stood on the international economic ladder.

Where do I position myself in this society? To a great extent I live here like a guest. Officially, I hold a temporary visa which clearly spells out my work rights and hence my economic status. Culturally, I notice the similarities and differences. I speak the language of gratitude and am thankful for people's kindness, concern and love. Should I decide to stay on here, however, my status would change. Events in India will lose some of their immediacy. I would become more affected by the here and now, by the workings of this society. I would speak the language of rights and responsibilities. What kind of participation would that be? How do immigrants, who it seems to me, live between two worlds, define their social position? Who would be my allies? Would marginalization, of a different kind this time, be a source of understanding and power? That will be another story.

Acknowledgements

I would like to thank Helen and Linda Walter for their patience and thought-provoking comments while I was trying to articulate my experience of class, caste, religion and gender. Without them this chapter could never have been written.

Notes

1. The title of this chapter is taken from a popular folk song in Oriya. Traditionally this song was sung by young women when they left their mothers' home for their husbands. It symbolized the woman's entry into a hostile world where she would not have the protection and care of her mother. I have used the translated version from Susie Tharu and K. Lalitha (1993: 135).
2. *Dalit* literally means oppressed. The terms used in the Indian Constitution to refer to the less privileged are scheduled caste (SC), scheduled tribe (ST), and other backward classes (OBC). Mahatma Gandhi coined the term Harijan which meant God's people, to refer to the Untouchables.
3. The obsession with administrative services is typical of Orissa and some other underdeveloped states in India. In the absence of a strong agricultural or industrial base most educated young women and men were encouraged by their families to join the administrative services. Those jobs are open to graduates of any discipline and selection is based on national level tests.
4. Idd is the Muslim festival which follows the holy month of Ramzan. Mughlai, possibly a derivation from the word Mughal, is sometimes used to describe Muslim cooking.
5. Media reports and analyses of communal violence in India in the 1990s can be found in popular and academic writings of the period. See in particular various issues of *Economic and Political Weekly of India* and the detailed analysis of Bonner et al. (1994).

References

Bonner, A. et al. 1994. *Democracy in India: A Hollow Shell.* Washington, DC: The American University Press.

Diwan, P. 1990. *Dowry and Protection to Married Women.* New Delhi: Deep & Deep Publications.

Engineer, A.A. 1989. *Communalism and Communal Violence in India: An Analytical Approach to Hindu–Muslim Conflict.* New Delhi: Ajanta Publications.

Kishwar, M. 1996. Who Am I? Living Identities vs Acquired Ones, *Manushi*, 94, May–June, 11–12.

Kumari, R. 1989. *Brides are not for Burning: Dowry Victims in India.* New Delhi: Radiant Publishers.

Lateef, S. 1990. *Muslim Women in India: Political and Private Realities, 1890s–1980s.* New Delhi: Kali for Women.

Liddle, J. and Joshi, R. 1986. *Daughters of Independence: Gender, Class and Caste in India.* New Delhi: Kali for Women.

Roy, A. 1997. *The God of Small Things.* Melbourne: Flamingo.

Sarkar, T. and Butalia, U. (eds) 1995. *Women and Right-wing Movements: Indian Experiences.* New Delhi: Kali for Women.

Tharu, S. and Lalitha, K. (eds) 1993. *Women Writing in India.* Vol. 1, New Delhi: Oxford University Press.

CHAPTER FOURTEEN

Genealogies of class

Susan Hawthorne

> The upper class is despised, although their wealth and lifestyle is
> envied; the working class "battler" is glorified, although no one wants to
> be one; the middle class is considered boring, but most belong to it.

Class in Australia

The above epigraph summarizes the dominant culture view of class in Australia:
the country whose white history begins with political prisoners and petty crimi-
nals; made criminal by the British culture of the late eighteenth century; criminal
in a way we can barely understand today in our "historyless" society. They were
deported for stealing a loaf of bread or a horse, indeed for poverty, crimes which
today would incur a few days or weeks of community service. Of course, the
above epigraph probably does not describe the reality of any individual life, it
simply summarizes cultural attitudes.[1]

Australia has class divisions, but they are not as marked as they are in
Britain. There is also an ideology of egalitarianism, although in practice this falls
far short of its goal. Generational fluidity of class is quite common in Australia
and education and lifestyle can forge new external class positions. I use the term
"external" class positions, because internal identities are more resistant to shifts.
One tends to pick up subtle class behaviours at a young age and many of these
become integrated into one's social responses. A convict heritage, once considered social doom, is now highly regarded by the elites. A southern European
migrant background once made class mobility difficult, but with new generations educated into the culture there have been vast shifts in demographics. The
newer migrants from Asia will become the next generation of the middle class,
but in the mean time they predominate in the lower paid and lower status jobs.
With each wave of migration comes a new underclass, a new group who are

poor, struggling with linguistic and cultural disadvantage, and whose children will move away from the class into which they were born.

Class is perpetuated most readily through schooling. The well-off attend private grammar and church schools; those with fewer assets predominate in the state school system, although not entirely. Class is affected by profession, with lawyers and doctors most easily able to slip upwards in class, while the paid employee in the service industry is likely to be of middle-class or working-class origins. Education allows for rising class, and lack of it contributes to falling class. One's origins – and they relate to at least the two previous generations – are critical in determining where one's class trajectory begins. Urban and rural Aboriginal people who participate in the white market economy are perhaps the only cultural group with a stable class position over the past five or six generations: as members of the working class or the underclass. The position of Aboriginal people living in near traditional ways falls outside our Western notion of class, since class only becomes an issue in interactions with the white community.[2] With ever more government interference in Aboriginal affairs their underclass position is heavily overdetermined. Class does not work as a category to describe traditional forms of Aboriginal culture. What hierarchies exist are patterned on very different social structures. Australia's upper class come from a mix of rural and urban settings. They predominate in some farming regions, as well as in industry, the arts and the professions. As elsewhere, marriage can change a person's fortunes.

This chapter focuses most on the rural experience of class. The urban experience has its own pattern, marked frequently by the urban areas where particular classes live.[3] Inner urban areas used to be working class, but the past 50 years has seen a shift or drift to suburban and outer suburban areas for the working class, and a drift towards the centre for the middle and upper classes.

Class

When I examine the word class, I am trying to find what it is that distinguishes one class from another. My life has been marked by shifts in my personal economic fortunes or misfortunes. My student years were alleviated by a scholarship, not a huge income, but sufficient to share rent in flats and houses with two to five people. The most difficult periods financially were the years when I was unemployed, but I enjoyed the self-structured days, the freedom to read, to think, to write.

If I have to identify with a single class then middle-class is the term which fits. The markers of class vary across cultures and countries. One can be upper class, but cash poor; one can be working class and cash rich. One can be middle class and ill-educated; one can be working class and highly literate, an intellectual or an artist. And there are other permutations on this theme.

Class is a way of knowing the world and this knowledge is made evident in ways of speech and action. A working-class friend has said that I bear the mark of the middle class: confidence engendered by class. I am unaware of this, and am only aware that my mother projected a similar image.[4] Another has pointed out that the attitude to friendship and networking is different in middle- and working-class individuals.[5] As the editors of this volume have written elsewhere:

> The middle-class world is one with a particular culture and particular rules. Because it is taken for granted as the norm, the knowledge which is needed to negotiate it is rarely made explicit. Middle-class women usually do not know what they know in this respect (Mahony & Zmroczek 1996: 72).

Genealogies

As I write this I find the need to explain something of my parents' history.

My father was born in 1913 on the farm where we lived. The farm had come into his parents' hands a few years earlier. His father, and his father's brother had come from Central Victoria, where one branch of the family remains. Grandma Hawthorne, as my father refers to her, appears to have been a formidable character. He recently told me that they had travelled five days to visit her once when she was ill. Grandma Hawthorne and her descendants established a country department store which still exists. My grandfather, Jim, became important in local politics serving for 31 continuous years on the local shire council and as a founding member of the county council (Back to Ardlethan Week Committee 1985: 90). On my father's mother's side family connections were urban. My grandmother, Mardi, moved from Mosman, a North Sydney harbourside suburb to an isolated area of dry farmland.

My mother's mother's family were among the earliest white settlers in South Australia, in a region where the country is still marked by their presence. My great grandfather was a land-wealthy man, and even with nine children, seven of them girls, they were still well off in the following generation. My mother's relatives in Sydney, South Australia and Melbourne were all marked by something I read as upper class. In Sydney it was yachts on the harbour, original paintings on the wall and North Shore addresses; in South Australia it was a long history on the land, dating back to the 1840s and claiming large tracts of country; in Melbourne it was my grandmother's rooms in the Majestic Hotel in St Kilda.

My mother's father was a merchant sea-captain. He came from Bute, in the western isles of Scotland and his family had been seafarers for generations. I have no sense of what kind of class status this gave him. It is too far removed from the social context of Australia.

Both my parents came from families that were well travelled for the period. Two great aunts on the Hawthorne side travelled to Iceland in 1904 as part of their grand tour of Europe. My maternal grandmother had met my Scottish grandfather on a warship in the First World War, when she was a nurse and he a captain. In the 1920s all of my grandmother's sisters travelled to Europe; one remained in England for the rest of her life. And my grandmother was a frequent traveller, with a long sojourn in Germany just before the Second World War began, and during my childhood she visited both England and Japan. She was a cultured woman whose life ended tragically when I was nine. So my grand-parents had the necessary elements for class and social status: assets – especially land, money, education, culture and mobility.

Coming closer to my parents' class position and attitudes: theirs remained much the same as their parents'. The farm I grew up on was around 4,000 acres. This was large for the district, and the average acreage for the region would be around 1,000 acres. The soil was poor, the rainfall erratic, but a good year could make up for the deficiencies of the bad.

My parents employed others to work for them, and in difficult years my father did subcontract work building dams on other properties. The families who came to work on our land lived in small houses on the farm. Most frequently it was the man who had a formal job, while the woman or children might help out at very busy times with work such as droving, shearing or similar. And we too would be drafted into such work, pushing the sheep through the races for marking, or moving sheep up to 4 or 5 miles from the paddocks to the yards.

In the early 1950s the families who worked on the farm tended to be dis-placed refugees from the Second World War. I know that Baltic and East Euro-pean families were among those who came, but I do not remember them. In later years they were replaced by Anglo-working-class families.

My parents were well educated in terms of their generation, although neither had attended university. My father was a highly decorated pilot in the Second World War and had flown VIPs and generals in his plane. My mother had been very bright at school, but left at an early age to attend art school in Sydney. She worked briefly as a secretary to the Department of Agriculture in Melbourne, and later as secretary to a high ranking officer in the army.

My mother was very active in community organizations, such as the Country Women's Association (CWA) and the local golf club. My father, like his father before him, was a member of the local shire and county councils and once stood as a candidate for pre-selection for the Country Party which was the forum of the farmers primarily. My recollection is that he stood in 1967, the year in which Aboriginal people were voted to full citizenship in a referendum. Among the people who surrounded me, there was very little dissension from this view. My parents' politics ranged from small "l" liberal views (they expressed horror at Apartheid in South Africa, voted for Aboriginal citizenship and my mother supported independence for women) to big "C" conservative views (they ex-pressed equal horror at any suggestion of socialism, or at almost any Labor Party policy). All this has left me with the knowledge that not all those who vote conservatively hold monstrous views on everything. It does make me more patient with the people, but I remain impatient with the views. In my early teens I thought everyone over the age of 20 voted for either the Country Party (the conservative farming party) or the Liberal Party (the conservative urban party). It was a shock to discover that some people's parents voted for the Labor Party (the left-wing urban party). Indeed, I spent a great deal of energy in my late teens arguing against almost everything my parents and their friends espoused. I think I was about 17 when I decided I would vote for the Labor Party when I could, and I have done so ever since.

My parents were pillars of the community, and they were involved. They were both confident public speakers, and I was especially proud the day my mother was selected to hand out the sports ribbons at the District Schools Sports Day.

Because several members of my father's family had settled together, in addition to our farm, nearby were also farms owned by his brother and his cousin, both living within a mile of our house. This meant we had cousins and that there were enough of us to make me feel as if we were important in the district. It was a surprise to discover much later that my family were relative latecomers to the district.

During most of my childhood we had some live-in help. The women who filled these positions were hugely different from one another. There was Mrs Hood, an older woman, whom we baited, but whose Golden Syrup dumplings, apple crumbles and chocolate puddings we loved. At the other extreme, Carma, a young woman of 18, Dutch, a single-mother of a four-week-old son came to work for us when I was seven. We thought she was fantastic. She became our friend. She taught us to rock-and-roll in the kitchen. She taught us about looking at the world differently. We gave her cheek and she challenged us back. She dealt directly with us. She stayed for about two years. I don't remember why she left, but perhaps to get a life of her own again.

The local school, Ardlethan Central School, serviced an area of perhaps 40 to 60 square miles, and included children from a wide range of families: town and rural working class, including children from Italian migrant backgrounds, as well as children of middle-class farmers, or professionals such as bankers, stock and station agents, retailers. The school had around a hundred students ranging in age from five to fifteen. There was Ted, the son of the bus driver, Valerie the daughter of the butcher, Margaret, whose older siblings had already gone away to boarding school, Maria, the tiny Italian girl, Sharon whose parents worked as farm hands for a friend of my mother's; there were children of share-farmers, train drivers, tin miners, milk bar owners, bakers, publicans, mechanics, rabbit trappers and telephone exchange workers. Anyone with sufficient money to send their children to boarding school did so, since the alternative was to finish school at 15 with few prospects for further education.

During the 1950s it was not uncommon for rural itinerants, swaggies, to come by our farm. Since we lived 6 miles from the nearest town on one side and about 30 miles from the next nearest, they usually called in to our place. They would come to the back door and ask for food. They were always given sustenance, and sometimes shared a cup of tea on the back step. There was generosity, but the rules were strict, they were never allowed inside. Much later, my mother told me that when she had first come to live in my father's house in the late 1940s, other women of the district left their calling cards before visiting. This formality was dropped by the time I came to notice social mores, but many others remained until well into the late 1960s. A recent meeting with a locally born woman who married an Indonesian man in the early 1970s confirmed this impression. The insularity of the town meant that he was given a hard time until he'd been around long enough to gain gradual acceptance.

The isolation, racism and conservatism of rural Australia in the 1950s meant that I was not exposed to other styles of living (there was no TV, and radio simply reflected the cultural norms). But the advantage of a country upbringing is that one is exposed to a range of different class positions constantly and one is able to observe them over long, slow periods of time. I would watch my father move through the different interactions he had with farm workers. There was a camaraderie "up the paddock" or "in the pub" or in the event of a breakdown on the road. But put him in a suit for some formal function and I would see a very different man. My mother also walked through these transformations. She was one of the few women to hold the qualification of wool classer, a role which determines the price a bale of wool can fetch on the international market. The wool classer judges the quality of the wool produced by feeling, looking, smelling the fibre. Rubbing and twisting the wool gives the classer the ability to test the strength of the fibre, and therefore what class the wool is allocated. She also held an endorsed truck licence which gave her licence to drive an articulated semi-trailer. Again, few other women in the district held endorsed licences. During shearing time she became a sheep drover when she would become "one of the boys", easy going, blasting out her piercing whistle which the dogs understood perfectly. On other occasions she moved between the more usual roles of women, from mother and gardener when she visited her women friends, to the society woman at the picnic races in the big town nearly 70 miles away or in Georges, the Harrods of Melbourne, where she would go once a year to buy something special. I had quite a range of options to choose from when modelling my own behaviour as a child and adolescent. My grandmothers, on both sides, were not nearly so flexible in their outlook. They were staunchly big "C" conservative all the time, although both were independent women of independent means.

The concept of class, however, came to me quite late. My first conscious recognition of it was when my mother tried to tell me that I shouldn't play with some children. At around age ten I was puzzled by this and it changed my outlook. I continued to play with the same children, but a distance had been put between us and I could not return to the blissful state of not knowing or not noticing class in this community. I tried to figure out the rules, but the only one that worked was attached to the ability of the parents to afford to send their children to boarding school.

During my childhood I had had a sense of my place in the world. It was a class sense, even in the years before I recognized it. This sense of position took some buffeting when I was finally sent away to boarding school in Melbourne. By then I knew we were middle class, I even had fantasies that maybe we were upper class. But when I met other girls with families who could afford *anything* they wanted, *then* I wondered. Had I placed my family too far up the scale? Granted, the school I attended attracted some of the upper class, and I don't think I had really encountered that previously. The very wealthy "establishment" girls at the school were daughters of big industry, legal practitioners, the Church of England hierarchy, and farmers who could also afford a city residence.

Land wealth had given my family class privilege. But my parents still depended on the weather for their sustenance and as the mid-1960s saw a devastating drought in southern New South Wales, there was little cash available to give me a sense of importance in terms of class status during my adolescence.

The lack of cash was compounded by my own personal shock when I went to boarding school. All of a sudden I was a small fish in a big pond. No longer could I count on being one of the two top students in my year. I became very much a middling student. "Susan could do better, try harder, concentrate more," said one teacher after another in my school reports.

The shock continued for the first four years of my six-year stay at the boarding school. I also discovered that my relative status in class terms depended very much on who was looking on. I stayed with day girls on weekends whose parents had two-storey city houses, swimming pools and lots of cash; I shared rooms with girls who had open accounts at the big department stores, who could book up smoked oysters for the annual midnight feast; I stayed with friends who had beach houses. But I also stayed with friends whose farming parents were struggling to pay the bills to keep their children at school. There were class divisions even between those of us who were boarders. Some were clearly descendants of the squattocracy. They were descendants of mostly British settlers from the early 1800s who "squatted" on large tracts of land. My father's family bought the land they held at Ardlethan, but it is possible that my mother's grandfather in South Australia may have squatted. My historical understanding, however, is that squatting occurred only in Victoria and New South Wales. One friend, whose parents ran a dairy farm, used the term squattocracy abusively against me on one occasion because my parents, although strapped for cash, owned a house and farm which gave the impression of inherited wealth. And that was what my parents wanted to convey. It was how they saw themselves. But my perception differed from theirs and I often felt embarrassed by their class snobbery.

Prior to going to the city and boarding school I had thought that social position was a given. The school I attended was one of several establishment schools in Melbourne, and the message I was being fed was that it was the best.

I still half believe this even though I now have critical distance. It was a good school, but it was too big for me – and perhaps too homogeneous.

By the end of my secondary schooling I thought I could enter any social setting and deal with it. Because of my poor performance in end of year exams I did not get into university and instead attended teachers' college, a much more mixed social environment in those days. And I began to rebel. I went out with boys from the western suburbs. In Australia "western" in front of an urban location tends to denote poor as, for cities on the eastern seaboard of Australia, west means suburbs away from the sea. A student recently pointed out to me that workers in the western suburbs drive to and from work directly into the sun's glare, whereas their eastern suburban counterparts – the wealthier classes – have the sun behind them.

In this period I also went regularly to the skating rink, St Moritz, and learned to skate, to dance, to race around the edge to blaring loudspeaker music. And not long after I went out with a truck driver. All of this was my rebellion against my own class. A rejection, however, which I could not sustain.

I chose rebellious friends, hippies. My parents scolded me for "slipping backwards" as they saw it. In fact, many of my new disreputable-looking friends were middle-class kids from private school backgrounds,[6] themselves rebelling against the stodginess of the previous generation. But my parents were not convinced. Nor had I realized my friends' backgrounds when we first met. But I suppose we shared a culture, without even realizing it.

Feminism

Then I became a feminist. And it wasn't long before I identified as a lesbian. The latter damaged my class status quite considerably. Not because I was instantly recognizable as a lesbian, but because coming out changed my sense of class for me. I had long familiarity with silence, as I had suffered from epilepsy all my life and had been told that silence was a necessary defence against social stigma. This new identity was another self-silencing among my parents' friends. It was one more thing I could not speak about in the community I'd grown up in. In self-defence I withdrew from family events, annual rituals and reunions. My mother was both relieved and horrified. The relief was that the women I entered relationships with were educated and middle class. Whereas the man I had lived with, although of middle-class background, was not well educated and worked as a driver. She was disappointed, of course, that the class shift of my partners had taken place at the expense of a heterosexual existence. The imagined marriage to a doctor would never happen; the grandchildren would never appear. The stages of a woman's life would not be met. In spite of this initial reaction, both my parents have accepted my decisions, and although they have not spoken of it openly, they have never denied it. This from two people who vote for the conservative Country Party is reassuring. On my mother's death in 1994, my partner's name was included in the notice in the local newspaper, and she has now also been included in the family tree.

But back in 1974 I knew that I could not any longer enter *any* social setting and feel comfortable. It knocked that illusion over forever. It also gave me a political means for understanding difference – of sexuality, of background, of disability, of class. Putting it together has taken a long time.

In the process of doing so, I have experienced some long periods of unemployment, which meant frugal living for some years, but I have never felt desperate, never felt that terror of not knowing where the next meal might come from, never felt the consequences of poverty having a direct impact on me. I am thankful for this. Instead, my periods of unemployment have been enriching times. And I think this is due to my basic sense of security. Like many other rebellious people I have lived at the edge of my means, I have hitchhiked to other cities and then, finding no place to sleep, have slept on newspaper in derelict houses or on the beach. In doing this I have known it is only for a night or two, it is not a life of homelessness. In a similar way, although there have been a few long periods when money has been short, I have always believed in its shortage as temporary. I find it hard to decide whether my tendency to live on less income than many of my friends is because of my middle-class background or in spite of it. To this day I have never earned more than a very average wage.

My working-class friend was right about my unknowable class privilege. One of the results of oppression is a thorough knowledge of the ways of the oppressor, what I have come to call Dominant Culture Stupidities (Hawthorne 1996). As a lesbian, a woman and as one who has felt the sting of an epileptic seizure in a public place, I understand the culture of heterosexuality, of men and of the rhetoric of the abled. And I have developed analogues. I will always be white, but I have fought for and supported a better deal for Aboriginal people. I will always be middle class, but I support the services for poor people and a better distribution of wealth through taxation. I will always be a woman, a lesbian, a sufferer from a despised illness – and despite the anger and frustration and sometimes the pain of that, I believe that they are the experiences that have made me more aware, more sensitive to the injustices of others' experiences.

When my novel *The Falling Woman* (1992) was published some readers asked how I felt about coming out as a lesbian; some asked how I felt about coming out as someone with epilepsy. My feelings depended on the context. As a lesbian, life in a country town can be difficult (Hawthorne 1995); in the city among writers and artists, having epilepsy is not exactly cool. But for me there was another coming out, going on. With the mass downward mobility of the left there were times when by omission I failed to mention my background, my solidly middle-class background. In some ways, in terms of my own peers, my novel was a class coming out – an acknowledgement of it. My mother worried about the lesbian content, some acquaintances mentioned the epilepsy, what I wondered was whether some friends would ignore me now because I had been to a prestigious boarding school.

Acknowledging who we are, where we come from, is important – and it can take a long time if one inhabits a hostile environment or one imagines a hostile response from one quarter or another.

These days I find the class distinctions harder to see. There are many filters – education is perhaps the most important; but perhaps that's the milieu I inhabit. In another milieu it might be money that filters the perception. The vast majority of my friends come from families with less wealth or status than my own, but we have finished up in the same social grouping. With rare exception my friends are lesbians, but now and then I find a heterosexual friend who shares a commonality. Above all, my friends are readers, women who think, women who protest injustice. Some are in paid work, some are unemployed, some are retired or on pensions, a few suffer long-term illness. These things too filter class position.

I still have a flare of excitement when I meet another woman who has attended a boarding school. It's a commonality. Similarly, finding others who share some distinct feature of my identity: a country upbringing, being Australian overseas, the experience of epilepsy, choosing to be lesbian, a writer and so forth. Whiteness is so prevalent in Australia and so much the dominant force, that it alone causes no frisson.

My experiences of class have had a profound effect on me, shaping my identity, my expectations, my whole way of social interaction. And yet I hope that I have also learnt sensitivity to other class positions. My intention is not to abuse the privilege I have received, and in many arenas I have acted to counter it. I cannot become working class or upper class. They are not my cultures. Indeed, when I have encountered such cultures and been the solitary other, I have found them confusing, not knowing quite what to do. But there are some middle classes where I feel just as uncomfortable for other reasons. Such middle classes would include those who are oriented towards money rather than education; or rampantly heterosexual middle classes which leave no room for lesbian existence. The middle classes I feel uncomfortable in are those which are not open to change and newness. Perhaps this is why I have never returned to live in the country. I do not like snobbery or prejudice of any kind. My own social group is very mixed with commonalities and differences along different dimensions. Perhaps my country upbringing with its mixture of classes has led me to another community, primarily the lesbian community, with its diversity across classes, cultures, disabilities, even politics.

Notes

1. The sentiments of the above epigraph and opening paragraph have been borne out since its writing. After this chapter was written Craig McGregor published his book, *Class in Australia* in which he writes of the upper class:

   Uneasiness about class labels even applies to the upper class. Fifteen or 20 years ago opinion polls found that many upper class Australians were reluctant to call themselves that, perhaps out of deference to the strong egalitarian ethos of the time and preferred to label themselves upper-middle class (1997: 6).

Of the working class:

although the Australian Labor Party was formed as a working-class party there has been an obvious desire on the part of its leaders to play down its working-class basis and to court the all important middle-class vote (ibid.).

2. For an analysis of women's positioning see Bell (1984).
3. For a discussion on the literatures which have emerged depicting both rural and urban lives, see Hawthorne (1990).
4. Personal communication with Phoebe Thorndyke.
5. Personal communication with Susan Holmes.
6. Rita Mae Brown wrote: ". . . the irony of downward mobility . . . is that they could *afford* to become downwardly mobile" (1974: 20).

References

Back-to-Ardlethan Week Committee (eds) 1985. *Poppet Heads and Wheatfields: A History of the Ardlethan and District, Wheat and Tin Centre of South-West N.S.W.* Temora: J.A. Bradley.

Bell, Diane 1984. *Daughters of the Dreaming.* Sydney: Allen & Unwin.

Bell, Diane and Klein, Renate (eds) 1996. *Radically Speaking: Feminism Reclaimed.* Melbourne: Spinifex Press; London: Zed Books.

Brown, Rita Mae 1974. The last straw, in Bunch, Charlotte and Myron, Nancy (eds) *Class and Feminism.* Baltimore, MD: Diana Press.

Hawthorne, Susan 1990. Working-class women's writing in Australia: on the margins of every margin?, in Hocking, Brian (ed.) *Australia Towards 2000.* London: Macmillan.

Hawthorne, Susan 1992. *The Falling Woman.* Melbourne: Spinifex Press.

Hawthorne, Susan 1995. Plotting circles in the mind, in Scutt, Jocelynne A. (ed.) *City Women Country Women: Crossing the Boundaries.* Melbourne: Artemis Publishing.

Hawthorne, Susan 1996. From theories of indifference to a wild politics, in Bell, Diane and Klein, Renate (eds) (1996), pp. 483–501.

McGregor, Craig 1997. What is class, *Sydney Morning Herald, Spectrum*, 26 April, p. 6. An extract from *Class in Australia.* Ringwood: Penguin Books.

Mahony, Pat and Zmroczek, Christine 1996. Working-class radical feminism: lives beyond the text, in Bell, Diane and Klein, Renate (eds) (1996), pp. 67–76.

CHAPTER FIFTEEN

Questioning correspondence: an Australian woman's account of the effects of social mobility on subjective class consciousness

Elizabeth J. Hatton

In terms of malestream analyses of class and social stratification based on the structure of the Australian workforce such as Western and Western's (1988), this chapter might straightforwardly focus on what it means to be a female member of the professional/managerial class in Australia. However, I argue these models are flawed and not just because of their failure adequately to capture women's classed and gendered oppression (Connell et al. 1982). It is also the case that the rationalist discourse on which they are premised omits consideration of the embodied, lived experience of class. Even where this dimension is taken into account, there is an assumption of correspondence between objective location and class consciousness. Drawing on themes that have been part of my lived experience of class, I demonstrate that this assumption does not adequately capture empirical reality, particularly for those who have experienced social mobility. Thus much of the complex lived experience of class is ignored or misunderstood. It is this dimension that feminist analyses of class must also capture to go beyond malestream analyses.

The mythical view of Australia is that it is a classless, egalitarian country typified by mateship. The reality of Australia is that it is a country stratified by, among other things, ethnicity, gender and class. Let me make a brief point on each of these. Stratification by ethnicity is a complex issue in Australia. Many, but not all, migrant groups experience racism and ethnocentrism and inequality. It is, however, indigenous Australians who are the most oppressed group in Australia. On any nominated inequality dimension (housing, health, education, employment etc.), indigenous Australians fare worst of any ethnic group. Secondly, not only does Australia have the dubious distinction of having the most sex segregated workforce of all OECD countries but sexism pervades the ethos of the country. Indeed, "egalitarianism" is still understood in Australia through the phrase "*Jack is* as good as *his master*" and "mateship" refers to the friendships between men, originally between men isolated in the bush. This latter point is quite ironic in a country in which homophobia is almost a national obsession (see Hatton & Swinson 1994).

Australia, like many Western countries including Britain and my country of birth, New Zealand, has been typified in recent years by greater inequality as the wealth of the country has been aggregated in fewer and fewer hands and poverty has been more widely shared in the community (see Lean & Ball 1996). This situation of inequity can be illustrated by a consideration of the shape of the class structure in Australia. Western and Western (1988) provide a four-class structure of Australian society based on the structure of the Australian workforce. It posits a traditional bourgeoisie who are the owners and controllers of the means of production. This group is approximately 5.8 per cent of the workforce. There is a professional/managerial class who are different from the bourgeoisie insofar as they lack formal ownership of the means of production and distinct from the working class insofar as they have a "privileged market situation, reflected in their possession of skills and services" which "is matched by material and non-material rewards" (Western & Western 1988: 83). This group is about 17.1 per cent of the workforce. There is also a petit bourgeoisie of shopkeepers and independent tradespeople which forms about 9.8 per cent of the workforce. The final and largest group is the working class who have historically consisted of two distinct fractions: the white-collar fraction of clerical and sales workers is about 24.6 per cent of the population and the blue-collar fraction which forms 42.7 per cent of the population. While this model is dated, and it overlooks those who live in poverty outside the workforce on social welfare, it serves to give some indication of the limited number of the population of Australians in whose hands wealth and high incomes are aggregated.

On Western and Western's model, given my work as a university lecturer, I would place myself as part of the privileged professional/managerial group, more privileged than some because my ethnic background is Anglo-Celtic in a country in which the dominant group is also Anglo-Celtic and because I belong economically to that class of women in Australian society for whom the benefits of feminist agitation for equality have probably had most effect. This chapter, therefore, might focus straightforwardly on what it means to be a female member of the professional/managerial middle class in Australia. The fact that my class of origin in Aotearoa/New Zealand,[1] where I was born and lived for the first 24 years of my life, was working class, would be incidental to the discussion which follows. However, rather than incidentalize it, this chapter attempts to shows the significance of my New Zealand working-class lived experience to my life as a female member of the professional/managerial middle class in Australia. Indeed, I attempt to show that malestream models are flawed not just because of their failure adequately to capture women's classed and gendered oppression.[2] The discourse about class on which they are premised also frequently tends to omit adequate consideration of the embodied, lived experience of being classed and gendered. Even where there is some attention to the embodied dimension of class it is often based on false assumptions.

There are two broad ways in which the lived, subjective dimension of class is treated in the literature both of which implicitly or explicitly assume that objective location and subjective consciousness correspond totally or significantly such that class of origin is assumed to be no longer significant in one's life. First, there is an explicit assumption of a correspondence between the two elements which this chapter calls into question. Consider, for example, Western and Western's discussion of Marx's theorizing on social class:

> ... there is general agreement that a Marxist concept of class contains two elements: an objective economic situation in which people at work can be located, and a subjective consciousness (Ossowoski 1963; Bottomore 1966). The first of these elements is defined in terms of the social relations of production, that is, the various relationships between people involved in producing economic goods and services. The second concerns the various understandings and conceptions that individuals in different classes possess about the nature of society, and the way in which these conceptions are tied to class struggle and social change. In other words, Marx's theory of class is one which attempts to explain "the interplay between the real situation of individuals in the process of production, on one side, and the conceptions which they form of their situation and of the lines of social and political action which are open to them on the other" (Bottomore 1966: 17) (Western & Western 1988: 51).

Second, there is an implicit assumption that economic location unproblematically corresponds with subjective class identification. At the very least, it is assumed that the important dimension in class analysis is objective economic location. Categorical models of social class such as that provided by Western and Western (1988) are typical. This arises because categorical models tend to ignore class as a lived process. In categorical models, "classes or strata are basically understood as categories: sets of individuals who all share the same attributes or possessions (such as level of income, type of occupation, ownership)" (Connell et al. 1982). Connell et al. argue, by contrast, that a more productive view is that of class as a lived process:

> It is not what people are, or even what they own, so much as what they *do* with their resources and their relationships, that is central. (Some of the things done with resources very much concern education.) Classes are not abstract categories but real-life groupings, which, like heavily-travelled roads are constantly under construction: getting organised, divided, broken down, remade. (Significant parts of this activity occur

in and around the schools.) At the same time, classes reflect terrible constraints in the lives of their members, for their making and remaking is done in the course of intransigent conflicts that arise in a deeply divided and unequal society (Connell et al. 1982: 33).

This view comes closer to the sort of understanding which I believe feminists ought to be pursuing. Moreover, Connell et al., unlike many class theorists, acknowledge that families can be internally divided by class given the different position of, and strategies pursued by, the two adults in the family. However, the issue of the lack of straightforward correspondence between objective class location and subjective consciousness receives no more attention in the work of Connell and colleagues than it does elsewhere.

While it is conceded that these assumptions are possibly most significant or obvious in their failure to capture the experience of those who have experienced upward or downward social mobility, they have consequences for the adequacy of feminist class theorization. Given the commitment of feminist researchers to the production of "unalienated knowledge", there is an obligation to capture and theorize the embodied experience of class, gender and ethnicity and the like (Stanley 1990: 12). And if the rejection of the theory/research divide in feminism seriously means "seeing these as united manual and intellectual activities which are symbiotically related" (ibid.: 15) then the lived experiences presented and explored in this chapter have clear implications for improved theoretical analysis, especially if differences are taken seriously.

What this chapter attempts, therefore, is to portray what it is like to have an economic and structural location in Australia's middle class and sufficient subjective identification with the working class to disrupt comfortable subjective identity both within my own occupation and within the wider class or category to which I belong. Drawing on personal experience, I will direct attention through discussion of a number of themes to illustrate the way in which identification with my working-class background intrudes in my middle-class occupational setting and life in ways which disrupt seamless subjective middle-class identification. While education acted to alienate me from my family in my youth (explored under the subheading, "I became a stranger in my own family"), it will be shown that another dynamic of interruption/dislocation is apparent in my occupation and within my wider class situation. The themes used to explore this dynamic include my enduring guilt and unease about being privileged ("I'm a working class girl gone wrong"), the feelings of alienation I have within privileged situations ("Am I really one of these pampered, overindulged people?"), the alienating emotional response I have to middle-class feminist academic analyses which fail to capture the experiences of the women I knew as a child ("Where's my mother in all of this?"), and the heightened sense of the ridiculous I have in esoteric academic situations ("If my mother/father heard this what would she/he say?"). Thus despite my economic location as middle class, my subjective identification/consciousness, I will suggest, is frequently disrupted by the powerful experiences of growing up working class to the degree that seamless subjective identification is rendered impossible. The themes, it will be suggested, explore an ignored emotional dimension to classed and gendered experience which is significant especially for those who have experienced social mobility. It is this lived dimension which feminist analysts of class should capture if their analyses are to go beyond those of their malestream theorists. I provide some biographical notes to set a context for the themes I presently explore.

Biographical notes

I grew up as the second child of six (five girls and a boy) in an unruly, impoverished, extended Anglo-New Zealand working-class family in a country area. My mother was educated to age 15 and my father, who had barely finished primary schooling before having to leave school to help support his family, was barely literate. He struggled daily to make his way through the newspaper. My childhood was difficult: I learned well the lessons of poverty and came to fear every manipulative travelling salesperson who darkened our doors in case they talked my parents into a purchase which would not only plunge us into debt, but would also precipitate fierce family arguments over money.

I learned about the class war at the Formica kitchen table. My father taught me about "bosses" and "workers" and their connection with political parties with pepper and salt shakers used to stake out the different territory and interests of each. Each election night, from the time I was about eight, my job was to sit at home with the newspaper filling in, electorate by electorate, the results from the radio while my father and mother joined the party faithful at the local Labour Party headquarters. The next day, my labours would be examined minutely in exultation or despair.

Struggle was a daily part of our lived experience. I remember that as children, our parents' struggle became our struggle and in our own ways we attempted to help. Unexpected visits by relatives, for example, could be enough to throw the family budget into disarray. Sometimes there simply was no extra money to supplement what was in the house. We knew this, and the oldest of us would ensure that a FHB code (family hold back) was communicated to the youngest ones to ensure there was sufficient food to go around. In this way, our parents were saved embarrassment in front of relatives whose circumstances were less pinched than ours.

I recollect too the Christmas we spent without presents because my father had been seriously injured at work. He received no pay and his worker's compensation claim had not been processed. We did receive one present from my father's boss. It was an object called a googly ball; a weighted ball which behaved unpredictably. The receipt of this object caused my mother and father great anguish. My father was, at this time, a foreman at a metal crushing plant. His boss would phone him on weekends and ask him to do favours for him which would often steal a full day from Dad's weekend. There was never any extra pay for this. It was simply expected that he would do it. When Christmas came and the boss arrived with his paltry present to be shared among six children, the extent to which Dad was exploited and under appreciated was painfully obvious to us all.

My mother, who worked mostly in a part-time capacity, undertook most of the family battles with the "system" (which was virtually anything outside the family that might treat the family unfairly through procedures, sale of faulty goods, etc.). One of her more profound battles was with the surgeons who, after Dad's accident, simply wanted to amputate his arm. My mother, recognizing the implications of this for the family, fought until they agreed an alternative to amputation was possible.

I was struck during a recent visit to one of my sisters, who has by and large reproduced in her family life the struggles of my parents, at the closeness between her and my mother's *modus operandi*. Perhaps my sister's case is complicated by the racism she, her partner and children have encountered because my brother-in-law is Maori. Intermarriage between Maoris and *pakehas* (a non-Maori person, usually of European descent) in New Zealand is still problematic for some New Zealanders (see, e.g., Hatton 1994b; Hatton & Swinson 1994). The theme of struggle against the system, for my mother and my sister, is a lived reality. It permeates their lives in ways in which it has not characterized my adult life.

Growing up in my sprawling, sport-conscious family was made difficult by a bookish disposition; a disposition not shared by my siblings who revelled, as did my parents, in sports of various kinds. One constant battle I faced was to find a space in which I could read without interruption. Indeed, the only lavatory in the house became my favourite haunt for reading, much to the despair of the other eight occupants of the house. It gave me a seat, four walls around me and a space from which it was difficult to be ejected. There were other consequences given the access to ideas I gained through reading. I'll explore this notion presently through the theme of "I became a stranger in my own family".

After a two-year period of teacher training I joined the workforce at age 18 as a probationary primary school teacher; a career chosen not for its possibilities for mobility, nor even for commitment to young people, but as an insurance for my imagined future family against the poverty my own family had endured when my father was injured and unable to work. I remained in teaching until 1984 through my move to Australia in 1971. After teaching for many years it occurred to me that given the changes in teacher preparation, many of the new teachers I was inducting into the profession were poised for more successful careers than I could dream of given the value placed on their credentials compared to mine. At the same point in time my favourite aunt delivered me a rather severe tongue-lashing about my failure to extend or challenge myself in my life despite being intelligent. Simultaneously delighted and intimidated by what was the first show of faith in my intellectual capacities in adult life, I set about the process, rather uncertainly, of acquiring the qualifications and "track record" which resulted in my current position in the university.

Rather anxiously I enrolled initially in a local College of Advanced Education (CAE) as a part-time evening student to undertake an upgrade of my qualifications to a three year Diploma of Education. Ironically given my current position, I chose a CAE because I felt that a university was a place for people very different from me. Perhaps this view was inculcated unintentionally during my secondary schooling in New Zealand. Under the system in place in the 1960s you were able to go to university once you had passed University Entrance; a credential acquired through accreditation or examination in the fourth year of secondary school. However, to get a scholarship it was necessary to complete a fifth year of schooling. In the secondary school I attended only the students with relatively wealthy backgrounds took up this option. Students with backgrounds like mine tended to view the very few students doing the fifth year as strange, exotic and different. Moreover, it is interesting to look back on my secondary schooling in New Zealand and realize that university was never discussed or made familiar to me or my peers despite the fact that we all did well in school. It was as though the school also assumed that university was not for us. There was no concerted endeavour to make us mobile and thereby help us escape our working-class fates (Walkerdine & Lucey 1989; Walkerdine 1990).

During my CAE diploma experience I found that I enjoyed the taste of academic work I encountered and elected to continue on and do a degree. In the CAE, it turned out degree places were scarce and, to my horror, despite excellent academic results, I was not selected for one of them. So, despite myself, I had to turn to a university to continue. It was during this period, and particularly after I left teaching and took up a tutorship at the University of Queensland, that I had access to the full gamut of university culture and it was during that time of full employment in the tertiary sector and my change in status from primary school teacher to university academic that the issue of correspondence/dislocation between economic location and subjective identity emerged as an issue for me.

Disruption/dislocation themes

I became a stranger in my own family

It is sometimes claimed that access to formal education changes a person. For example, Lynch and O'Neill (1994), whose work I discuss below, would argue that one's habitus changes as a result of the acquisition of academic credentials. During this process cultural capital is acquired and integrated into the habitus. I am unsure about this in my case. I think, however, that the changes that happened to me were a product of access to ideas brought about by my own rather free-wheeling reading rather than my formal education which was on the whole sadly uninspired and through which I made fairly erratic progress. Moreover, I remember encountering and explicitly (sometimes angrily) rejecting class-based values and practices even in primary school. For example, daily baths were upheld by one of my teachers as essential to hygiene. I can remember sitting in class contemplating the size of the hot water system which would be required to enable the eight of us each to have a daily bath and still enable my mother and grandmother to get the mountainous daily washing done.

Many of the ideas which I gained over the years through reading, which were not part of my family's taken-for-granteds, did have an impact on me. Indeed, they tended to make me a stranger in my own home; a cuckoo in the nest. My father and I fought outrageous battles over them. This usually happened when he was sufficiently "in his cups" to stop being his everyday taciturn self. And as a young girl in a family in which the sexual divisions were profound, I was thrilled and flattered that my father seemed to want to talk to me. These sessions, which probably began when I was about ten, inevitably ended badly as we battled over issues and ideas. I remember trying desperately to convince my father that it was not homosexuals who constituted a sexual threat to my brother or that a conscientious objector who went to war despite his beliefs was not as brave as a conscientious objector who was interned in a prison camp and who had to face the social rejection that went along with this. I learnt at this point that education, understood broadly, for someone like me was dangerous, alienating, dislocating; it interrupted my place in my family. Ironically, after becoming an academic a reverse dynamic of interruption/dislocation became apparent both in my occupation and within my wider class situation. The themes described below attempt to capture this.

I'm a working class girl gone wrong

One of the enduring aspects of unease about my life is the relative ease with which I am able to acquire the material goods I desire, to buy good quality food, to take part in cultural activities, to access good health care and the like. I am frequently overwhelmed by guilt and unease about being so privileged. I find it impossible to provide any adequate justification for my access to these things when my family and others like them had, and continue to have, so little. I look at my brother's life or my sisters' lives and cannot explain away my structural position through merit. My barely literate father was an intelligent man yet he was not able to live the privileged life I live and died a horrible death worn down by a life time of tough, outdoor manual work which made his health fragile. It is precisely because of my working-class background that this is an issue for me.

Am I really one of these pampered, overindulged people?

There is no question that I enjoy privileged situations – restaurants, good food, coffee shops. However, I often look around the assembled throng in these places and "read" the style of the people around me. I find their look alienating, foreign, over-pampered, over-indulged. I have often caught myself doing this and have been forced to confront the fact that economically at least, and probably in terms of style, I am one of them. I contemplate this with horror. However, I would argue that the fact that I am engaging in "reading" style as other and outside of me is again attributable to having been part of, in the early years of my life, another very different group which was distinctively different in style and which did not have a sleek, pampered aura.

Where's my mother in all of this?

Perhaps one of the most dislocating emotional responses I have in the academy is when I sit in on the analyses of middle-class feminist academics and realize the oppressed category "women" about which they speak fails to capture the experiences of women such as my mother and her friends. Indeed, I experience their generalizations about women based on the experiences of women like them, as distinctly classist. These analyses impact on me like a class slur. This type of experience is alienating, marginalizing and acts as a constant reminder of the fact that the backgrounds of many of my contemporaries are very different to mine. There is a sense in which this induces a feeling of being in, but not of, the academy;[3] of being marginal in a way that makes my class of origin omnipresent.

If my mother/father heard this what would she/he say?

As I write this chapter and imagine myself presenting it as a paper to an academic audience, I know that it would occasion in me some feelings of discomfort/dislocation. Indeed, I would undoubtedly feel, to some degree, the heightened sense of the ridiculous which I often have in very esoteric academic analyses. This is not to say that I gain no pleasure from them. The reverse is true. It is simply that my comfort in these situations is usually disrupted by a sense of how bizarre and ridiculous my parents would find the production and presentation of a piece of "work" such as this. Again, there is a sense in which familiarity with the working-class culture in which I was raised acts again to make my class of origin omnipresent. Although the dislocation/interruption has been a part of my lived experience as an academic, it has remained until this project undiscussed within the academy.

It is worth pointing out that I do not mean to suggest that the knowledge produced by academics and that produced by working-class people have different values with middle-class academic knowledge being inherently more valuable than that produced by working-class people. Indeed, my own research with working-class parents has shown me that working-class people are equally capable of producing knowledge and insights which are valuable in informing the academy (see, e.g., Hatton 1994b; Hatton & Swinson 1994). However, it is undoubtedly the case that my knowledge of working-class responses to certain forms of "packaging" of ideas will result in a sense of marginality.

Correspondence or dislocation/interruption?

The literature on academics with working-class backgrounds is relatively sparse. Nevertheless there are some accounts (see, e.g., Ryan & Sackrey 1984; Walkerdine & Lucey 1989; Walkerdine 1990; Tokarczyk & Fay 1993). Lynch and O'Neill (1994) provide an interesting, albeit flawed, relatively recent discussion of the issue of education, social mobility and the working class focused on, among other things, academics who were once working class. The context for discussion is a concern about middle-class academics colonizing, for their own professional purposes, the oppressions and inequalities suffered by working-class people in their education, a situation they argue that has been "greatly facilitated by the nature of the scholastic context itself" since working-class people lack both the "intellectual legitimacy" and the "freedom from the urgency and necessity of survival" (Lynch & O'Neill 1994: 307) to "document their social analysis of their world" (ibid.). Moreover, and importantly for the concerns of this chapter, they add that working-class people occupy a structurally contradictory role in relation to education. Specifically, they point out that "social mobility requires that they be well educated. Yet if they are to succeed in the education system they have to abandon certain features of their class background. They cease to be working class at least to some degree" (ibid.: 318).

Lynch and O'Neill initially appear open to the view that not all aspects of a class background are lost when education results in social mobility. However, as their discussion proceeds, this seems to become less important and it is in this respect that their argument seems to me to be flawed. They say that "to participate in the academic definition of their own class culture, working class people must become part of the colonizing/mediating group; they must become credentialised *via* higher education". While they initially claim that "this does not mean they abandon their class identity", they then assert "that, by virtue of the lengthy process of participating in education, they will be 'contaminated' if not converted to middle class culture" (ibid.). They cite, in support of this view, Aronowitz and Giroux (1991: 163) who suggest that one of the functions of schooling is to "erase the memory of self-representing popular culture" and suggest:

> The objective of schooling, conscious or not, is among other things to strip away what belongs to the student, to reconstitute his or her formation in terms of the boundaries imposed by hegemonic individuals acting for the prevailing social order. The students who succeed in these terms must be stripped of their ethnicity, race and sex; if they are of working class origin, their submission to their curriculum already signifies probable social mobility (Lynch & O'Neill 1994: 318).

Lynch and O'Neill go on to argue that "working class people have to abandon certain features of their background class habitus (that is their modes of thought, perception, appreciation and action, Bourdieu and Passeron, 1977, pp. 40–41) in

220

a way that is not really true for other socially mobile groups" (Lynch & O'Neill 1994: 318). Once educated, they suggest their defining identity in social class terms is changed in a way that does not hold true for any other marginalized group: "they will cease to be working class in a way that a woman, no matter what her social position, will never cease to be a woman; a person who is black will never cease to be black, and those with a major physical disability will never be without it" (ibid.).

The result of this, Lynch and O'Neill claim, is that the structural relationship working-class people exercise in relation to education is fraught with difficulties and dilemmas:

> As long as they remain outside of the formal credentialised system of education, they are excluded from challenging that very system. If they are to become credentialised, however, they generally cease to belong to their class of origin, at least in so far as their access to credentialised cultural capital has changed (and maybe even their access to embodied and social capital through the styles of living and learning one engages in and the social contacts that one makes in education) . . . In addition, their occupational status may change due to the credential acquired. While such contradictions and dilemmas arise for all groups who are not male, white and middle class in education, they do not arise for all members of any of these groups. Middle class women, middle class blacks and middle class disabled people are not in this position [since their cultures are not defined in totality as being structurally inferior and inadmissible in education]. At least in their middleclassness they can be at home in education at certain times and at certain stages (Lynch & O'Neill 1994: 318–19).

The claim for the distinctiveness of working-class experience in education has its appeal. However, the problematic aspect of this analysis lies in the assumption that a working-class habitus is overwhelmed by a middle-class habitus or, put differently, that having acquired credentialized capital and a middle-class objective location, one's embodied and social capital is sufficiently changed so that an academic who was once working class can no longer adequately capture a working-class voice . Their argument, it seems, is flawed because they overemphasize the extent to which a new class habitus overrides a previous class habitus.

The question is whether the acquisition of cultural capital can totally change one's habitus to the extent that the remnants of one's remaining working-class habitus are so insignificant that correspondence with the subjective identity of the professional/managerial class is totally secured. It is the argument of this chapter, developed through the themes of disruption/dislocation which have been part of my lived experience as an academic member of the professional/managerial class, that this is unlikely. For those who are socially mobile, a professional/

managerial class habitus, for example, is unlikely totally to override and replace the system of dispositions which have mediated structures and practices through an earlier, and often tougher, life. Rather, those remnants are likely to play a disruptive, dislocating role which make seamless subjective identification problematic. Likewise those who are downwardly mobile are likely also to experience difficulties with seamless subjective identification because remnants of their old dispositions will act to disrupt and dislocate it.

Perhaps what is illustrated by the foregoing discussion of themes which are part of my lived experience as an academic, is the fluid and dynamic nature of social class identification which encourages me on occasions such as I have described through these themes to feel marginal to my economic class and, on others, to be totally comfortable within it. Context seems to make a difference here. When I am not in situations in which there is any form of interruption (through exclusionary discourses, through the style of the setting etc.) my class identification feels seamless. Sometimes, however, there is a stronger feeling than the marginality to my current social class occasioned by disrupting/ dislocating themes. There are occasions when I have been working with very oppressed Maori and *pakeha* (or Anglo-New Zealand) working-class parents in New Zealand and others when I have been working with Aboriginal and Anglo-Australian parents when the feeling I have is of strong identification with the working class. It is almost as if, at that time, I have shrugged off my current class position and returned to my class of origin as though I had never left it. Their struggle is my struggle, their oppression is my oppression.

On some occasions this dynamic identification may perhaps be viewed as debilitating, undermining. I suspect, for example, that my career trajectory may have been different if I had been born to a more privileged class and acquired the "born to rule" gloss that appears to underpin the career moves of some of my contemporaries in Australian universities. On other occasions, it can be viewed as a positive force which has underpinned my teaching and research with a concern for social justice. Certainly, it is this dynamic that has enabled me to cling tenaciously to the significance of the concept of *class* through the period in which many feminists were rejecting it in favour of the primacy of gender in shaping women's subjectivity. I know my multifaceted subjectivity can only be understood adequately by attending to my ethnicity, my gender and my class. To focus on one of these dimensions, to the exclusion of the others, would be to omit crucial understandings.

Feminist class analyses must therefore turn to lived, embodied experience of class in the lives of specific people and specific groups of people to ensure that their analyses go beyond those based on rationalistic discourse which fails to attend to the body, or only talks about it in abstract terms. The experiences of those who cross class boundaries, but who do not definitively "pass out of one class into another" (Tokarczyk & Fay 1993: 5) because their lives are marked by their trajectories, provide paradigmatic instances of the significance of this endeavour.

Acknowledgment

This chapter has benefited from discussions with Katie Maher and John Tulloch and helpful suggestions from the editors.

Notes

1. The use of Aotearoa/New Zealand signals the dual country heritage of my country of birth.
2. Western and Western's model, and others like it, are flawed in part because they are based on the workforce experiences of men. Connell et al. draw attention to the reason for their rejection of a categorical approach in their study of schools, families and social divisions:

   > conventional ideas of class as category practically always defined it via status in the workplace or the marketplace (for example, type of occupation, ownership of capital). People who weren't in either – notably school pupils and housewives – could be given a class "location" by labelling them with the status of their nearest adult male. The inadequacy of this became very obvious when we met families that were divided internally along class lines; where for instance, a wife had a different class identity, was pursuing different strategies, and stood in a quite different relation to the school, from her husband (Connell et al. 1982: 33).

3. The academy in Australia is very much the preserve of those from privileged backgrounds.

References

Aronowitz, S. and Giroux, H. 1991. *Postmodern Education: Politics, Culture and Social Criticism*. Minneapolis: University of Minnesota Press.

Bottomore, T. 1966. *Classes in Modern Society*. London: Allen & Unwin.

Bourdieu, P. and Passeron, J. 1977. *Reproduction in Education, Society and Culture*. London: Sage.

Connell, R.W., Ashenden, D.J. Kessler, S. and Dowsett, G.W. 1982. *Making the Difference: Schools, Families and Social Division*. Sydney: Allen & Unwin.

Hatton, E.J. (ed.) 1994a. *Understanding Teaching: Curriculum and the Social Context of Schooling*. Sydney: Harcourt Brace.

Hatton, E.J. 1994b. Exclusion: a case study, in Hatton, E. J. (ed.) (1994a), pp. 221–34.

Hatton, E.J. and Swinson, S. 1994. Sexual orientation, policy and teaching, in Hatton, E.J. (ed.) (1994a), pp. 279–91.

Lean, G. and Ball, G. 1996. UK most unequal country in the West, *Independent on Sunday*, 21 August, p. 1.

Lynch, K. and O'Neill, C. 1994. The colonisation of social class in education, *British Journal of Sociology of Education*, 15(3), 307–24.

Ossowoski, S. 1963. *Class Structure in Social Consciousness*. London: Routledge & Kegan Paul.

Najman, M. and Western, J.S. (eds) 1988. *A Sociology of Australian Society: Introductory Readings*. South Melbourne: Macmillan.

Ryan, J. and Sackrey, C. 1984. *Strangers in Paradise: Academics from the Working Class*. Boston, MA: South End Press.

Stanley, L. 1990. Feminist praxis and the academic mode of production, in Stanley, L. (ed.) *Feminist Praxis: Research, Theory and Epistemology in Feminist Sociology*. London: Routledge, pp. 3–19.

Tokarczyk, M. and Fay, E. 1993. *Working-Class Women in the Academy: Laborers in the Knowledge Factory*. Amherst: University of Massachusetts Press.

Walkerdine, V. and Lucey, H. 1989. *Democracy in the Kitchen: Regulating Mothers and Socialising Daughters*. London: Virago Press.

Walkerdine, V. 1990. *Schoolgirl Fictions*. London: Verso.

Western, M.C. and Western, J.S. 1988. Class and inequality: theory and research, in Najman, J. and Western, J. (eds) (1988), pp. 50–91.

CHAPTER SIXTEEN

Spilling the caviar:
telling privileged class tales

Laurel Guymer

When I was asked to write of my experiences of growing up in the privileged classes I accepted reluctantly, for fear of exposing an identity that I have spent many years trying to hide and deconstruct. But, it is time someone spilled the caviar so to speak. My class/life education consisted of learning to tell the difference between those who were educated to "pass" and those who were so-called "born and bred". The irony is that there are many more similarities than differences between those "born and bred" and those who have "learnt". For example, the many markers of class are actively taught over an entire lifetime. In order to provide some background information I begin this chapter with a brief overview of my family and schooling. I describe how I was actively taught class and my ongoing resistance.

The bigger picture

My experiences shape my understanding of class. They represent a part of the bigger picture in which men as a social group have a vested interest in maintaining and sustaining class distinctions which perpetuate their privileged patriarchal world. Radical feminists Robyn Rowland and Renate Klein put women's experiences of oppression at the centre of their theory and practice while acknowledging the differential nature of that experience by virtue of "race and culture boundaries, as well as those of class and other delineating structures such as age, sexuality and physical ability" (Rowland & Klein 1996: 18). My connections to radical feminism have greatly affected my understandings of class. While it is undoubtedly the case that "men benefit in concrete and material ways from their oppression and exploitation of women" (ibid.: 21), there is no doubt that some women benefit from patriarchal privileges. This helps to explain why they reinforce the system that ultimately oppresses them as individuals and as women.

Who am I?

I was born in 1963, adopted at eight weeks old to grow up in the upper or privileged class where the class position and money had been carried down through generations of medical practitioners. As the youngest of three, the only daughter, I was given a private school education, 12 years at Presbyterian Ladies College, with all the trimmings of ballet, speech classes and music lessons. To this day, I still have nightmares about ballet and music lessons, the restraint of the movements, the white frock and the quiet shoes reinforcing the myth that "young ladies" should be seen and not heard – look beautiful but be silent.

Nevertheless, knowing I was not "born" but obviously "bred" made me feel uncomfortable and at times inadequate compared with girls at the school and women from the "real" privileged class. Biological arguments were used to alienate me at school. "Oh Laurel! You are an unknown quantity. Your father might be a doctor but who knows where you are really from?" Comments like this from other students were common. They thought they could destabilize anyone who was other, that is, not from a long line of wealthy medical or law families, not born with the right genes. So, my fears that everyone around me was better, escalated. Even though I knew that the school I attended actively expelled those who did not make the intellectual grade, the stereotype or tale was perpetuated that wealthy people were clever – and maybe I was not.

Through what I can only describe now as brainwashing, I learnt that some people were valued more than others and at the time I never questioned it. I had no concept that my privileges were at the expense of others until later when I realized that the power resulting from privilege was only accorded to men as a social group and that my access to it was directly related to my father. It became clear to me, once an awareness of radical feminist theory had entered my life, why my entire education thus far had revolved around learning to "pass". Not only was I a direct reflection of my father but how I behaved would have a direct link to whom I married (something I rejected totally). It was this which would secure me access to the patriarchal privilege that I had grown up assuming was mine.

The notion of "belonging" is crucial in understanding my experience of growing up knowing I was adopted, "special", "chosen from all the others", not "born" into the privileged life, but "bred". I was taught to pass – bred – so I would not be discriminated against for having the wrong accent, not knowing the table rules or what to wear. I was bred to be safe from ridicule, so safe, that I was unaware of how the privileged class are despised or that, really, I did not fit in. My world view revolved around that of my parents and peers and never for one moment included the possibility that I, as a member of the privileged class, was in fact the one who was "other". This is a glimpse of privileged class arrogance which is not easily left behind. For example, in refinancing a mortgage, I held out for a lower interest rate knowing that as the consumer one has the upper hand. Instead of fearing the institutions, the privileged classes know how to play the game so that the rules work for you. Class arrogance is hard to shed totally because it is such a useful tool for manipulating situations in the way you want them. It is important to reveal some of the ways I was actively taught class so as to expose them for what they are: mechanisms of power and discrimination.

Privileged class rules: learning what to do and how to do it

For Tracey Reynolds, class has many signifiers:

> occupation type, level of education, speech and dialect, body language, manner of dress, spatial locality and even the type of housing someone resides in are used to judge a person's social class (Reynolds 1997: 8).

Similarly, in Australia, markers of class begin with what you look like, where you went to school, what your *father* does for a living and where you live. These are questions I was taught to ask when I met someone for the first time, no matter the context, in order to ascertain the answer to a bigger question: "Do I want to know you or not?" Acceptance into the invisible club of the privileged class depends on many things, their answer and their accent (see Hey 1997). Accents are only invisible if you are silent. My accent exposed my class every time I spoke and unlike Kim Clancy who felt "discomfort [when] realising the 'a' in 'bath' and 'path' was not pronounced in the same way as the 'a' in 'bat' or 'pat'" (Clancy 1997: 49), I was supposed to feel powerful and more important because I could pronounce the words correctly. The way the spoken English language was taught and reinforced was not out of context either – don't raise your voice, act submissive but confident, smile, don't answer back, agree with men, remember that assertiveness can be misconstrued as aggressiveness but, most importantly, do not disagree with men as they are your direct link to class privilege.

Another signifier of the privileged world is occupation, that is the power and prestige that certain occupations accrue. Again, what your father does is crucial. It was not going to be good enough for me just to work, I needed to do a certain type of work which would make me stand out from the crowd. If I was going to attract the right sort of man I had to do the right sort of work. This was rein-forced when a friend expressed a desire to be a hairdresser. Everyone, including teachers, parents and peers actively prevented her from even contemplating such a so-called menial job. She was at the Ladies College and the expectation was that she would pursue some sort of prestigious, well-paying occupation such as law or medicine. She was threatened with expulsion and told regularly by teachers that "Your parents aren't paying all this money for you to end up a mere hairdresser." This of course had lasting effects on me and even when my marks were not high enough to get me into the prestigious Melbourne University, hairdressing did not even enter my mind. For only the "dummies" did hairdressing.

Another assumption was that if you went to the Ladies College you must be clever. The privileged class cannot see their own power – a phenomenon Susan Hawthorne calls "dominant culture stupidity" (1996: 493). Nevertheless, it was a simple argument that was reinforced over and over – why would clever people do manual and repetitive jobs, or worse, live in poverty? In retrospect it is clear to me that it had such an impact because it presupposed some sort of choice in the matter, choice which I and my peers had but, unbeknown to us, others did not. Perhaps we believed that any woman could decide to be a brain surgeon, earn lots of money and be part of the privileged world. Such naivete ignores power differences and assumes that we are all born – or bred – with the same resources or opportunities. Even if you happen to be the student who never studies but achieves high results or you are born and bred into the privileged class there is still the issue of the majority. Privileged individuals rarely make the connections between their so-called good fortune and their impact on others less privileged, yet by reinforcing the power of the privileged class they also reinforce the oppression of the majority.

Racism: not that you marry but whom you marry

In most countries the dominant culture has created a hierarchy based on class, race, sexuality, ability and age (Clunis & Green 1988). At age ten I was forbidden to play with an Italian boy in my neighbourhood. This open racism was typical of the time and demonstrated fear of anyone who was "different". It was never acknowledged that with the exception of Aboriginal peoples we Australians were all the descendants of one-time immigrants to Australia. Constantly being told that I must not talk to this person or that person, that I was only to make friends with the "right kind of people", isolated me from most of society. The wrong kind of people included anyone who was of minority ethnic origin, or poor, or uneducated. In fact, it included anyone not "one of us", not part of our elite world. Even when I lived in the US as an exchange student, I was told not to make friends with black people because as a consequence I would be ostracized from society, i.e. from the white patriarchal world.

For a long time it remained a mystery to me why I had been prevented from associating with the Italian boy. I can only surmise that my parents feared I might marry him or that I would begin to infringe the rules I had been so carefully taught. Perhaps they thought I would learn bad table manners or forget how to be "ladylike" – use your knife and fork this way, don't scoop up the peas – carefully place them into softer foods, hold the cup by its handle, wait till everyone is served before you start eating, and make sure the men have bigger serves. All of which were presented as important life skills necessary to be included in the privileged world of power.

Dress: not what you wear but how you wear it

"What to wear or dressing for the occasion has been a constant preoccupation" for women from working-class backgrounds now in middle-class occupations (Mahony & Zmroczek 1996: 73). Similarly, I was taught that it was not just what you wear but how you wear it. There are many examples; a scarf wrapped around your neck (like you are preparing to brace a storm) was "common", "ladies" on the other hand "draped" their scarf elegantly over one shoulder; a pair of earrings, one in each ear, was elegant but two in one ear was "cheap"; your hat should be worn forward subtly covering your brow not tipped back as it "looks like you are working on the farm" and so on. I am still confined by these rules of dress to the extent that when I visit my parents I try to dress in "Camberwell clothes".[1] Moreover, at the end of a recent visit, my anxieties were rekindled when my mother commented, "Wearing your rags today?" Instead of the usual silk shirt and tailored pants, I wore shorts and a T-shirt with holes. All this unnecessary anxiety stems from the classist rules that plague my mother. What you wear is a crucial marker of where you belong.

For me belonging was crucial and still is to a degree. I have felt a strong need to belong, so I wear the "Camberwell" clothes when I visit my parents, go for job interviews, to work, travel on planes or meet the bank manager, so as not to be excluded. I know that in the bigger picture dress codes exclude people, particularly women and those who cannot afford to conform. Dressed "incorrectly" for the occasion means in the privileged world that you are not worthy and do not deserve entry into the club or institution concerned. Fear of exposing "the purely bred" to having to mix with the common majority reinforces discriminations of class, race, sexuality and age. Discrimination takes many forms and for the privileged class asking the question, "Where do you come from?" indicates clearly that there is thought to be a "right" part of town and a "wrong" one. In sum, to be part of the privileged class means that if you do not have the right accent, right clothes, live in the right place and your father is not a professional, you will be thought to be and dismissed as "stupid". Nevertheless, all these signifiers that I have identified are difficult to remove.

Resistance: rejecting patriarchy

I strongly believe that anyone can unlearn classist, homophobic, racist, ageist, heterosexist and ableist behaviours but also, that there is a price to pay. The price is loss of power. Power is hard to give up, which probably explains why the long fight against patriarchy is still ongoing. Why would those with power want to give it to someone else so that they themselves might be oppressed (Clements 1996)? The maintenance of power was another tactic reinforced during childhood with admonitions of "Remember who you are – never fear anyone else – you know you are better than them." Although I was told these lines over and over I still questioned them. Who am I? But I am fearful – of those who are bigger and stronger than me and of those who have more money. I am not better than the next person. Needless to say, I did not gain the confidence I should have, growing up in such an environment. But, as I learnt the arrogance that comes with passing, no one knew I lacked confidence.

Such confidence can so easily also be arrogance. At a recent book launch I knocked over a stack of books without even noticing. My partner grabbed me and in a part embarrassed, part exasperated tone whispered, "You are so middle class. Pick the books up." It is hard to shed the class arrogance that I have learnt over an entire lifetime of education and socialization. I have spent the best part of 15 years trying to de-program the classist, racist, homophobic views inscribed on me as I was growing up, but they are still there. To the keen eye (those with working-class origins), it will always be there. Another issue is money or economics. Class can seem quite separate from economics to those of us with more than enough family money behind us to support us and buy us the privilege to think money irrelevant. But to many it is inextricably linked because money means power, and thus it is obvious that money is not entirely irrelevant. The privileged class use money to gain power over one another and waiters may be paid a substantial tip, not in order to show appreciation of their work or even in recognition that in many places wages are so low that they depend on them, but because next time better service and a better table will be guaranteed. The privileged classes have clubs and schools that are out of the price range of the majority but even then you cannot just pay to enter, you must be part of their world to be allowed in.

Opportunities are endless for members of the privileged class and that is why it is so difficult for those of us brought up as part of it to reject the whole thing. The class issues are so intertwined with patriarchy that survival revolves around working with both or in fact rejecting both. For example, if you went to the Ladies College in Melbourne you were guaranteed a job, just because of the school you attended. There is an unspoken language in the privileged class that trusts and encourages the few. What school you went to and what your father's social standing is are crucial factors in opening doors which remain closed to the majority of women.

The segregation of classes is more than the privileged class trying to make itself feel more important. I was constantly told how bad others were in an attempt to raise my own position in the world. The inadequacies of my class are disguised by maintaining the simple myth that they are better than everyone else regardless of their classist, racist, homophobic attitudes to life. In fact it is more complex than this. Class discrimination is about power, one group asserting power over another. It is about a mindset, an arrogance, an attitude taught very subtly as you grow up. Annette Kuhn argues that

> Class is not just about the way you talk, or dress, or furnish your home;
> it is not just about the job you do or how much money you make doing

it; nor is it merely about whether or not you have 'A' levels or went to university, nor which university you went to. Class is something beneath your clothes, under your skin, in your reflexes, in your psyche, at the very core of your being (Kuhn 1995: 98).

I agree with Annette Kuhn that class is an impression, an indentation in your mind, bound up with a sense of self that restricts or gives you the confidence to do anything. For this reason feminist debates and research around issues of class have to begin with women's experiences, albeit within a theoretical framework (Mahony & Zmroczek 1996). As Shulamit Reinharz says:

One shared radical tenet underlying feminist research is that women's lives are important. Feminist researchers do not cynically 'put' women into their scholarship so as to avoid appearing sexist. Rather for feminist researchers females are worth examining as individuals and as people whose experience is interwoven with other women. In other words feminists are interested in women as individuals and as a social category (Reinharz 1992: 241).

My life now is totally different from the one in which I grew up. The people who are my closest friends come from many different classes and groups. And I now belong to an invisible minority of lesbians. This was difficult for my family to accept initially, mostly because of their concern with "what the neighbours and in-laws will think". However, with time (nearly ten years) my partner, who is working-class, has been accepted into the family as "one of us". Whether she wants this is, of course, another question. I have learned that just because I was taught that this family is an important unit in society, it does not mean that others will place the same emphasis on belonging to it.

I was taught from childhood how to be successful as a woman in a patriarchal society – that it is fine to "think differently" as long as no one knows. I stick to my long curly blonde hair, a heterosexual disguise if ever there was one. This has disadvantages as it often means being invisible within my own lesbian community because I do not look like a lesbian (even though it is not clear what a lesbian is supposed to look like). But the advantages are overwhelming and it is clear to me that I have actively kept my blonde curls, my accent and dress so that when I choose, I can participate to some extent in the privileged world of patriarchy. In my case, this is limited by being born female. I am only able to access it via my father (or if I had one, a husband) and this stands in tension with wanting to be an autonomous woman, a radical lesbian feminist who spends her life working to break down the oppressive world for women. Now a lecturer in women's studies, I challenge the classist, racist, homophobic world, the "dominant culture stupidity" that has discriminated against women for too long.

Debunking the myths: rejecting the labels

In writing this chapter, I felt extremely challenged by the fact that as I described how I was "taught class" and tried to analyze it, I actually found that I had kept many parts of the behaviours I was critical of, those that served to maintain my power and privilege. I might not have been "born" but I had been "bred" to pass. Questioning the nature and extent of my resistance and my active attempts to de-program myself from my childhood has brought some painful realizations. Nevertheless, it is an important step and one I want to share with others.

I define myself now as part of the majority – the Australian middle class – and feel as though I have been fighting all my life to escape the ridicule, the elitism and isolation of the upper class. But it was not until I was much older and had experienced the company of strong radical feminists that I felt free to ignore the rules of this patriarchal privileged world and mix with all the "wrong" sorts, the majority, the "wild types" (Hawthorne 1996).

Acknowledgements

Thanks to Renate Klein, Susan Hawthorne, Christine Zmroczek, Pat Mahony, Suzanne Bellamy, Susan Clements and Liz Crock for their support.

Note

1. Camberwell is an eastern suburb of Melbourne where predominantly middle- and upper-class families live.

References

Bell, D. and Klein, R. (eds) 1996. *Radically Speaking. Feminism Reclaimed.* Melbourne: Spinifex Press.

Clancy, Kim 1997. Academic as anarchist: working-class lives into middle-class culture, in Mahony, P. and Zmroczek, C. (eds) (1996), pp. 44–52.

Clements, Susan 1996. Nurse's experiences with horizontal violence: A feminist exploratory study. Unpublished MA thesis, Deakin University, Geelong, December.

Clunis, Merille and Green, Dorsey 1988. *Lesbian Couples.* Seattle: Seal Press.

Hawthorne, Susan 1996. From theories of indifference to a wild politics, in Bell, D. and Klein, R. (eds) (1996), pp. 483–501.

Hey, Valerie 1997. Northern accent and southern comfort: subjectivity and social class, in Mahony, P. and Zmroczek, C. (eds) (1997), pp. 140–51.

Kuhn, Annette 1995. *Family Secrets: Acts of Memory and Imagination.* London: Verso.

Mahony, Pat and Zmroczek, Christine 1996. Working-class radical feminism: lives beyond the text, in Bell, D. and Klein, R. (eds) (1996), pp. 67–76.

Mahony, P. and Zmroczek, C. (eds) 1997. *Class Matters: "Working-Class" Women's Perspectives on Social Class*. London: Taylor & Francis.

Morley, Louise 1997. A class of one's own: women, social class and the academy, in Mahony, P. and Zmroczek, C. (eds) (1997), pp. 109–22.

Reinharz, Shulamit 1992. *Feminist Methods in Social Research*. Oxford: Oxford University Press.

Reynolds, Tracey 1997. Class matters, 'race' matters, gender matters, in Mahony, P. and Zmroczek, C. (eds) (1997), pp. 8–17.

Rowland, Robyn and Klein, Renate 1990. Radical feminism: critique and construct, in Gunew, S. (ed.) *Feminist Knowledge: Critique and Construct*. London: Routledge.

Rowland, Robyn and Klein, Renate 1996. Radical feminism: history, politics and action, in Bell, D. and Klein, R. (1996), pp. 9–36.

Index